Email to the Universe

and other alterations of consciousness

Email to the Universe

and other alterations of consciousness

Robert Anton Wilson

Illustrations by
Richard Rasa

Introduction by
R. Michael Johnson

Afterword by
Paul Krassner

HILARITAS
PRESS

First Edition 2005
Second Printing 2008
Third Printing 2011
eBook Version 1.0—2017, Hilaritas Press

Hilaritas Press Print Edition ISBN-10:0-9987134-0-6

Cover Design by amoeba
eBook Design by Pelorian Digital

Hilaritas Press, LLC.
P.O. Box 1153
Grand Junction, Colorado 81502
www.hilaritaspress.com

to Arlen,

dove sta memora

It is dangerous to understand new things too quickly.
— Josiah Warren, *True Civilization*

Email to the Universe

CONTENTS

Part III: In Defense of the Damned

Part IV: Q & A

Part V: On My Way Out

Introduction

By R. Michael Johnson

The genesis for this book — half of which consists of a compendia of fugitive writings by Robert Anton Wilson spanning 1959-2003 — may seem non-ordinary, so here goes: In the mid-to-late 1990s a devoted coterie of Robert Anton Wilson fans (etymology from "fanatics") met each other digitally and virtually on the old Usenet group alt.fan.rawilson, and we exchanged at times our own extended, multi-paragraphed views on "RAW." At one point, I mentioned the interview in the library reference book *Contemporary Authors*, in which Wilson guessed he'd sold 1500 (or was it 2000?) articles for various print publications, beginning in 1959. He added he'd rather be "rhino gored" than to see some of those articles re-surface. On alt-fan-rawilson, we began to wonder about all those "lost" articles; we loved Wilson's writings so much we agreed that even his ephemera would be pretty good, but RAW had never published an exhaustive bibliography, so we had to guess at some likely small periodicals, based on hints from his published books.

Mike Gathers soon notified me that he'd found some of RAW's lost work by using "Robert Anton Wilson" as a keyword on eBay, so I started doing the same. We'd buy old issues of magazines like *Oui, Cavalier, Green Egg, Gnostica, Critique: A Journal of Conspiracies and Metaphysics, New Libertarian, Spit In The Ocean, Heavy Metal, Spin, Neurolog, Starship, Future Life, High Times, Way Out, No Governor, The Realist, Fact, Mattachine Review, Fortean Times, Conspiracy Digest, Journal of Human Relations, The Thresher* and *Magical Blend*, among *many* others. I found Wilson's first published article from 1959, from the *James Joyce Review* (included in this volume: see "Joyce and Daoism") via interlibrary loan.

As we announced our finds, other Wilson fanatics stepped in to add they had some rare or obscure Wilson material that had never made it into his books. For this Gathers and I have to thank Eric Wagner, Dan Clore, Marc Lutter, and Ted Hand. Jesse Walker often cited where other articles could be found and later pitched in with his own Wilson ephemera, but I don't think any of it made it into this book.

Mike Gathers then decided, and we all agreed, that these pieces should be digitized and shared, and Gathers did yeoman service on what turned out to be rawilsonfans.com (now rawilsonfans. org), stocked with previously-lost articles, interviews, and other unpublished writings that one of us had found on Internet. Indeed, we thought the dredged articles were of high quality, some of it of exceedingly fine merit. Our sole purpose was to share with RAW fandom worldwide and at large, for free.

It turns out Wilson had a contract, circa 2002, with New Falcon for a book called *The Tale of the Tribe*, which looks to have been an abundantly ambitious work that he'd been thinking about and making notes for, for a long time. (To get a glimpse of the *précis* for this book, see the last pages of Wilson's *TSOG: The Thing That Ate the Constitution.*) Wilson never finished his intended *Tale of the Tribe.*

However, around the year 2000, Wilson (b: 1932) began experiencing debilitating health issues related to his bout with polio as a child. Muscle cells in his legs had been damaged and his Post-Polio Syndrome symptoms began to haunt him. He'd suffer falls. He was in constant pain. His body temperature felt 15 degrees colder than it "really" was.

In an effort to fulfill his contractual obligations, he'd spied many of those long-lost pieces that we'd put up at rawilsonfans. com.

It turns out there were plenty of Wilson articles there that didn't make him feel like he'd rather be "rhino-gored," and soon his publisher politely asked Gathers to take those selected ones down, and Gathers complied. Many of us think these old pieces rank among his finest non-fiction writing.

As RAW writes on the first page of this book:

I wrote these polemics, poems, neurolinguistic experiments and assorted meanderings over a period of about 45 years; they represent part of my life's work not-previously

Email to the Universe

available in book form — a part that I would now like preserved in that (relatively) Hard Copy.

As I recall, Gathers got a free copy of *Email To The Universe* from this. The rest of us were delighted that we'd inadvertently helped Wilson compile another book to add to his massive *oeuvre*.

The new, original material for the book consists of the series of haiku, "Old Man on a Balcony: Scenes From Monterey Bay." He enjoyed a wonderful view from his condominium's balcony overlooking the Pacific near Santa Cruz, smoking cannabis (which he had been dedicated to for decades, but now it helped with his post-polio syndrome immensely). Also included are one or two page pieces that often addressed his world in 2003. This is where RAW utilizes Ezra Pound's ideogrammic method to stellar effect. I'd point to his extended piece on his own political party, the Guns and Dope Party, which contains a type of humor that Wilson once referred to as like the literature of the Russian Decembrists: RAW juxtaposes movie quotes, short paragraphs about an issue, Guns and Dope party platform positions, quotes from historical figures, play with fonts and typeface size, absurdist humor and satire, coded language for insiders, odd photos, open-ended questions, obscure allusions, neologisms, and, well see for yourself. The "Guns and Dope Party" essay might be classified as surrealist/neo-Decembrist pamphlet literature, even a sort of samizdat. One of RAW's favored forms of rhetoric was using humor to make very serious points. At this he was a master.

But RAW really did run for Governor of California under this party, joining his old friend Timothy Leary, who'd run for the same office in 1969, against Ronald Reagan.

Besides his pieces from the early aughts, there are a few articles that he published online including "Language, Logic and Lunacy" and "Shocking Hidden Facts About Male Non-Violence", from the online 'zine *Backlash!*

Many of Wilson's revived pieces had their titles altered from the original; in addition, he lightly edited many of the older pieces and liked to add *post-scriptum*-like footnotes as further commentary.

Some notes on the origins of a few of the resurrected articles:

"The Passion of the Antichrist," came from maverick publisher Ralph Ginzburg's *Fact,* March-April 1964. Even in the years since this was re-published in *Email To The Universe* it's taken on a new significance in that we gain a profound perspective on what Madelyn Murray went through as an open atheist in early 1960s U.S., compared to the astonishing traction the so-called New Atheists (Richard Dawkins, Sam Harris, Bill Maher, Daniel Dennett, Christopher Hitchens, et.al) have enjoyed since the 9/11 attacks.

"The Celtic Roots of Quantum Theory" (original source unknown at time of press) provides a link to the Irish mathematical genius William Rowan Hamilton and his role in quantum theoretical thought, which is usually overlooked in books written on the origins of quantum theory.

One day an e-Bay purchase arrived and it was a little self-pressed magazine I'd never heard of called *Neurolog*, which is where "The Relativity of 'Reality'" came from. This 1978 piece still seems quite avant-garde, and as I write in the first month of the Trump Presidency, I can't help but think if more people read this short gem of an article, the world would be a safer and saner place. The article was embedded among other writers' works, and I've often wondered if Wilson got paid at all to write it; *Neurolog* seems quite obscure and looks like one of the thousands of 'zines published in the late 1980s/early 90s. The topic of "reality" was always a major issue with Wilson, and only now, when the President cites *The National Enquirer* as a reference to bolster claims and the President and others claim media outlets they don't like as "fake news," Wilson seems to be avant here too.

"Left and Right: A Non-Euclidean Perspective," first ran in *Critique: A Journal of Conspiracies and Metaphysics*, in 1988. It has since appeared in many places on the Net, and for good reason: it's writing about political thought that is so lucid and creative and sane it would inevitably be forwarded all over the Net, as geopolitics became crazier and more unstable under the acceleration of information in Western culture that RAW called "The Jumping Jesus Phenomenon." It's still stark staring germane, and you will probably want to force this into the hands of a friend or colleague, because, surely, 'tis not an ill wind yet blows many minds.

"Black Magic and Curses" originally appeared in the hard-copy version of *The Thresher* in 2003.

Some of the topics Wilson addresses in this book are well-known to Wilson readers: atheism, model agnosticism, quantum theory, the many problems of hard-core ideologues, androphobia, James Joyce, dreams and Carl Jung, Korzybski and neurose-mantics, magick, Vico and "theotopology," the subconscious mind and movies, psychedelic drugs and expanded perception, Nietzsche and self-perception, the labyrinthine enigmas and conspiracies involving a small church in the south of France and Vatican banking conspiracies and the Mafia, drug-dealing and modern European fascism; Philip K. Dick, anarchism and liber-tarian thought, Timothy Leary, Einstein, the erroneous percep-tion of what's commonly referred to as "normal," multi-valued logics, alternative economic ideas, literary modernist figures, sexual magick, the occult and secret societies, and the poverty of Euclidean "Left-Right" framing in political thought. Earlier in his career Wilson wrote about longevity and human immortality; in this work he writes about death.

Near the end of the book RAW included snippets of interviews he did from 1977-2002, the last of which was conducted by his longtime friend Paul Krassner in 2002; Krassner brought in Wilson for his legendary countercultural satire magazine *The Realist* in 1959, when Wilson was 27, giving Wilson his first regular writing platform with a column titled "Negative Thinking."

In addition, there are heaping doses of what RAW once referred to as "guerrilla ontology": a zany and Erisian mix of verifiable facts, absurdities, fiction disguised as fact and vice-versa, footnotes, a melange of Joyce, Flann O'Brien, H.P. Lovecraft, dense allusions, parodies of living epistemologists he perennially disagreed with, and the late 20th century serious-but-joking "new religions" of Discordianism and the Church of the Subgenius, of which "The Horror of Howth Hill" includes all this and seems to defy classification.

The form of the book is left for the Reader to discern; Wilson wrote in an at-times gnomish fashion about the subconscious effects of the Form of books. In this he was heavily influenced by the Modernist tradition of Joyce and Pound.

For the reader willing to go the whole nine, pay very close attention to the very first pages of the book. Two brief notes on the section titled "Note" . . .

1.) RAW admits to a variant of a stance of "Intelligent Design." Have you seen this particular take before?

2.) In Wilson's acknowledgment of the "debt" he owes to meta-modes of thought promulgated by Remy de Gourmont, Korzybski, Fuller, Bandler, Shannon and Wiener, and Ezra Pound, it is my own personal experience, and that of many others with whom I've come into personal contact, that each of these ideas or *any one of them* can be studied and implemented by the Reader/Writer/Artist for a lifetime, without exhausting them. These meta-models for thinking and acting creatively can be thought of as disciplines in the sense that yoga or learning a musical instrument is a discipline.

Wilson was the epitome of the freelance writer: outside academe, free to roam across multiple disciplines, not beholden to any Institution and so free to write what others shied away from, astonishingly erudite, seemingly the ideal thinker who sees more and so has a fuller view of the world than journalistic/ academic/ThinkTank thinkers; he was one of a group of thinkers that the Father of the Sociology of Knowledge, Karl Mannheim, called the *freischwebende Intelligenz*, or "socially unattached intelligentsia" — a rare writer/thinker/artist who, because of his or her "situated-ness" in the social scheme, has views less occluded than usual intellectuals and offers novel and nuanced takes on social reality because of this.

— R. Michael Johnson
Penngrove, CA
4 February, 2017

Note

This book intends to change your way of perceiving/conceiving the world, without drugs or drums or Voodoo, simply by using words in certain special ways.

I wrote these polemics, poems, neurolinguistic experiments and assorted meanderings over a period of about 45 years; they represent part of my life's work not previously available in book form — a part that I would now like preserved in that (relatively) Hard Copy.

I hereby acknowledge the debts my works owe to Remy de Gourmont, for his method of **dissociation of ideas**; to Alfred Korzybski, for his formulations of **General Semantics**; to Richard Bandler, for his invention of **neurolinguistic programming**; to Buckminster Fuller for his synergetics; to Claude Shannon and Norbert Weiner for their studies of **control and communication** between animals and/or machines; and to Ezra Pound for **Ideogrammic Method**.

None of them deserve any blame for my errors and blunders.

I don't believe anything, but I have many suspicions. I **strongly** suspect that a world "external to," or at least independent of, my senses exists in some sense.

I also suspect that this world shows signs of intelligent design, and I suspect that such intelligence acts via feedback from all parts to all parts and *without* centralized sovereignty, like the internet; and that it does not function hierarchically, in the style an Oriental despotism, an American corporation or Christian theology.

I somewhat suspect that Theism and Atheism both fail to account for such decentralized intelligence, rich in circular-causal feedback.

I more-than-half suspect that all "good" writing, or all prose and poetry that one wants to read more than once, proceeds from a kind of "alteration in consciousness," i.e., a kind of controlled schizophrenia. (Don't become alarmed — I think good acting comes from the same place.)

I sometimes suspect that what Blake called Poetic Imagination expresses this exact thought in the language of his age, and that visits by "angels" and "gods" state it in even more archaic argot.

These suspicions have grown over 72 years, but as a rather slow and stupid fellow I do not have the *Chutzpah* to proclaim any of them as certitudes. Give me another 72 years and maybe I'll arrive at firmer conclusions.

PART I

BRAIN GYM — SIMPLE EXERCIZES

neuro-semantic challenges to such readers who
think they know who they "are," where they "are"
and what the hell "is" going on around here

NUMBER SIX: I "am" not a number! I "am" a free man!
— *The Prisoner*

NUMBER FIVE: No malfunction! Number Five is alive!
— *Short Circuit*

HANNIBAL LECTER, M.D.: A census taker tried to
quantify me once. I ate his liver with some fava beans and a
nice Chianti.

— *The Silence of the Lambs*

Old Man On A Balcony:
Views Of Monterey Bay #1

Clear blue bay at sunset
And I am stoned and placid—
Free of grief. almost.

The Passion of the Antichrist

Article II. As the Government of the United States of America is not, in any sense, founded on the Christian religion; as it has in itself no character of enmity against the laws, religion, or tranquility, of Mussulmen; and, as the said States never entered into any war, or act of hostility against any Mahometan nation, it is declared by the parties, that no pretext arising from religious opinions, shall ever produce an interruption of the harmony existing between the two countries.

> — TREATY WITH TRIPOLI written by John Adams, vice-president, 1796; passed by Congress 1797; signed by John Adams, president, 1797.

*If you ever believed our founders intended this nation to "be" a Christian country — i.e., to **enforce** Christianity on all citizens and residents, even agnostics, Buddhists, Jews, Muslims, atheists, Daoists, Sihks, etc. — perhaps you should read some of our early history. I suggest that you start with the above treaty, then take a look at the First Amendment to the Constitution, and then read the Jefferson-Adams correspondence 1812-1826.*

__De jure__, this is not a Christian nation.

Of course, this has become a Christian nation __de facto__, by hook and by crook — mostly by crook. This means that non-Christians theoretically have the same legal rights as Christians but in fact they have to fight every hour of every day of every year to prove it, in a system where almost all judges and politicians either "are" Christians or prudently pretend that they "are."

I wrote the original of this in 1965 for a now-defunct journal called __Fact__. It seems worth resurrecting 40 years later because, with Bozo in the White House, the Christians have gotten rambunctious and downright ugly again . . .

For four years, Baltimore endured an atheist in its midst. Not just any atheist, mind you, but the most infamous atheist in America: Madalyn Murray, the woman who filed a lawsuit and got the Supreme Court to kick monotheistic prayers out of the public schools. Ever since the lawsuit brought her to their attention, the good people of Baltimore strove to get rid of Madalyn Murray, and in June 1964, they finally did it. As a result of the methods they used, Madalyn lives now in exile in Hawaii, her arm is partly paralyzed, her hair is almost white at 44, her organization — The Free Thought Society of America — has been wrested away from her, her brother is unemployed, and her son is under a psychiatrist's care. The worst victim of all, however, has been the U.S. Constitution, which has emerged from the affair even more battered than the Murray family.

Those people traditionally concerned about civil liberties have not protested much about the Madalyn Murray case, probably because they find it simply incredible. When I visited Hawaii and spoke to Madalyn Murray's present — day lawyer, Hyman Greenstein, he frankly told me that he himself did not completely believe Madalyn's story when he first agreed to represent her. "She was a human being in trouble," he said. "That was obvious. But I was sure she was exaggerating and dramatizing what had happened. I just didn't believe these things could happen in the United States. Then I went to Baltimore and investigated the facts. Believe me, Jack Ruby didn't face worse prejudgment in Dallas than Madalyn Murray has faced in Baltimore."

In fact, to understand the Madalyn Murray story, one must first understand the City of Baltimore and the State of Maryland, and nothing in America prepares a person for such an understanding. If the founders did not intend this to "be" a Christian *nation*, Maryland remains emphatically a Christian *state*.

Imagine Spain, in the days of the Inquisition, transferred within our borders. Maryland is named for the Virgin Mary; it was founded by Catholics; it is still predominantly Catholic; 17% of all property in the State belongs to the Catholic Church, which pays no taxes on it. Maryland is the only state in the Union that demands a religious qualification for judges; the only state that demands a religious qualification for jurors; the only state that demands a religious qualification for witnesses. Madalyn Murray literally could not testify in her own behalf in any trial there, nor could any other atheist testify for her.

In addition, the legal code has not been substantially revised since 1789, and it perpetuates many old English common-law punishments that have been abolished elsewhere. Particularly crucial to Madalyn Murray, who is under indictment on eight counts of assault against policemen (she charges that the police actually assaulted her), the Maryland laws do not fix a maximum sentence for the crime of assault. The judge can make the prison term as long as he wishes — and Baltimore judges are not noted for their partiality to Madalyn Murray.

If Maryland's laws are Medieval, its folk culture, with its persistent violence, deserves to be called Fascist. It is part of the South: the stink of hatred permeates the air like smog in Los Angeles and grime in New York. Negro homes have been bombed in the past year. Talk to a cabdriver in Baltimore about the "color" problem and hate sprays from him like odor from a skunk — in three minutes he will improvise 90% of the tortures it took de Sade years to dream up, with "Martin Luther Coon" as the principal victim and [U.S. Supreme Court Chief Justice] Earl Warren next in line.

A celebrated lynching in Baltimore not so long ago ended with the hanged man's toes and ears being hacked off by a member of the mob. The ears and toes are probably on somebody's mantelpiece today, and the owner is probably proud of them. Bet on it. He shows them to guests: "Got these babies fighting Communism."

In this little pocket of 13th-century life, Madalyn Murray stood up and declared herself an atheist, an anarchist, and an integrationist. Here she started, and fought to a Supreme Court victory, a suit to end prayers in the public schools. Here she took into her home, and into her Freethought Society of America, Mae Mallory, a feisty Negro militant wanted by the authorities in North Carolina,

And here, Madalyn Murray, after winning her school-prayer case, started a lawsuit to force the United States government to tax church property the same as any other property.

In the March-April 1964 issue of *Fact*, I wrote the first profile of Madalyn Murray to appear in a major magazine. In it I described some typical reactions to Madalyn's activities:

— Day after day the letters from holy people pour in...
"You should be shot!" "Why don't you go peddle your slop in
Russia?" "YOU WICKID ANAMAL" "I will KILL you!"

— The day before Christmas a rock was thrown through the
window, causing $67 worth of damage...

— The phone calls are a barrage of insult, obscenity, threat and
psychotic rambling...

— Her elder son, Bill, now 17, has been beaten up by gangs of
Catholic adolescents more than 100 times.

— Her younger son Garth, who is 9, has begun to have
nightmares because of frequent assaults by other boys.

— Sitting in her office interviewing her I heard a school bus go
by. Every child stuck his head out of the window and shouted,
"Commie, Commie, Commie!"*

~•~

*Only possible in the dark days of McCarthyism and
witch-hunts . . . Forty years later, the American people have grown
and matured. The kids today would shout "Arab-lover."

~•~

My article appeared on the newsstands on April 1, 1964. A few
weeks later, Madalyn Murray wrote to me to say that reporters
from *Time* and *Life* were coming in squads and battalions to
interview her, carrying my article and asking their questions
from it.

(Both *Time* and *Life* later swiped my title, "The Most Hated
Woman in America")

"They're all trying to find errors in your *Fact* piece," Madalyn
told me. "They're sore as hell about *Fact's* expose of errors in
Time and they want to get even." They never found any errors,
although once they thought they had. A Mr. Michael McManus,
of *Time's* Washington office, called Madalyn and announced
that she had lied to me about her Army career. "You weren't
on Eisenhower's staff," he crowed, or croaked, "you never left
North Carolina."

Madalyn's maiden name was Madalyn Mays, and *Time* had
gotten ahold of the WAC record of a different Madalyn Mays.

The *Time* article appeared on May 15, and Madalyn wrote to tell me that now *Esquire* and the *Saturday Evening Post* were doing stories on her. Baltimore, more and more, found itself spotlighted as the nation's atheism capital, and Baltimore did not like it.

Madalyn's cat was strangled.

A series of letters, postmarked Baltimore, became progressively uglier:

"You had better read this carefully! It may be the last one you read. Somebody is going to put a bullet through your fat ass, you scum, you masculine lesbian bitch!"

"You will be killed before too long. Or maybe your pretty little baby boy. The queer looking bastard. You are a bitch and your son is a bastard."

"Slut! Slut! Slut! Bitch slut from the devil!"

Madalyn files all such letters in a folder which she someday hopes to publish under the title, *Letters from Christians.* But the growing murderousness of the correspondence, as national publicity about her increased, began to get under her skin, and she bought Tsar, a large German shepherd, and trained him to attack on command.

Meanwhile, somebody in the Baltimore Post Office began systematically underlining the first three letters in her name, so that all of her mail reached her insultingly addressed, "*Mad*alyn Murray." Madalyn complained to the Baltimore Postmaster and was told that an investigation had failed to unearth the culprit, although her mail continued to arrive disfigured.

Then, suddenly, all mail stopped. Madalyn complained to the Baltimore Postmaster and to the Postmaster General in Washington, with no immediate results.

Then an unidentified Communist* called and told her that her mail was being delivered to the Communist Party of Maryland. The C. P. leaders, having a long-standing grudge against Madalyn "(All Communists have a long-standing grudge against all anarchists," Madalyn says), had not bothered to notify her that they were receiving her mail. Madalyn again complained to the Postmaster General and soon began to receive her mail anew. Not long after, the "_Mad_alyn Murray" underlinings were resumed.

~•~

*Yes, Virginia, real Communists roamed the land in those days, and Senator Joseph McCarthy didn't imagine them all. He just invented the technique of using "Communist" as a label for anybody he didn't like, knowing that the Terminally Gullible (who cannot distinguish between labels and persons labeled) make up a majority in many voting districts.

~•~

The good Christian people of Baltimore devised other harassments.

The garbage cans at Madalyn's office were dumped onto the ground every day, before they could be collected. Her son Bill received traffic tickets almost every time he went out driving.

Somebody entered the backyard of her home at night, was attacked by Tsar, and rammed a piece of wood down the dog's throat.

Coming into her office one morning, she found two officials of the City zoning board going through her correspondence, and when she tried to have them arrested for trespassing, no judge would issue a warrant.

Each of Madalyn's efforts to cope with these harassments brought on further difficulties. To handle the garbage problem, she boned up on Baltimore law and found that a business firm could use its own incinerator if the incinerator was a specific legal size. She bought an incinerator that met the requirements, but the first time she used it several fire trucks rushed to the scene with sirens blaring and extinguished the blaze.

When Madalyn quoted the law to the fire chief, he informed her that in his judgment the incinerator was unsafe.

Madalyn picked the most flagrant of Bill Murray's traffic indictments and fought it in court. Although two witnesses, one a policeman's son, testified that Bill had not committed the violation (driving through a red light), the court found him guilty.

Madalyn Murray continued to fight back. Her lawyer at that time, Leonard Kerpelman, found in his law books that a citizen unable to obtain redress from a judge could appeal directly to a grand jury. Madalyn persuaded him to make this last attempt to register charges against the zoning-board inspectors who had been caught in her office.

A few hours later, Madalyn received a frantic phone call. Kerpelman was in jail. He had knocked on the office door of the grand jury and was immediately arrested for contempt of court. Rushed before Judge T. Barton Harrington, Kerpelman was quickly convicted and fined $25. Having only $24.78 in his pockets, Kerpelman was taken to jail.

Madalyn paid his fine and got him out, but he was shaken by the experience and began to show increasing disinclination to represent her further. He also was worried that Madalyn's enemies might use the contempt conviction to try to have him disbarred. To head this off, he appealed his case. Strangely, he was represented by William L. Marbury and Marvin Braiterman. Marbury acted as the attorney for the Roman Catholic Church in Madalyn's "tax the churches" suit, and Braiterman as the attorney for the Episcopal Church in the same suit.

They appeared before Judge Michael J. Manley and persuaded him to drop the case against Kerpelman. This was the first, and only, case ever won in the City of Baltimore by anyone associated with Madalyn Murray.

Kerpelman subsequently broke with Madalyn and is now publicly working against her.

The next act of the melodrama began, like the Fall of Troy, with a runaway girl. The fair Helen in this case was 17-year-old Susan Abramowitz, who met Bill Murray in high school. Bespectacled, timid, and "intellectual," Susan soon became emotionally involved with Madalyn's elder son.

What happened after that remains subject to dispute. Susan's parents, Leonard and Jeanne Abramowitz, charge that the Murrays "induced Susan to abandon her Jewish faith" and to move into the Murray household. Susan claims that her parents beat her cruelly for associating with Bill, broke her glasses, cracked her teeth, and blackened her eyes, and that she sought refuge in the Murray home only after her own parents threw her out of theirs.

The Baltimore papers printed all of the charges made by Mr. and Mrs. Abramowitz, but not a single word of the countercharges by Susan and the Murrays. When Madalyn complained, an editor told her that her charges were libelous and that he could be sued for printing them. (Actually, the charges against Mr. and Mrs. Abramowitz are legally protected against libel action, being contained in a brief filed by Susan Abramowitz, William Murray, and Madalyn Murray in the Criminal Court of Baltimore, under Article 26, Sections 91-101 of the Baltimore Code. Among other complaints of cruelty, this document charges, on Susan's testimony, that her father struck her on one occasion so hard that he fractured a bone in his own hand.)

The Abramowitzes obtained an order from Judge James Cullen on June 2 placing Susan in custody of an aunt and uncle. Susan immediately fled to New York City and took refuge with a friend. Two weeks later, she and Bill returned to Maryland and were secretly married.

Then they returned to the Murray household on June 20. A neighbor recognized Susan and called the police. "You'd think it was Dillinger they were after," Madalyn says. "A whole fleet of squad cars came racing to our house." In their haste, the police forgot to obtain a warrant for Susan's arrest, so the Murrays refused to open the door. The police tore open a screen door and rushed in.

What happened next is again a matter of dispute. The Murrays charge that they were brutally beaten by the police. According to the police version, Madalyn Murray singlehandedly assaulted eight policemen. (The next day, only five policemen claimed to have been assaulted by her, but two days later three additional policemen pressed charges.)

Madalyn's mother, Leddie Mays, an elderly woman suffering from arthritis, is accused of assaulting still another policeman. Mrs. Mays admits touching a policeman. "He had Bill on the ground and kept clubbing him, so I grabbed his shoulders from behind and yelled at him to stop. 'You're killing the boy!' I said." For her crime, 73-year-old Mrs. Mays was promptly knocked unconscious by the club of another guardian of the peace.

When I asked the plump 44-year-old Madalyn how in the world she managed to assault eight armed policemen, she grinned. "You didn't know I was such an Amazon, did you?"

More seriously, she said, "I bet every hood in the country will migrate to Baltimore when word gets out that eight of their policemen can be assaulted by one overweight, middle-aged housewife."

Madalyn was taken to University Hospital for injuries, her mother was taken to Union Memorial Hospital, and Bill was taken to jail, where he claims the police beat him all night long while one of them read the Bible aloud to him. "We'll make a Christian out of you yet, you cocksucker," he quotes one of his tormentors as saying.*

~•~

*And you thought it only happened in Iraq?

~•~

The next day the Murrays were released, and they carefully hid a tape-recording that Bill had made of the tussle, in which Sgt. Charles Kelly is clearly heard admitting that the police had no search warrant. The matter of the warrant apparently began worrying the authorities at this point, for State Attorney W.J. O'Donnell suddenly called a press conference to explain that the police do not need to have a warrant in their possession when entering a house if they have reason to believe a warrant has been issued.

This legal theory appears startlingly new. I called the Attorney General's office in Washington to inquire about this and was told, "I never heard of such a doctrine." When I asked if I could quote this, my informant hastily added that the Attorney General's office does not officially utter opinions on the law for the press and suggested that I call the American Civil Liberties Union.

At the A.C.L.U., Mr. Alan Reitman, a lawyer, stated flatly, "There is no such doctrine in American law. If a search is to be made, the police must have a warrant."

Madalyn's Hawaiian lawyer, Hyman Greenstein, says bluntly, "O'Donnell's doctrine wouldn't last as long as a snowball in hell in any court outside Maryland. Even in Maryland, it wouldn't

Email to the Universe

stand up against anybody but Madalyn Murray."*

~•~

* Regard these legal facts as dated 1965 — i.e., 35 BB. [before Bozo].

~•~

Madalyn and her family held a conference. Considering her 100% record of defeat in all Baltimore courts, they decided that if she remained in Baltimore she would undoubtedly be convicted on assault charges. They recalled that the prison sentence for assault, in Maryland, can be as high as the judge chooses to make it. That night the Murrays, with Bill's new wife, Susan, drove to Washington and took a plane to Hawaii.

Baltimore was at last rid of its atheist.

The holy folk of Baltimore were not satisfied yet. Leo Murphy, a Baltimore artist who had done a drawing for the cover of Madalyn's magazine, *American Atheist,* began to receive phone calls from people threatening to kill him or to throw acid in his face and blind him.

An Ida D. Collins wrote gleefully to the *Baltimore Sun,* "Madalyn Murray took the wrong route when she left us this week. Instead of Hawaii, she should have taken a 'slow boat to China' and do us all a favor and stay there." The insurance company cancelled the insurance on her house and, although the mortgage payments were up-to-date, the bank began court action to foreclose because the house no longer was insured. And in Hawaii, Madalyn watched her son Bill begin to slip into a mental breakdown.

Bill had taken his share of punishment during the previous four years with Spartan solidarity. After his night in the Baltimore jail, however, he suddenly broke into screams before Judge Joseph G. Finnerty and shouted, "You Christian, you Catholic, I won't go back to that cell and be worked over again!" In Hawaii, Bill began to sit for long periods in his room, utterly silent. Occasionally, he would come out of his stupor and attack his mother verbally, saying she had ruined his life by getting him mixed up in the school-prayers case. Then he locked himself in his room and refused to talk to anyone for nearly a week. He is now under the care of psychiatrist Linus Pauling Jr. He has come out of his silent depression, but retains a violent hatred of his mother, whom he blames for all his troubles.

Back in Baltimore, Madalyn was tried *in absentia* for contempt of court and sentenced to one year in jail. The Baltimore authorities also got busy and created a new law that fixed a minimum 20-year sentence for each count of assault against a policeman. Madalyn Murray, the *Baltimore Sun* announced, now faces at least 160 years' imprisonment if she ever returns to Baltimore. I asked Madalyn's lawyer, Hyman Greenstein, about this: "Doesn't the Constitution prohibit such *ex post facto* punishments?" "Yes," he said, "but the Constitution also prohibits trials *in absentia*, and Baltimore has already done that to her." He added: "Assault, you know, is a misdemeanor. If they get away with it, she'll be the first American ever to serve life for eight misdemeanors."

Meanwhile, a gang of people moved into Madalyn's business office, announced that they were the "Freethought Society of America," and tried to use the bank account Madalyn kept under the society's name. Madalyn's fight against *the coup d'etat* has followed the traditional pattern in Baltimore courts: She has lost every single hearing.

Heading the group occupying Madalyn's office is Lemoin Cree, a 26-year-old biologist who works at Fort Detrick, where the U.S. Army carries on research in the creation of artificial bubonic-plague epidemics, anthrax and other methods of biological warfare. Mr. Cree and his associates insist they were appointed by the "board of directors" of the Freethought Society. Madalyn Murray insists there is no board of directors of the Freethought Society, and showed me the by-laws to prove it.

Madalyn is convinced that Cree and his group are "Catholic agents." A friend of mine, who knows the atheist movement the way Clark Kent knows the inside of the phone booth at the Daily Planet, laughed at this. "Madalyn is breaking under the strain," he said.

"The Church has given her such a hard time, she's beginning to see priests everywhere." According to this informant, Lemoin Cree and his associates are actually atheists, but atheists whose politics are Right-wing and who are embittered by the fact that Madalyn Murray, the only atheist to achieve national publicity, is conspicuously Left-wing.

Since the office contained several hundred dollars worth of furniture belonging, not to the "Freethought Society of America," but to Madalyn's mother, Leddie Mays, Madalyn sold this furniture to her friend, Mae Mallory, who thereupon tried to obtain a robbery warrant against the group in the office. A Baltimore judge ruled that the bill of sale was not legal. The bill of sale had been witnessed by a notary public in Hawaii, and the judge declared that, under Maryland law, it had to have been witnessed by a clerk of a Hawaiian court, not by a notary public.

Lawyer Joseph Wase, representing Mae Mallory in this matter, insists there is no such Maryland law.

According to Miss Mallory, however, the judge involved had said of Madalyn, "That atheist doesn't have any rights in this State."

Yes, all this is happening in Baltimore, Maryland, in the United States of America, in the Year of Their Lord 1965.

Going from Baltimore to Honolulu must be like ascending from the "nethermost" or darkest circle of hell to the pinnacle of paradise. In every way, Hawaii seems the antithesis of Baltimore. It is the most cosmopolitan of American states, and the most tolerant. Racial harmony is so good that even the year-long parade of tourists — with its high percentage of Legionnaires, werewolves, warlocks, Storm Troopers, monsters, and miscellaneous Ugly Americans — does not undermine it.

Shortly after her well-publicized arrival in Hawaii, Madalyn telephoned lawyer Greenstein and asked to see him. Hyman Greenstein is a legend throughout Hawaii. Everybody told me he was the model for Lieutenant Greenwald in Herman Wouk's *The Caine Mutiny*, that he is a fanatical devotee of sports-car racing, that he loves "impossible" cases, and that during World War II he won so many "impossible" courts-martial that Admiral Halsey personally intervened to have him transferred out of the Pacific area.

In one notorious court-martial, the president of the court lost his head and called Greenstein "a son of a bitch." Greenstein calmly turned to the court clerk and asked, "Did you get that down?" Court was immediately adjourned. It reconvened a few minutes later to dismiss the charges against Greenstein's clients.

A short, soft-spoken man, Greenstein always wears green bow ties and his office is decorated in shades of green. Madalyn warned me, "The green is some kind of personal symbol to him. He is not amused when somebody says, 'Oh, are you Irish, Mr. Greenstein?'"

When it became known that Madalyn had called for an appointment, Greenstein's staff was dismayed. His secretary told the lawyer, "Everybody wants to know if you're going to take that awful woman's case." Greenstein called the entire staff into his office and left the door open. "That door is always open to people in trouble, whatever their beliefs," he said. "Does anybody want to quit?"

Nobody did.

Mr. Greenstein has prepared a blockbuster of a brief against Madalyn's extradition. He charges that "No court in the State of Maryland is legally constituted" because of that State's religious qualifications for judges, juries, and witnesses, and that, therefore, "The entire judicial system of Maryland is in violation of and repugnant to the Constitution of the United States." He further argues that Maryland's failure to prescribe maximum penalties for assault is "barbaric, outmoded; and repugnant to the Constitutional guarantees against cruel and unusual punishment."

Not only has Madalyn found a conscientious and capable lawyer in Hawaii, but she has also come upon some truly good Christians. Eighteen Hawaiian clergymen, including a Catholic priest, signed a petition urging Governor John A. Burns not to approve the extradition of Madalyn back to "religious persecution in Maryland." In fact, as soon as she landed on the island she was offered help by a church. The Rev. Gene Bridges, of the Unitarian Church, called her on the phone to ask if she had found a home yet. When he learned that she hadn't, he invited her whole family to spend the night in the back room of his church. Mr. Bridges immediately thereafter started calling the board of directors of his church for approval. The board has 15 members. After calling eight and receiving 7 approvals, he invited the Murrays to stay until they found a home. They remained in the church for two weeks.

"Madalyn has mellowed a lot, due to the Unitarian Church," one Unitarian told me. Madalyn now attends the Unitarian services every Sunday and sends her son Garth, 10, to the church's Sunday School. I attended services with Madalyn at Mr. Bridges's church one Sunday. It began with some recorded music by Dizzy Gillespie, then Mr. Bridges read selections from Anne Morrow *Lindbergh's Gift From the Sea* and e.e. cummings's *I: 6 non-lectures*. Madalyn listened enthralled and said to me as we came out, "Isn't he wonderful?"

That afternoon, Madalyn and I visited the largest Buddhist church in Honolulu and she picked up several free pamphlets of Buddhist sermons. "You're not getting religious, are you?" I joked.

"Hell, no," she said. "I'm just curious."

For Madalyn Murray remains unshakable — and unsinkable. Sitting on the veranda of her little rented house at 1060 Spencer Street on the side of Punchbowl Volcano, with the panorama of Honolulu and the looming whale-like hump of Diamond Head spread before us, she told me eagerly of her plans in the "tax the churches" suit.

"We're going to subpoena the Archbishop of Baltimore, Lawrence Sheehan," she said, "and make him tell how much money the church collects from its property in Baltimore, how much of that remains in Baltimore, how much remains in the United States, and how much goes to Rome. That information has never been available before, but it will be now. People can add and subtract, you know. Wait 'til the American public starts figuring out how low its taxes would be if all that untaxed money weren't flowing out of the country."

Madalyn is also planning to run for Governor of Hawaii, on a platform in which a fourth branch of government — the economic — would be added to the executive, legislative, and judicial. She is broke, in debt to the chin, the Baltimore courts won't let her use her bank account, and she is still riding "at a gallop, high in heart."

The other victims are less buoyant. Bill Murray is still under psychiatric care. Garth, Madalyn's other son, has frequent nightmares about "seven-foot tall cops" beating his Mommy. Old Mrs. Mays is subdued and anxious. Madalyn's brother Irving, 48, gave up a good factory job, not wanting to be the only Murray in Baltimore and a standing target for the remaining hatred, and he has not found a new job yet. As for the victim that has suffered most — the U.S. Constitution — it is not flesh and blood and, hence, doesn't feel its wounds, but if it could speak it would probably whimper softly.

Postscript: Madalyn Murray disappeared in Texas in 1995 and police found her buried body about two years later. Murder. The Texas cops say another atheist did it.

All of the "shocking" and unconstitutional persecutions she faced have become legal and normal now, thanks to the War on [Some] Drugs, the War on [Some] Terrorists and the U.S.A.PATRIOT Act.

But don't fret; the targets of choice all seem mid-eastern: Muslims or those who "look like" Muslims to the ignorant, including some Sihks and Hindus.

Old Man On A Balcony:
Views Of Monterey Bay #2

After the fog lifts.

A naked beauty: blue sky

with buttermilk clouds

The One "Law" of Economics

I have read a great deal of economic *theory* for over 50 years now, but have found only one economic "law" to which I can find *NO* exceptions:

Where the State prevents a free market, by banning any form of goods or services, consumer demand will create a black market for those goods or services, at vastly higher prices.

Can YOU think of a single exception to this law?

THOUGHTS TO PONDER

First of all, if the State takes upon itself the right to kill, then inevitably those who oppose the State will arrogate to themselves the same right. Revolutionaries and terrorists do in fact use that argument with some sincerity. "If the State can take life, then we can also take life." After all, they generally claim that they represent the people and that the State doesn't. I am opposed to the cheapening of human life created by that rhetoric on both sides.

Sean MacBride

Where memory dwells*
Love takes its Throne

— Guido Cavalcanti [1260-1300]

~•~

* dove sta memora

~•~

Old Man On A Balcony: Views Of Monterey Bay #3

Lights across the bay —

White jewels scattered, shattered

In a deep black box

The Celtic Roots of Quantum Theory

The reality of metaphysics is the reality of masks.
— Oscar Wilde

We lived in Los Angeles and I thought I had a movie deal when I wrote this for an Irish magazine c. 1990. As far as I remember, they never paid for it and, probably, never published it . . . But I think it deserves an audience, and it seems appropriate for a volume of guerrilla neurolinguistics.

The movie deal dropped dead, or went into coma, too.

According to "conventional wisdom," and/or conventional folly, the ontological roots of Quantum Mechanics lie in German Idealist philosophy of the 19th Century. I dare to offer a different view here.

The day in 1982 when my wife, Arlen, and I arrived in Ireland we tried her battery-operated radio to listen avidly to whatever we might find: our way of dipping our toes in the new culture before plunging in to its alien waters totally. By the kind of coincidence that I don't regard as coincidental, we found an RTE* interviewer discussing local legends about the pooka with a Kerry farmer. As a longtime pookaphile, I found the conversation spellbinding, but the best part came at the end:

"But do you believe in the pooka yourself?" asked the RTE man.

"That I do not." the farmer replied firmly, "and I doubt much that he believes in me either!"

~•~

* RTE = Radio Telefís na hEirenn, the State-owned but feisty and independent radio-TV monopoly.

~•~

I knew then that I had indeed found my spiritual homeland, wherever I may otherwise roam, and that Yeats and Joyce and

O'Brien had not risen out of a vacuum. We had planned to stay six months; we eventually stayed six years.

Anthony Burgess once argued that English English, American English and all the other varieties of Anglophonics have become rational and pragmatic (closure-oriented), but Irish English remains ludic and esthetic (open-oriented). The rest of us speak dry prose; the Irish speak playful poetry.

While I see some truth in that formulation, I would prefer to describe all-other-English as belonging to what Neurolinguistic therapist Dr. Richard Bandler calls the meta-model (statements we can logically judge as true or false), and Irish English as belonging to the Milton-model (statements not containable in true-false logic but capable of seducing us into sudden new perceptions).

The Milton-model, named after Dr. Milton Erickson — "the greatest therapeutic hypnotist of the 20th Century," in the opinion of his peers — contains no propositions subject to proof or disproof, uses language the way that Kerry farmer did, and can cause both intellectual and physiological transformations. Because of his many successes in curing the allegedly incurable, Dr. Erickson often became proclaimed "the Miracle Worker."

Oddly, most of Dr. Erickson's patients did not think they had undergone hypnosis at all. They just remembered having a friendly chat with an unusually sympathetic doctor.

According to the Korzybski-Whorf-Sapir hypothesis, **the language a people speak habitually influences their sense perceptions, their "concepts" and even the way they feel about themselves and the world in general.** "A change in language can transform our appreciation of the cosmos," as Whorf stated the case.

The clinical record of Erickson and his school indicates that language tricks can even make us ill or make us well again.

The Irish neurolinguistic system illustrates these theorems uncommonly well.

Whether you call it ludic language, Ericksonian hypnosis, or the verbal equivalent of throwing LSD into the linguistic drinking water, Irish English even in the professional hands of all of Ireland's greatest writers shows the same non-Aristotelian "illogic" or Zen humor as that Kerry farmer.

Witness:

> Death and life were not
> till man made up the whole,
> Made lock, stock and barrel
> out of his bitter soul
>
> — W.B. Yeats

Try taking all literary, scientific, theological and philosophic connotations out of "death" and "life" see them merely as two predicaments of grammar — and then — ?

"Men are born liars." — Liam O'Flaherty, in the first sentence of his autobiography.

Logicians call this an Empedoclean paradox. To an Irish stylist, it does not appear Empedoclean nor paradoxical, but merely another pregnant bull. Since O'Flaherty belonged to the class of all men, he lied; but if he lied, his statement does not carry conviction, so maybe he told the truth . . .

"Are the commentators on *Hamlet* really mad or only pretending to be mad?" — Oscar Wilde.

> Thy spirit keen through radiant mien
> Thy shining throat and smiling eye
> Thy little palm, thy side like foam —
> I cannot die!
>
> O woman, shapely as the swan,
> In a cunning house hard-reared was I:
> O bosom white, O well-shaped palm,
> I shall not die!
>
> — Padraic Colum

(A Romantic poem, in style; anti-Romantic in content — whether you think of the female as a human lady or a symbol of Ireland *a la* Cathleen ni Houlihan, Dark Rosaline or *shan van vocht*, Colum still will not die for Her.)

"Durtaigh disloighal reibel aighris dogs." — Myles na gCopaleen

(It only makes sense if you pronounce it as Gaelic, and then it becomes ordinary English, expressing an ordinary English attitude toward "their Hibernian neighbors.)

"They shall come to know good." — James Joyce. (Read it silently, then read it aloud.)

"There is in mankind a certain *************************** *Hic multa* *** ********** *disiderantur* ********************************** *******. And this I take to be a clear solution of the matter." — Jonathan Swift [all expurgations in Swift's original text.]

"I considered it desirable that he should know nothing about me but it was even better if he knew several things that were quite wrong."— Flann O'Brien

Or, to take a few examples that lend themselves better to condensation than quotation:

Consider Swift's "pamphlet war" with the astrologer Partridge, in which Swift claimed Partridge had died and Partridge vehemently insisted on his continued viability. Swift won hands down by pointing out that just because a man claims he's alive does not compel us to accept his uncorroborated testimony.

Or: Bishop Berkeley, proving with meticulous logic that the universe doesn't exist, although God admittedly has a persistent delusion that it does.

Or: the scandalous matter of Molly Bloom's adulterous affairs in *Ulysses*, which number between one (Hugh Boylan) and more than thirty (including a few priests and Lords Mayor and one Italian organ grinder), depending on which of Joyce's 100+ narrators one chooses to believe. This grows more perplexing when one realizes that some of the "narrators" seem more like styles than persons: styles masquerading as persons.

Or maybe the ghosts of departed stylists, in the sense that Berkeley called Newton's infinitesimals the ghosts of departed quantities?

Colonized and post — Colonized peoples learn much about text and sub-text; and Yeats did not develop his mystique of

Mask and Anti-Mask out of Hermetic metaphysics alone. In my six years sampling Dublin pubs (1982-88) I overheard many conversations in the form:

— I saw your man last night.
— Oh? And?
— All going well there.

Who the devil is "your man"? Does this concern hashish from Amsterdam for the Punk Rock crowd, gelignite on its way to Derry, or just ingrained habits Masks and Anti-Masks — shaped by 800 years of Occupation? After all, the speakers might simply refer to tickets for a soccer game . . . (You will find a similarly oblique dialogue in the second section of the "Wandering Rocks" montage in *Ulysses*, except that "your man" has become "that certain party." Palestinians have probably become that "Irish" by now.)

I do not claim that Sassanach conquest alone produced Ireland's elusive wit and ludic poesy; but it sharpened tendencies already there as far back as Finn Mac Cumhal. Yeats says somewhere that Ireland was part of Asia until the Battle of the Boyne; but that dating merely represents W.B.'s reactionary Romanticism. Joyce knew that Ireland remained part of Asia; *Finnegans Wake* explicitly tells us it emerged from "the Haunted Ink bottle, no number, Brimstone Walk, Asia in Ireland."

You can test one level of truth in this by simply asking directions in both Tokyo and Dublin. In either place you will encounter old-fashioned politeness and friendliness unknown in most of the industrial world, and you will get sent in the wrong direction. Hostile humor? I think not. Asiatic languages, including Irish English, simply do not accommodate themselves to Newtonian grids, either spatial or temporal.

Arlen and I used to play a game in Dublin: whenever we saw two clocks we would compare them. They never agreed.

In Cork, the four clocks on the City Hall tower always show four different times; locals call them "the Four Liars."

The sociologist may class this as "post-Colonial syndrome" — based on the baleful suspicion that the English invented time to make a man work more than the Good Lord ever intended — but Joyce noted that the only three world-class philosophers of Celtic genealogy, Erigena, Berkeley and Bergson, all denied the reality of time (and only Berkeley lived under English rule).

A Dublin legend tells of an Englishman who, noting that the two clocks in Padraic Pearse station do not agree, commented loudly that this discordance "is so damned typically bloody Irish." A Dubliner corrected him: "Sure now, if they agreed, one of them would be superfluous."

Even more in the Daoist tradition: Two Cork men meet on the street. "Filthy weather for this time of year," ventures the first.

"Ah, sure," replies the second, "it isn't this time of year at all, man."

Compare the Chinese proverb, "Summer never becomes winter, infants never grow old." Einstein's relativity and Dali's melting clocks belong to the same universe as these Hiberno-Chinese Eccentricities.

In County Clare and the West generally one often hears the grammatical form, "My uncle was busy feeding the pigs one night *and* I a girl of six years . . ." (One also hears this in Synge's plays — all of them.) Elsewhere in the English-speaking world one would hear, "My uncle was busy feeding the pigs one night *when* I was a girl of six years . . . " The Irish English retains the grammar of Irish Gaelic, but it thereby retains the timeless or Daoist sense of a world where every now exists but no now ever "becomes" another now.

Nor does this neurolinguistic grid — or reality-tunnel — only manifest in Irish speech and literature. William Rowan Hamilton, one of Eire's greatest mathematicians — probably the greatest of all — made many contributions, but two have special interest for us here:

One — Hamilton invented non-commutative math, which I shall try to explain. In arithmetic, $2 \times 3 = 3 \times 2$, or they both equal 6 (if you haven't raised too many pints that night). Ordinary algebra, the only kind most of us ever learned in school, follows the same rule: $a \times b = b \times a$. Everybody knows that, right? Well, in Hamilton's algebra, $a \times b$ does NOT $= b \times a$.

More "Asiatic" influence? More of the Celtic Twilight? Well, in Pure Mathematics, you can invent any system you want as long as it remains internally consistent; finding out if it has any resemblance to the experiential world remains the job of the physicist, or the engineer. It required about 100 years to find a "fit" for Hamiltonian algebra, and then it revolutionized physics. Hamilton's math describes the sub-atomic (quantum) world, and ordinary math does not.

The reader may classify Hamilton's feat as a variety of precognition, or maybe just as more of the Hibernian compulsion to challenge everything the Saxon regards as unquestionable.

Two — Physicists of Hamilton's day endlessly debated whether light travels as "waves" like water or as discrete "particles" like bullets. He supported both *totally contradictory* models, although in different contexts. Among Fundamentalist Materialists, they call this the Heresy of "perspectivism," but again, after 100 years, it became part of quantum mechanics, although usually credited to Niels Bohr, who only rediscovered it. Perspectivism also haunts postmodern literary theory, cultural anthropology and, especially, the Joyce Industry, as more and more Joyce scholars realize that all of the 100+ narrative "voices" in *Ulysses* seem equally true in some sense, equally untrue in some sense, and equally beyond either/or logic in any sense.

Quantum Mechanics owes a second huge debt, and a perpetual headache, to another Irish physicist, John Stewart Bell.

Bell's Theorem, a mathematical demonstration by Dr. Bell published in 1965, has become more popular than Tarot cards with New Agers, who think they understand it but generally don't. Meanwhile it remains controversial with physicists, some of whom think they understand it but many of whom frankly admit they find it as perplexing as Mick Jagger with his guitar hopping around like a chicken on LSD in the middle of a Beethoven string quartet.

In a (hazardous) attempt to translate Bell's math into the verbal forms in which we discuss what physics "means," Bell seems to have proved that any two "particles" once in contact will continue to act as if connected no matter how far apart they move in "space" or "time" (or in space-time). You can see why

New Agers like this: it sounds like it supports the old magick idea that if you get ahold of a hair from your enemy, anything you do to the hair will affect him.

Most physicists think a long series of experiments, especially those of Dr. Alain Aspect and others in the 1970's and Aspect in 1982 have settled the matter. Quantum "particles" (or "waves") once in contact certainly seem "connected," or correlated, or at least dancing in the same ballet . . . But not all physicists have agreed. Some, the AntiBellists, still publish criticisms of alleged defects in the experiments. These arguments seem too technical to be summarized here, and only a small minority still cling to them, but this dissent needs to be mentioned since most New Agers don't know about it, and regard Bell's math with the same reverence Catholics have for Papal dogma.

The most daring criticism of Bell comes from Dr. N. David Berman of Columbia, who believes he has refined the possible interpretations of Bell down to two:

(1) non-locality ("total rapport") and

(2) solipsism.

We will explain non-locality below, but Dr. Berman finds it so absurd that he prefers solipsism. ("Is The Moon There When Nobody Looks?" *Physics Today*, April 1985. He says the moon, and everything else, doesn't exist until perceived; Bishop Berkeley has won himself one more convert.)

Among those who accept Bell's Theorem, Dr. David Bohm of the University of London offers three interpretations of what it means:

> It may mean that everything in the universe is in a kind of total rapport, so that whatever happens is related to everything else; or it may mean that there is some kind of information that can travel faster than the speed of light; or it may mean that our concepts of space and time have to be modified in some way that we don't understand. [London Times, 20 Feb 1983.]

Bohm's first model, "total rapport," also called non-locality, brings us very close — very, very close — to Oriental monism: "All is One," as in Vedanta, Buddhism and Daoism. It also brings us in hailing distance of Jungian synchronicity, an idea that seems "occult" or worse to most scientists, even if it won the endorsement of Wolfgang Pauli, a quantum heavyweight and Nobel laureate. You can see why New Agers like this; you will find it argued with unction and plausibility in Capra's *The Tao of Physics*. It means atomic particles remain correlated because everything always remains correlated.

I suggest that physicists often explain this in Chinese metaphors because they don't know as much about Ireland as they do about China, and because they haven't read *Finnegans Wake*.

The strongest form of this non-local model, called super-determinism, claims that everything "is" one thing, or at least one process. From the Big Bang to the last word of this sentence and beyond, nothing can become other than it "is," since everything remains part of a correlated whole. Nobody has openly expressed this view but several (Stapp, Herbert, et al.) have accused others, especially Capra, of unknowingly endorsing it.

Bohm's second alternative, information faster-than-light, brings us into realms previously explored only in science fiction. Bell's particles may be correlated because they act as parts of an FTL (faster than light) cosmic Internet. If I can send an FTL message to my grandpa, it might change my whole universe to the extent that I wouldn't exist at all. (E.g., he might suffer such shock that he would drop dead on the spot and not survive to reproduce.) We must either reject this as impossible, or else it leads to the "parallel universe" model: I'm here in this universe, but in the universe next door the message removed me, so I never sent it there. Remind you, a bit, of that Kerry farmer?

Even more radical offshoots of this notion have come forth from Dr. John Archibald Wheeler. Dr. Wheeler has proposed that every atomic or subatomic experiment we perform changes every particle in the universe everywhichway in time, back to the Big Bang. The universe becomes constant creation, as in Sufism, but atomic physicists, not Allah, serve as its creators. Yeats again wakes? (He would, of course, place Bards as the creators, not *mere* measurers and calculators, but still the human mind has "made up the whole.")

Dr. Bohm's third alternative, modification of our ideas of space and time, could lead us anywhere . . . including back to the Berkeleyan/Kantian notion that space and time do not exist, except as human projections, like persistent optical illusions. (Some think Relativity already demonstrates that . . . and some will recall Mr. Yeats again, and that Kerry farmer . . .) All particles remain correlated because they never move in space or time, because space and time only exist "in our heads."

Meanwhile, a Dr. Harrison suggests that we may have to abandon Aristotelian logic; i.e., give up classifying things into only the two categories of "true and real" and "untrue and unreal." In between, in Aristotle's excluded middle, we may have the "maybe" proposed by von Neumann in 1933, the probabilistic logics (percentages/gambles) suggested by Korzybski, the four-valued logic of Rapoport (true, false, indeterminate and meaningless), or some system the non-Hibernian world hasn't found yet. The Kerry farmer would handle all of this better than the typical graduate of any university outside Ireland.

And so we see that two Irishman, Hamilton and Bell, have the majority of physicists arguing about issues that make them sound like a symposium among Berkeley, Swift, Yeats, O'Brien and Joyce. Through their literature, speakers raised in Irish English have transformed the printed page; now their mathematicians, raised in the same neurolinguistic grid, have revolutionized our basic notions of "reality," which in the light of what we have seen, badly needs the dubious quotes I just hung on it.

Afterthought 2004: Two of the giants of quantum math, Schrödinger and Dirac, both spent time at the Institute for Advanced Studies in Dublin. Schrödinger, in fact, wrote his most important non-mathematical book there, What Is Life? (1948), in which he defined life as a function of negative entropy. This thought seemed so radical and far-out that nobody began to grasp it until Wiener and Shannon showed that information also behaves like negative entropy. Information = that part of a message you didn't expect; the unpredictable part.

Or, as Wiener once said, great poetry contains high information and political speeches contain virtually none. And, therefore, Life = negative entropy = high information = surprise and initial confusion = tuning-in the previously not-tuned-in . . .

Got it?

THOUGHTS TO PONDER

The challenge before us today, the challenge before our nation and the world is whether we accept the beneficence of Lincoln's Prayer to create ". . . a government of the people, by the people and for the people," or whether we timidly accept the economic, social and political consequences of a government of the corporations, by the corporations and for the corporations.

— Dennis J. Kucinich

Old Man On A Balcony: Views Of Monterey Bay #4

"Weep, weep!" cries a bird

Lost somewhere in fog and mist.

Sunrise with no sun.

Schrödinger's Other Cat

A review of Dirk Gently's Holistic Detective Agency by Douglas Adams

I just found this in the "saved" file on my computer; I think I wrote it around 1982 in Ireland and it probably got published somewhere.

Maybe.

Some people may wonder what a holistic detective agency does, but this new book by Douglas Adams, author of the famous *Hitchhiker's Guide to the Galaxy*, will explain that for them, with such transcendental clarity that the mind, as in Dante's *Paradise*, is nearly blinded by the light.

Can you believe that the disappearance of a cat in London seven years ago cannot only "be" caused by, but equally "be" the cause of the miraculous appearance of the music of J. S. Bach more than two hundred years earlier?

If this thought is incomprehensible to you, then you should either study quantum physics or read *Dirk Gently's Holistic Detective Agency*.

Mr. Adams not only explains the relationship between the missing cat and the Goldberg *Variations*, but also demonstrates how a sofa can get wedged into a stairwell in such a way that you not only cannot get it out, but mathematized computer analysis will prove that it never could have gotten wedged in that position in the first place. Not in this universe, anyway.

Oddly, there is no fantasy in this book. Dirk Gently is as logical as Sherlock Holmes, and all the macoronic inter-connections he masters are necessary parts of the world of modern physics.

It may seem startling to contemplate probability matrices in which everything "is" the cause of everything in one sense and nothing "is" the cause of anything in another sense, but such is the probable world in which we probably live according to current science, and if in one probability matrix Dirk Gently has to move a sofa through a solid wall (and incidentally save humanity from extinction — for which he does not charge extra), the missing cat is then located.

Unfortunately, the cat is dead.

But that's only in one probability matrix. In the matrix next door, the cat is probably alive, but we've seemingly lost Bach. While cat-lovers and music-lovers ponder that conundrum, at least the matrix in which humanity is destroyed has been avoided.

But the damned couch is still stuck in the stairwell, in the probability matrix where we lost Bach and saved the cat.

Alas, I fear that those who talk of "holistic medicine" have little inkling of how holistic sub-atomic physics can get. I can only urge that all who wish a glimpse of how our probable universe probably operates should rush right out and buy this marvelous book, which works equally well as a thriller, a mystery, a farce and the most scientific novel of the year.

Old Man On A Balcony:
Views Of Monterey Bay #5

Bay like blackboard grey

Monterey lost in white fog

Shortest day draws nigh

THOUGHTS TO PONDER

nothing matters but the quality
of the affection —
in the end — that has carved the trace in the mind
dove sta memora

— Ezra Pound, Canto 76

Paranoia

A few pages back, I wrote;

> Where the State prevents a free market, by banning any form of goods or services, consumer demand will create a black market for those goods or services, at vastly higher prices.

Remember?

Those who profit continually from this black market will never, never, never, of course, contribute financial aid or other goods and services to the politicians whose prohibitions and inhibitions prevent the lower prices of the previous free market.

Of course not.

That "is" a Conspiracy Theory, and all Conspiracy Theories "are" whacko.

Of course.

And Saddam Hussein made all those Wicked Weapons of Mass Destruction disappear by sprinkling them with fairy dust.

Of course.

Old Man On A Balcony:
Views Of Monterey Bay #6

MIDNIGHT HAIKU

Mottled blueblack sky.

A sudden moon — briefly! Then:

Blueblack mottled sky ...

Black Magick & Curses

Secrets of ye Dark Arte call'd Ducdame

Zounds! I was never so bethump'd with words
Since I first call'd my brother's father dad.
> — The Bastard in King John Act 11, Scene 1
> by Wm. Shakespeare

People sometimes ask me, "Doctor Bandler, do you have to use that kind of language?" And my answer is "Fuck, yes!"
> — Dr. Richard Bandler, Neuro-Linguistic Programming
> Workshop, Los Angeles, 1999

Dr. Harold Garfinkle, a UCLA sociologist, has written a whole book recounting experiments that demonstrate that it takes remarkably little breaching of local Game Rules before subjects begin to show disorientation, anxiety, anger, panic, delusions, "inappropriate" emotions, etc. — *wigging out*, or *going ballistic* in lay language.

Even standing with your nose closer to a person's face than the social norm for conversation can provoke remarkable uneasiness with remarkable alacrity; it may even trigger "homosexual panic." Doc Garfinkle did experiments to prove it.

To treat one's parents with the politeness and formality usually given to landlords and landladies can produce memorable freak-outs, sometimes involving pleas for psychiatric intervention. Etc. (More experiments: See Garfinkle, *Studies in Ethnomethodology*, Prentice-Hall, NJ, 1967.)

Garfinkle's data demonstrates that **humans at this primitive stage of terrestrial evolution** have so many taboos that they cannot remember or articulate most of them; but they quickly become physiologically "disturbed" when even one of the rules seems even temporarily suspended. This disturbance may culminate in serious injury, or death.

Thus, when I first moved to Santa Cruz, the world capital of

Moral & Political Correctness, I made the mistake of quoting a George Carlin routine at a party. One line of this shtick goes, more or less:

> Why, why, why do all the women you see at anti-abortion protests look like nobody would want to fuck them in the first place?

A psychiatrist standing nearby said to me, sourly, "I don't like cursing." This caused me considerable confusion. I had obviously violated a local taboo, but I did not know which one, and worse yet, I had never considered "fuck" as a curse or malediction. I felt like a guy who wanders into the local branch of Al Qaeda under the impression that he has found the Department of Motor Vehicles, or — even more — like a ginkus who opens a door in his own house and finds The Three Stooges in a phaser-gun shoot-out with Darth Vader and Mother Teresa.

I feel grateful to that psychiatrist now, of course. Mulling over how he came to classify "fuck" in the category of curses, led me to review all that I knew about the art and science of effective Cursing and about Black Magick in general. The results of my meditations will appear as we proceed. (Thanks, Doc!)

This sort of head-banger or mind-bender happens more and more in our postmodern & multicultural world, especially if you travel as much as I do. A basic sociological and anthropological law holds that while *every culture (and every sub-culture) has different Game Rules regarding speech and behavior, each tends to believe that its own tribal rules represent the only "correct" way for humans to interact with each other.* Among savages, you must learn the local taboo system quickly or your life may pay for your ignorance.

Of course, as Veblen pointed out long ago, among the Higher Barbarians, they will not take your life but only your liberty; yet because confinement in a cage causes much suffering in all mammals, including humans, this threat terrifies the majority as much as the threat of death.

Among the Politically Correct, milder reprisals for taboo-breakers vary from economic arse-kicking (denial of tenure) to cruel & unusual punishments (compulsory

"Sensitivity" Training).

I first experienced this sociological phenomenon when, after three years in Ireland, I had a lecture-tour in the United States. I found that taboo systems had changed rapidly in some places but not in others: no city on the trip prepared me for the Game Rules in the next city. E.g., in Dallas, they still thought it polite to hold a door for a lady and boorish not to, but in New York they thought it insulting to hold the door for a lady, thereby making it necessary for me to navigate with extreme delicacy to avoid either holding the door or allowing it to slam rudely in her face.

If you fully understand the anthropological significance of the above, you know enough to write a whole book on black magic. Otherwise, read on. I will reveal the secret inner dynamics of how to hurl a truly nefarious curse — knowledge previously reserved only to the greatest Adepts of the Art called Ducdame.

We all, to some degree, think in "magical" categories. Books on anthropology have sold better than any others in social science because they all shed as much light on our own tribal taboos as on whatever so-called "primitives" they depict. We need to understand Magick to understand ourselves.

What do we mean by Magick?

As Aleister Crowley, Epopt of the Illuminati, 97th degree Order of Memphis and Mizraim, 33rd degree Scotch Rite, 10th degree Ordo Templi Orientis, "Baphomet" to the profane and "Phoenix" within the Sanctuary of the Gnosis, the Great Beast 666, etc. wrote:

> MAGICK is the Science and Art of causing Change to occur in Conformity with Will.
>
> . . . Illustration: it is my Will to inform the World of certain facts within my knowledge. I therefore take "magical weapons," — pen, ink and paper; I write "incantations" — these sentences — in the "magical language," i.e., that which is understood by the people I wish to instruct; I call forth "spirits," such as printers, publishers, booksellers, and so forth, and constrain them to convey my message to those people . . .
>
> -- *Magick*, by Aleister Crowley, Weiser, 1997, p. 126

In other words, the distinction between "magick" and "communication" exists only in our traditional ways of thinking. The uncanny Egyptians attributed both inventions to a single deity, Thoth, god of speech and other illusions.

In the existential world — in the sensory-sensual continuum — Thoth still reigns and language still has magick. All communication contains sorcery and/or hypnosis, because humans use howls, snarls, yaps, purrs, gargles, gurgles, etc. — noises of many sorts — to create a neuro — semantic "grid" projected upon all incidents and events. We generally call these grids *languages*.

We literally "see" incidents and events only as they register upon that grid.

If I use certain words that cause you to have certain predictable neuro-somatic reactions, I have cast a *spell* upon you. I have *enchanted* you. I may even have *cursed* you.

(Sure you want to know more about this?)

My method of spellbinding or enchanting or cursing may not involve the traditional drums and rattles of the tribal shaman, but the laws of neurolinguistic programming governing the transactions do not differ. I once triggered widespread scotoma, primate herd panic and psychoclonism in one nut cult called CSICOP simply by ridiculing them. They thought of themselves as Rationalists, but I "magically" turned them into terrorized savages acting exactly like the ancient Irish kings who ordained death for any Bard writing satire against them. (No applause, please.)

To understand the language of magick one must first understand the magick of language.

Let me define certain key terms. It may help disperse the fog of ignorance and superstition that has covered this subject for centuries.

By the *sensory-sensual continuum* I mean all that humans can **experience**, as distinguished from those "things" (or non-things, or nothings) that they can only make noises or chatter about.

Examples: [A] I can say "If you open that box of candy, you will find three chocolates inside." Going to the box and opening it, in the sensory-sensual continuum, will quickly confirm or refute my statement, because you will inevitably find [1] fewer than three chocolates, [2] exactly three chocolates, or [3] more than three chocolates. Results [1] and [3] refute my statement; [2] confirms it.

But [B] I might also say "Opening God for similar investigation, you will find three persons inside," as, in fact, Romish Magick does say. No investigation of the sensory-sensual manifold can ever confirm or refute this. Scientific philosophers generally describe such statements (about things beyond confirmation or refutation) as "meaningless". Without speaking that harshly, I venture that we cannot fathom our situation in space-time if we habitually confuse ourselves by mixing type [A] statements with type [B] statements. We may never achieve Total Clarity (short of infinity), but we should at least have the ability to distinguish between what humans can experience and what they can only blather about.

Distinguishing between these two types of statements seems necessary for sanity and survival, because all forms of illusion, delusion, mob hysteria, hallucination, etc.; dogma, bigotry, "madness," intolerance, etc.; "idealism," ideology, idiocy, obsession, etc. depend upon confusing them. The people who released poison gas in the Tokyo subways, the Nazis, the Marxists, nut-cults like Objectivism, Heaven's Gate, Scientology, CSICOP, etc. represent some of the horrors and curses unleashed by mixing Class [A] statements with Class [B] statements.

All forms of Black Magick therefore depend on confusing and mingling these two classes: the nonverbal experiential and the verbal nonexperiential.

By *the neuro-semantic field* I mean the total vocabulary, grammar, syntax, logic, etc. by which an extremely rapid system of feedbacks synergetically links the verbal centers of the brain to the neuro-muscular, neuro-chemical, neuro-immunological, neuro-respiratory, etc. systems of the organism-as-a-whole. In other words, I explicitly reject, not only the traditional verbal division between "magick" and "communication," but the equally fictitious splits between "mind" and "body," between "reason" and "emotion," between "thought" and "reflex," etc.

All words transmitted as sonic or visual signals--sound waves or light waves — rapidly become photons, electrons, neurotransmitters, hormones, colloidal reactions, reflex arcs, conditioned or imprinted "frames," physiological responses, etc. as they impact upon the total synergetic organism.

Let's take that a bit slower:

All words transmitted as sonic or visual signals — sound waves or light waves —

rapidly become photons,
electrons,
neurotransmitters,
hormones, colloidal reactions,
reflex arcs,
conditioned or imprinted "frames,"
physiological responses,
etc.
as they impact upon the
total
synergetic organism.

"Perception" consists of a complex series of codings and decodings as in-**form**-ation trans-*forms* itself through successive sub-systems of the organism-as-a-whole.

(Please re-read the last two sentences.)

We never *experience* "thoughts," "feelings," "perceptions," "intuitions," "sensations," etc. We invent those categories after the fact. What we experience, nanosecond by nanosecond, consists of continuous synergetic reactions of the organism-as-whole to the environment-as-a-whole, including incoming verbal signals from others in the same predicament. These incoming verbal signals also produce in us reactions of the organism-as-a-whole sometimes culminating in a return signal.

That much seems simple neurobiological savvy.

But suppose I point a shamanic death-bone at you? Or utter a Magick Word that alarms and threatens you as much as a simple "fuck" threatened that Santa Cruz psychiatrist?

We never "know" organismically all that we know

theoretically. Parts of us remain simian, childish, "ignorant," murky, inertial, mechanical, etc.

Illustration #1: Consciously and will-fully remind yourself that you can tell the difference between a "movie" and "real life." Then go to see the latest ketchup-splattered horror/slasher classic and pay attention to how many times the director "magically" tricks you into real gasps, internal or overt cringe-reflexes, dry mouth, clutching (seat-rails, coke can, companion's arm, etc.), or other symptoms of minor but real (polygraph-diagnosable) anxiety and short-term near-panic, sometimes verging on vomit-reflex.

Illustration #2: With the same conscious and will-full reminders about the difference between "movies" and "real life," rent a hard-core XXX porno DVD. Observe how long it takes before physiological responses indicate that parts of you at least have lost track of that distinction.

To repeat an earlier point, in Neurolinguistic Programming (NLP), Dr. Bandler makes a distinction between the "meta-model" and the "Milton model." The *meta-model*, continually revised, updated and expanded, consists of the class of all scientifically meaningful statements available at this date. We should revise our meta-model every day, by keeping in contact with others in the same predicament. Since Scenario Universe always and only consists of — as Bucky Fuller said — *non-simultaneously* apprehended **events** (coherent space-time synergies), such continuous feedback appears necessary.

If everything happened at once, we would know Absolute Truth at once; but since space-time events happen **non-simultaneously**, we need feedback.

The "*Milton model*," on the other hand, named after Dr. Milton Erickson, "the greatest hypnotist of the 20th Century," consists of the class of all scientifically meaningless statements that "magically" make us feel much better, or much worse — or, in occult language, the class of all blessings and all curses.

(General Semanticists call it the class of all **purrs** and all **snarls**.)

This Heap Big Magick, *bwana*. You can fucking kill a guy with this stuff. And, of course, if you have Dr. Erickson's compassion, you can repeatedly heal the seemingly helpless.

Four score and something years ago, Drs. Ogden and Richards, in *The Meaning of Meaning*, brought forth a distinction between the **denotation** of words and the **connotation** of words.

In the *denotation*, any word or group of words belongs in the meta-model if it conforms to the test of the model; *viz.* scientifically meaningful reference in the experiential-phenomenological world.

And in the *connotation*, any word or group of words belongs in the Milton model if it conforms to the test of that model; *viz.* again, scientifically meaningless reference to nothing-in-particular and everything-in-general so packaged as to make us feel better, or worse.

Our major problem, in the elementary blessing and cursing game called social conversation, lies in the fact that quite often — very, *very* often — the same word may have "objective" denotations in the scientific meta-model but also have "emotive" neurosemantic connotations in the magical Milton model. In other words, we hypnotize ourselves, and one another, with remarkable ease. In only a few minutes, a dedicated dogmatist can have you heatedly shouting something in the form of the Primary Magick Theorem, which declares that *any non-verbal incident or event encountered and endured "really" "is" some noise or grunt we choose to label it with.*

(One corollary holds that sticking pins in a doll will hurt the person sharing the doll's label, and a second states that throwing darts at an image of the Enemy Leader will "help the war effort.")

Illustration: By persistent reiteration of medieval logical forms, the anti-choice people in the abortion debate have hypnotized the pro-choice people into interminable haggling about whether one non-verbal event inside a woman "really is" (the noise or grunt preferred by my side) and "really" "is" ***not*** (the gargle or gurgle preferred by the other side). Since the various noises, grunts, gargles, gurgles, etc. have no experiential or experimental or phenomenological or existential referents in the sensory or sensual or instrumental space-time manifold, this contest transpires in the Milton model, each side trying to hypnotize the other.

But, even more nefariously, this has the structure of what Watslavick called, in *Pragmatics of Human Communication*, the Game Without End. This Game — which word "really" "is" the non-word — gives great entertainment and self-esteem to those who really like that kind of thing; but it causes Kafka-esque and "nightmarish" sensations throughout the organism-as-a-whole among those who want to get out of the Game and go back where language made sense, but nonetheless remain *spellbound* & "cursed" for the seemingly infinite length of the Game Without End.

The Game Without End begins with the attempt to decide which bark or howl "really" "is" a nonverbal existential event.

None of this represents abstract theorems. The role of magick in all language transactions has very concrete and exhilarating/terrifying implications:

Well-documented case of a man literally killed by a shaman's curse and a "death-bone." (*The Psychobiology of Mind-Body Healing*, by Ernest Lawrence Rossi, Norton, 1988, page 9-12.)

Equally well-documented case of another man, a cancer patient, "miraculously" blessed by remission and recovery due to a placebo (with tumors shrunk to half their previous size), then cursed back into critical condition when learning of deaths of others receiving the same placebo. (Same book, page 3-8.)

Robert Houdin, often called the greatest stage magician of the 19th Century, once said, "A magician is only an actor — only an actor pretending to be a magician."

Similarly, what French anthropologists call *participation mystique* ("at-one-ness" or even "holy union") — a state allegedly limited to "savages" — occurs every day, in every modern city, in nonpathological forms, at our theatres and movie houses, and on our TVs, VCRs and DVDs.

This mystic trance, in which (for instance) Laurence Olivier becomes "Hamlet" right before our eyes, only mutates to the pathological if we cannot *break the spell* — if we continue to see, and relate to, Lord Olivier as Hamlet even if we chance to meet him in a pub: "I say, old bean, you seem to suffer from compulsive rumination, as the shrinks call it. Just kill the old bugger and make a run for the frontier."

Here the Milton model has replaced the meta-model in the wrong space-time locale (territory *not defined* as play-acting space). Madness lies but one step further.

My mother never stopped hating Charles Laughton for the sadistic glee he projected in the punishment sequences of *Mutiny on the Bounty*. She'd never look at another movie with Laughton in it.

Orson Welles, with considerable experience as both actor and stage magician, said "I have been an acting-forger all my life." He said it in his last film,* a fake documentary about a partially fake biography of a totally fake painter — *F For Fake*, based on a seemingly true but partly bogus biography called, even more bluntly, *Fake!*

~•~

* Not the last film he acted in, just the last film in which he had control as writer/producer/director/actor.

~•~

Some of us have become postmodern whether we like it or not. As the Poet wrote,

> I saw a man upon the stair,
> A little man who wasn't there;
> He wasn't there again today,
> Gee, I wish he'd go away!

Of course, we all clearly understand that the little man who "wasn't there" simply "*wasn't there*" and hence can't go away, but the structure of Indo-European grammar so spellbinds and enchants us that we illogically feel that the spooky little bastard *should* go away, just to conform to the syntax.

Whosoever speaks in any tongue gives birth to blessings and curses, & if the uncanny Egyptians made Thoth the father of both language and magick, the canny Greeks made Hermes the god of both language and fraud.

Old Man On A Balcony:
Views Of Monterey Bay #7

Dolphins in the bay

Playing, sporting, having fun —

World without money!

THOUGHTS TO PONDER

The hand that stocks the drug stores rules the world.

— Bokonon

Shocking Hidden Facts About Male Non-Violence

*I wrote this piece in April 1996 for a mag called **Backlash**, and have rewritten it only slightly. It should prove interesting not only to those in a currently scapegoated group, but to those NOT in such a group, because in the accelerating modern world we all eventually get assigned to the Shit-on role.*

Did you know that over 98 percent of the men in the United States today have never been convicted of any violent crime or served time in prison?

— That, even though the U.S. imprisons a higher percentage of its citizens than any other nation, over 98 percent of our men have never been convicted of rape, murder, child molestation, assault, battery, breaking and entering, or any kind of violence?

— And almost half of the men who do land in prison are convicted of non-violent crimes.*

~•~

* Usually medical, religious or recreational Heresy — i.e., deciding for themselves which herbs, vitamins and compounds to use, instead of allowing a Tsar to decide for them. See my *TSOG: The Thing That Ate the Constitution.*

~•~

These basic statistical facts about male nonviolence have been hidden from us by an ideology/mythology which I call androphobia — fear and hatred of the male. Androphobia has also hidden such facts as these:

Important Feminists of the past include such males as Clarence Darrow, John Stuart Mill, Henrik Ibsen, Robert Dale Owen, James Joyce, and Bertrand Russell.

Psychologists who measure IQ have never found any statistical difference between the intelligence of men and women. High, middle, and low IQs are found in both sexes! There is no scientific proof of male inferiority! *The mythology of male brutishness and stupidity has been spread by the androphobes without a single shred of statistical evidence.*

Do you believe men are innately brutal? When no other human being was willing to nurse the lepers on Molokai Island, it was a male, Father Joseph Damien, who went there to care for those unfortunates.

Consider these further suppressed facts about maleness:

Although they were men, Michelangelo, Sir Christopher Wren, and Frank Lloyd Wright are almost universally considered great architects.

The first Feminist pamphlet published in this country was written by a man — Tom Paine (who also wrote the first anti-slavery pamphlet).

The most original music of this century, Jazz, was created almost entirely by Black males.

Free public libraries, which made more knowledge available to more people than any invention before Internet, were founded on gifts made by Andrew Carnegie, who was not just male but a **rich white** male — the accursed of the accursed . . .

Leonardo da Vinci made hundreds of great contributions to both science and art despite the triple handicaps of being Gay, left handed and male.

Men including Martin Luther King Jr., Mahatma Gandhi, and Sean McBride have played important roles in the struggle for world peace.

Even though Shakespeare, Dante, and Homer were males, they wrote poetry generally considered as good as anything by Amy Lowell.

Beethoven, Mozart, and Bach were men and yet they wrote music at least as good as that of Hildegarde of Bingen.

Males such as Newton, Einstein, and Archimedes made contributions to science as important as those of Marie Curie.

The cure for yellow fever, saving the lives of millions, was found by a man, Major Walter Reed.

Despite the androphobic mythology/ideology, at no time in history except the present was maleness considered a shame, a disgrace, or a sign of inferiority.

All the "major" religions (those having millions of followers) were founded by males born in Asia (Confucius, Lao-Dzu, Buddha, Moses, Jesus, Mohammed).

Men were responsible for such discoveries as the sailing ship, the compass, the steam engine, the electric light, the AC generator, the computer, and many others. And males created over 90% of mathematics.

All of this sounds strange, bizarre, almost unbelievable, I know. We have all had so much brainwashing by the androphobic meme that we scarcely can believe males have ever done anything but shoot one another, rape women, and blow people up. Androphobia remains the one respectable bigotry — the only form of group-libel that nearly everybody considers "politically correct" and which therefore goes unchallenged almost everywhere. Male achievements, thus, have been systematically excluded from "the universe of discourse" — i.e., what "nice" people talk about.

Let us clarify the ideology of androphobia. I define androphobia as the transfer to **all males** of the negative stereotypes that the Ku Klux Klan and other neanderthal types assign **only to black males**:

— mental inferiority, of course;

— emotional childishness, or "inability to think rationally";

— brutality — i.e., sub-human status;

— criminality;

— sexual violence, etc.

You see? All the old racist clichés — except "a great sense of rhythm."

I thus regard androphobia as merely a transmutation from racism to sexism, an "advance" that is not an advance at all.

Let me make this very clear. I do not oppose Feminism;

on the contrary, I reject all forms of group stereotyping and dehumanization. Androphobia (or male-bashing) has no intrinsic or necessary link with Feminism, and many Feminists utterly reject androphobia. To use an analogy, Marx said that "anti-Semitism is the socialism of fools." Similarly, I regard androphobia as the Feminism of imbeciles.

I oppose androphobia as psychological gendercide. I believe it underlies the widespread male depression (which psychotherapists recognize as "epidemic"), and also explains much of the soaring suicide rate among boys and young males.

The suicide rate among boys aged 16 to 19 runs four times higher than that of females, and the suicide rate of men between 20 and 24 soars to six times that of females (according to the U.S. Department of Health Statistics).

This self-destructiveness has increased steadily, among males, for 30 years — since the rise of the androphobic ideology. Few want to grow up male in a society where maleness is defined as a sign of incurable inferiority or criminality.

Androphobia has created the kind of tension that psychologists call a "double-bind." A classic double-bind, as Gregory Bateson defined it in his pioneering work on the subject, *Communication: The Social Matrix of Psychiatry*, involves:

(a) an impossible choice one cannot escape, and,

(b) just as crucial, a social rule that forbids verbal comment on the impossibility of the situation.

Gays, blacks, Hispanics, and all other minorities retain the freedom to comment on their situation — even to comment angrily or to protest in the streets.

However, one cannot comment on androphobia these days. It is not only "politically incorrect" but virtually unthinkable. To talk about the subject at all remains under a very big taboo — while millions of boys and men stagger from depression to suicide annually.

For instance, in 1979, psychologist Roy Schenk attempted to give a workshop on men's oppression at the annual conference of the Association for Humanistic Psychology. He announced in advance that the seminar would investigate what it does to the psyche of boys and men to grow up "being perceived as morally inferior to women." The AHP would not allow the workshop.

This year, I tried again, offering a similar workshop at a New Age conference that had had me as workshop leader several times in the past. They also would not allow this subject to be discussed at all.

Consider the "logic" of androphobia, and how it deliberately contradicts known facts. Remember: 98% of the men in this country have never been in prison or committed a violent crime, but the androphobe insists that all men are "violent." Some of the most tender, beautiful music in the world was written by men such as Bach, Mozart, and Beethoven, but the androphobe insists all men are "insensitive." To repeat: all the major religions based on justice and love were founded by men (Asiatic men, in fact) but the androphobe insists all men are "greedy" and "competitive." This kind of "logic," based on totally ignoring all inconvenient facts, seems common to all forms of racism, xenophobia and bigotry.

In fact, if you listen to the rantings of any leading androphobe (such as Carol Hemingway, Andrea Dworkin, or Robin Morgan) and mentally change the word "male" to "Jew" every time it appears, the result would be totally indistinguishable from the rantings of Hitler, because the "logic" of bigotry remains the same in all cases.

It is the "logic" of ascribing one essence to a miscellaneous group, which is only possible when all sensory space-time facts become replaced by fungible abstractions; but this flight into abstraction is "politically correct" and virtually nobody dares to challenge it.

Thus, the "evil" of maleness in our society today, like the "evil" of witchcraft in medieval days, is beyond debate or discussion. The "no comment" taboo applies, leading directly to the double-bind that triggers mental breakdowns. Males, thus, have become the only minority that can be slandered and demeaned with any and all group stereotypes, in "respectable" media, and with no rebuttal allowed. All other minorities can "fight back" against group libel, but men who try to fight back against stereotypes and group libel are regarded as crazy, or "in denial," or beyond the bounds of reasonable discourse.

Fortunately, this is beginning to change — a little. We look forward to a day when sanity and common sense triumph over bias, and all men and women, all people of all races, are judged one at a time and not condemned by group stereotypes. Meanwhile, anti-Semites (and most other bigots) can only circulate their lunatic rantings through ill-written URLs with infrequent visitors, while the androphobes still have free access to all major media and can endlessly spout the most idiotic forms of sexism while claiming to oppose sexism.

As Shakespeare said (with a few minor revisions and updates):

I am a man. Hath not a man eyes? Hath not a man hands, organs, dimensions, senses, affections, passions? Fed with the same food, hurt with the same weapons, subject to the same diseases, healed by the same means, warmed, and cooled by the same winter and summer, as a woman is? If you prick us, do we not bleed? If you tickle us, do we not laugh? If you poison us, do we not die?

Old Man On A Balcony:
Views Of Monterey Bay #8

Flock of gulls appears

And suddenly — disappears

Going God-knows-where . . .

Language, Logic & Lunacy

*Another piece for **Backlash**, from around the same time as the previous Blasphemy . . .*

Kung Fu Dzu, called Confucius among the Higher Barbarians, said, "The first rule of politics is to use the language precisely. Otherwise, nobody understands anybody else, and everything falls into chaos."

Some commentators regard the ideograms about using language precisely — **ching ming** — as the single most important concept in Confucian philosophy.

ching as noun means officer or court official; as verb it means to correct errors or to regulate one's actions; cf. Catholic "examination of conscience," or cybernetic "feedback."

ming = mouth + moon — "moony" language, floating abstractions, vague generalities, meaningless propositions, etc.

ching ming = be sure brain turned on before setting mouth in motion.

In creating a defense league against the rabid androphobia of Steinem & Company, we need to notice which misuses of language create the logical chaos that reinforces and perpetuates the androphobic lunacy. I offer two small corrections of language here.

"White men still own all the corporations." I heard this from a Hispanic radical on local TV recently. This sentence can serve as a perfect example of how sloppy language habits create warped reality-tunnels, because it looks almost true at first, but it actually contacts an enormous Nazi-like Big Lie.

Leaving aside the facts that, internationally, many corporations belong to nonwhite males, and that, even nationally, a few corporations belong to females, let us assume that, within the US, the statement contains maybe 95 percent accuracy. In other words, let us assume that per- haps 95 percent of all corporations active here have white male owners.

This statement obviously differs vastly from "95 percent of all white males own corporations." In fact, even the Hispanic radical quoted above, if he opened his eyes, could see many, many white males working at lowly and menial jobs in this part of the country. These poor whites do not own corporations. Neither do many others who don't even have lousy jobs and survive by begging on the street.

"White men own all the corporations" does tend to get confused with "All white men own corporations." Listen closely to radicals in general, and Radical Feminists in particular, and you will hear, over and over, how this self-hypnosis works. They leap from the first partly true statement to the second totally false one without even noticing that they have reversed their logical terms in the middle. They can literally walk past a homeless white man sleeping in an alley and not observe how his existence contradicts their racist/sexist ideology.

Note that the same confusion existed in the foundation of the Nazi madness. "The Jews own the international banks" has lower accuracy than "white men own all corporations," but even if it fit 100 percent — or at least 95% — which it doesn't — of all banks, it still would not mean the same as "all Jews own international banks." Nonetheless, the Nazis somehow managed to convince themselves that it did; the Holocaust followed.

As semanticists like Korzybski and Bourland have pointed out, this type of confusion, and the bigotry it perpetuates, results from the very structure of our language. "White men" and "Jews" can serve as subjects of many sentences, but they do not mean the same in all sentences.

Thus, "White men came down the path" refers to a definite number at a specific occasion; "White men own corporations" refers to a larger, but still smallish number, a statistically tiny segment of all white men; and "White men are not eligible for affirmative action" refers to all white men in the U.S. today.

We tend to confuse these various meanings, unless we modify the key expression at once — e.g. "**Three** white men come down the path," "**5,000** white men own corporations," "**100 million** white men are not eligible for affirmative action." (These figures represent estimates, or guesses, to convey the idea. They do not claim to represent statistics I have not collected.)*

~•~

* I have elsewhere suggested that when generalizing without statistics we should use the term "sombunall" — *some bu*t *n*ot *all* — in every single case where we have not in fact examined all members of a set or class. Where you feel more sure of yourself than I usually do, you may use "mosbunall" — *mos*t *bu*t *n*ot *all*. But remember to encourage (not-**dis**courage) feedback and never neglect examination of conscience.

~•~

Consider next "the Patriarchy" against which we have heard so much heated rhetoric in recent decades. Does this term really fit our society? The Rad Fem crowd repeats over and over that it does fit, but I suggest that it does not.

In a Patriarchy, a man continues to have custody of his children after a divorce. In the U.S. today, the wife gets custody in about 90 percent of all cases, as noted by John Sample in the February 1996 *Backlash*. That seems to place us closer to Matriarchy than to Patriarchy.

More important, however, since males in our society die seven years younger than their wives, most families that own most of the wealth fall under female domination eventually. And, of course, contrary to Rad Fem propaganda, even while the males remain alive, most of them share decision-making with their wives on many important occasions; they probably share decisions with their mistresses also; and women do most of the shopping and spending. The men only earn the money; the women dispose of it.

I think we can only accept Oligarchy as the proper name for that system — not Matriarchy, as Philip Wylie wickedly suggested in the 1940's and not Patriarchy, as the Feminists have insisted since the 1960's. A group of rich families, not merely the males, make all the important decisions. This type of system has existed in every post-tribal society in history, including the ones that call themselves democratic, socialistic or even communistic. Oligarchy virtually means the same as "civilization." Ignoring this fact, and picking out some scapegoat group like Jews or males, utterly confuses our political thinking and can lead to nothing but madness.

Finally, my own take on the Angry White Males who allegedly caused the recent Republican *risorgimento*: as a boy, I learned to believe (as all my family believed) that the Republicans represented the Orangemen (English and Dutch banking families) and the Democrats represented all the rest of us, but especially us Irish Catholic working people. As my life took me further and further from that background, I lost all affiliation with Catholicism but retained an ethnic/class identification, of sorts, with the Irish and the working class.

If the Democrats have truly lost the Irish and the workers, I can only think they have done it by getting too cozy with Steinemism — too tightly associated with those racist and sexist pseudo-radicals who don't remember, or want to remember, that not all white men own corporations or meet weekly with David Rockefeller at the Patriarchy Club to make all the decisions for our society.

Old Man On A Balcony:
Views Of Monterey Bay #9

MIDNIGHT HAIKU #2

Dancing in the bay—

Dolphins again? No, better:

Reflected moonlight.

Dreams of Flying

*Another article from my Los Angeles period (**Magical Blend** 1988) . . . Arlen's illness had not begun yet, and for the first time in my writing career I kept earning enough every year to stop worrying about money. . . almost . . . (Once you hit bottom economically, as I did in 1972, you never earn enough to really stop worrying . . .)*

I have recently read a most enjoyable novel called *The Dream Illuminati* by Wayne Saalman (New Falcon Publications, Santa Monica, 1988). Mr. Saalman has found an epic theme — dreams of flight, and the achievement of flight.

Historically, dreams of flying appeared in the collective unconscious before the reality of flight existed in technology, and I suspect that if we understood our dreams better we would use our technology more wisely. Our machines manifest our **dreams in matter crafted to coherence**, and a psychoanalysis of our culture could easily derive from an examination of how we use science to materialize our fantasies and nightmares.

Mr. Saalman's science-fantasy made me wonder: Why have we always dreamed of flying, and why have we built flying machines? This question seems "eminently" worth pondering in a world where 200,000,000 people pass through Kennedy International Airport every year, flying the Atlantic in one direction or the other.

To understand the profound, it often appears helpful to begin with clues that seem trivial. I suggest that we contemplate what our children look at every Saturday morning on TV. One of the most popular jokes in animated cartoons shows the protagonist walking off a cliff, without noticing what he has done. Sublimely ignorant, he continues to walk — on air — until he notices that he has been doing the "impossible," and then he falls. I doubt very much that any reader has not seen that routine at least once;

most of us have seen it a few hundred times.

It might seem pretentious to see a Jungian archetype adumbrated in crude form in this Hollywood cliché, but follow me for a moment.

When Hollywood wishes to offer us the overtly mythic, it presents Superman, who can "leap over tall buildings in a single bound," and a more recent hero named Luke Skywalker.

The Tarot, that condensed encyclopedia of the collective unconscious, begins with the card called The Fool, and the Fool is depicted walking off a cliff — just like Donald Duck or Wily Coyote in the cartoons.

Funny coincidence, what?

A Greek legend (which James Joyce took as the archetype of the life of the artist) tells us of Daedalus and Icarus: Daedalus who, imprisoned in a labyrinth (conventional "reality"), invented wings and flew away, over the heads of his persecutors; and Icarus, the son of Daedalus, who flew too close to the Sun Absolute and fell back to Earth. Like Porky Pig walking off a cliff, Icarus' fall contains a symbolism many have encountered in their own dreams.

The Sufi order employs as its emblem a heart with wings (and the Ordo Templi Orientis employs a circle — symbolizing both emptiness and completion — with wings). The Egyptian god of wisdom, Thoth, had the head of a winged creature, the ibis; his Greek equivalent, Hermes, was portrayed as more human, but had bird's wings on his sandals.

The Wright Brothers, who made flying possible for all of us, remain beloved figures in the folk imagination — but how many readers can name the inventors of such equally marvelous (but earthbound) devices as the television, the vacuum cleaner, the computer, the laser, or the modern indoor toilet?

Yet while other geniuses seem "forgotten by the masses," the classic put-down to satirize any conservative who sets limits to what human craft can accomplish remains "I told Wilbur and I told Orville, you'll never get that crate off the ground."

You see? We even remember their first names.

I suspect that part of the function of flight consists in

destroying our concept of limit, opening us to the insight Dr. John Lilly expressed so eloquently in *The Center of the Cyclone:*

> In the province of the mind, what is believed to be true is true or becomes true, within limits to be found experimentally and experientially. These limits are further beliefs to be transcended. In the province of the mind, there are no limits.

The poet Hart Crane, trying to describe what Wilbur and Orville Wright meant to his generation (he died in 1932), wrote that from Kitty Hawk onward, be sensed "the closer clasp of Mars." By 1938 people tuning in on an Orson Welles radio program after the drama started, believed they were hearing a newscast and the Martians were already here. A quantum jump had occurred in the limits of our social imagination. Humanity had, like the poet, sensed the "closer clasp" of Mars.

Just slightly more than 30 years later, Neil Armstrong walked on the moon, like a character in the fiction of Jules Verne, and ten years later, our instruments invaded the Martian desert already familiar to "us" through the visions of Edgar Rice Burroughs and Ray Bradbury. If this does not confirm William Blake's notorious claim that "Poetic Imagination" should be considered another name for "God," it certainly suggests that Poetic Imagination may function as another name for Logical Destiny.

Perhaps we should ponder more deeply on the fact that Daedalus means "artist" in Greek. Daedalus, designer of labyrinths, imprisoned by those he served in a labyrinth he himself built — Daedalus, inventor of wings that took him from the Earth to Outer Space — why does he represent Art, instead of Science?

Well, to understand this we must remember that the ancient Greeks did not distinguish "Art" from "Science" as we do. The genius of an artist, Aristotle says, lies in his **texne**, the root from which we get our word "technology"; but **texne** basically means skill or craft, or the ability to make things that never existed before. Negative entropy, i.e., information.

In our age, by contrast, Stravinsky was regarded as "witty" or "paradoxical" (or deliberately enigmatic) when he called himself a "sound engineer." An artist who considers himself a kind of engineer? That is a hard thought for us to grasp.

Yet a few moments reflection will show that as much precise structural knowledge can be found in Stravinsky's music as in Roebling's blueprints for the Brooklyn Bridge — that edifice (considered "miraculous" when it was new) which Hart Crane took as a symbol of the unity of Art and Science.

The Occidental obsession with dichotomized and dualistic thinking has been denounced so often lately that I hardly need to labor this point. I would prefer to suggest a possible common origin of both art and science.

The musician and the architect, the poet and the physicist — all inventors of new realities — all such Creators may be best considered late evolutionary developments of the type that first appears as the shaman. Please remember that shamans in most cultures are known as "they who walk in the sky," just like our current shaman-hero, Luke Skywalker.

It should not be regarded as accidental or arbitrary that Swift put Laputa, the home of the scientists, in the sky, in order to disparage the wild-eyed and Utopian scientists of his time for not having all four feet on the ground; Aristophanes put Socrates in the clouds, to similarly disparage speculative agnostic philosophy.

Outer Space seems the natural home of all descendants of the shaman, whether they be called artists, philosophers or scientists.

The ironies of Swift and Aristophanes, and the myths of the fall of Icarus and Donald Duck, indicate that the collective unconscious contains a force opposed to our dreams of flight. This appears inevitable. As Jung, the foremost explorer of the collective psyche, often pointed out, an ineluctable polarity exists in the symbols of both dream and myth, a "Law of Opposites" which Jung compared to the Chinese concept of yin and yang energies.

Jekyll contains Hyde; love easily becomes hate; Cupid and Psyche reappear as the Phantom of the Opera and Margaritta, and also as King Kong and Fay Wray.

In the present context, the Law of Opposites means that we yearn to soar, yet we fear to fall. Our "inner selves" are mirrored not just in Orville Wright rising like a bird from Kill Devil Hills at Kitty Hawk, but also in Simon Newcomb, the great astronomer who "proved" mathematically that such flight was impossible.

As I have elsewhere suggested, neophilia and neophobia — love of novelty and fear of novelty — result from the primal polarities of the first imprint of the newborn infant. In other words, what Dr. Timothy Leary calls the bio-survival "circuit" of the nervous system — the oral bio-survival system, I prefer to call it, since it includes the immune, endocrine and neuropeptide sub-systems as well as the autonomic nervous system — always and only imprints either basic explorativeness or basic conservatism very quickly. That explains, I think, why some babies "Chortle with delight" when tossed up in the air and caught, while others scream with terror. Infants who like this experience of flight, I suggest, already have the infophiliac imprint and those who act terrified have the infophobic imprint.

Of course, "the universe" can count above two (even if Aristotelian logicians cannot), and few of us are either pure neophilics or pure neophobics. Rather, we wobble about on a gradient between neophilia and neophobia — between joy and anxiety, between conservatism and experimentalism, between yearning to soar and fear of falling. At times we feel like Jonathan Livingston Seagull, convinced that "a true Heaven has no limits" and trying to fly higher and faster; other times we become the old Reaganite gulls, nervously warning that to fly too high too fast will ruin your brain and directly contradicts the traditional mores of the flock. ("Just say no to soaring").

We contain both Orville Wright leaping into the air toward a future "where no man has gone before" and Simon Newcomb proving that Orville will certainly fall and smash himself like Humpty Dumpty.

As Joyce so poetically writes:

> My great blue bedroom, the air so quiet, scarce a
> cloud. In peace and silence. I could have stayed up
> there for always only. It's something fails us. First

> we feel. Then we fall. I'll seen him come down on
> me now under whitespread wings like he'd come
> from Arkangels, I sink I'd die down under his feet,
> humbly dumbly, only to washup.

Despite the multiple dream-images here — the Irish rain falling to become the Irish river Anna Liffey, Lucifer and his hosts falling from Heaven, the falls of Adam and Eve and Humpty Dumpty, Mary receiving the divine seed from the Archangel, Magdalene washing the feet of the Saviour, the Paraclete descending as a dove to bring the Apostles the Gift of Tongues, a housewife washing up the breakfast dishes — Joyce primarily invokes our deep awareness that gravity "pulls us down," our deep yearning to break free of this "drag" and soar back to our home above the clouds.

In 1988, the ancient Egyptian and Gnostic belief that our origin and our destiny reach far beyond Earth no longer seems as quaint and queer as it did in recent generations. In books like Dr. Timothy Leary's *Info-Psychology*, Dr. Francis Crick's *Cosmic Panspermia* and Sir Fred Hoyle's *Evolution from Space*, there appears a body of evidence strongly suggesting that life did not begin on this planet but arrived here from elsewhere in space.

While the interpretations of these brilliant philosopher-scientists differ, their various kinds of evidence, from diverse fields of enquiry, do make a strong case that evolution is older and more universal than we traditionally think. One leaves their books suspecting that the orthodox biological view regarding Earthly evolution apart from Cosmic evolution results from unvoiced pre-Copernican assumptions about Earth's centrality and its isolation.

In addition to the sophisticated and learned works of Leary, Crick and Hoyle, we have also recently witnessed the growth of a vast body of "vulgar," or at least popular, literature arguing the proposition that Ancient Astronauts seeded this planet, not with all life, but merely with (post-Neanderthal) humanity. Instead of dissecting the flaws in the arguments of this seemingly "crank" literature, it might be more illuminating, I think, to wonder why this popular mythos provides the masses with an unsophisticated and anthropocentric form of the theories more soberly presented in works like *Info-Psychology, Cosmic Panspermia*, and *Evolution from Space.*

Why do we find both first-rate and second-rate minds suddenly preoccupied with extraterrestrial evolution, while ninth-rate minds increasingly embrace Pop UFOlogy?

And why, one may next wonder, does this theme also appear centrally in the most beautiful, the most "haunting" and the most often-revived science-fiction film of all time — Kubrick's magnificent *2001*?

When one Idea or Archetype appears in learned tomes, in tabloids, in folk-belief, in new cults, and in great art, all at about the same time, one suspects the presence of what Jung called, in his book *Flying Saucers*, "a shift in the constellation of the archetypes."

In terms of current neuroscience, what Jung means, I think, we can now state thusly: the DNA/CNS "dialogue" — the neuropeptide "language" between genes and cells — is preparing us for a new evolutionary leap.

In *The Dream Illuminati*, the hero says bluntly:

> I realized that l was only as free as I thought myself to be and that there was no limit to how high we can fly!

Here we see again that the Archetype of flight carries always an umbilical connection to the idea of the transcendence of all limits. ("What is believed to be true is true or becomes true . . .")

And we must wonder again if more than childish fantasy lurks in the concept of Donald Duck walking on air only until he "remembers" that this "is" officially "impossible" in our current reality-tunnel.

In 1904, when Einstein was starting to write his first paper on Relativity and the Wright Brothers were testing the airplane design that finally worked after many failures, Aleister Crowley, the most controversial mystic of our century, "received" — or created by Poetic Imagination — a document which he ever after claimed was a communication from Higher Intelligence. In this work, called *Liber Al* or *The Book of the Law*, there is contained what purports to be a message from Nuit, the Egyptian star goddess, interpreted in Crowley's commentaries as the supreme consciousness of the cosmos, or the sum total of all synergetically interactive intelligences throughout space-time. Among other things, this "entity" — or corporation — told Crowley:

> Every man and every woman is a star . . .
> I am above you and in you. My ecstasy is in yours. My joy is
> to see your joy . . .
> For I am divided for love's sake, for the chance of union . . .
> Put on the wings, and arouse the coiled splendor within you:
> come unto me!

Many interpretations of these verses are possible, of course. Of course.

Personally, after reading some of the current scientists who see evolution as both terrestrial and extraterrestrial, I cannot look at the words of *Liber Al* without thinking that, in some sense, the interstellar creators who planted life here may be sending us a signal to return to our home in the stars — that "great blue bedroom" which Joyce poetically invokes on the last page of *Finnegans Wake* and in which the astronaut, David Bowman, abruptly finds himself at the climax of *2001*.

Of course, the language of poetic myth, like that of dream, should always be considered analogical and allegorical, not literal; to see only one meaning here means that one will "fall into the pit of Because and perish with the dogs of Reason" (to cite Crowley again). The content of a true archetype contains an "infinity" — or at least a heap big finity — of mirrors.

For instance, my Dream Diary for 23 April 1968 records that when I woke in the morning I remembered the following images from my night's hermetic journey:

I am in a Chicago nightclub once patronized by John Dillinger. I find that the present patrons are also a group of gangsters. They regard me with hostility, and I become frightened. I try to leave; they try to stop me. I open a door.

I find myself on the IRT subway in New York. I am riding in the front car, watching the tunnel ahead of the train (as I did as a boy). Suddenly, I see a brick wall ahead and realize the train is going to crash into it and kill everybody aboard, including me.

I am out of the subway and walking in Cicero, Illinois. An angry mob surrounds me. They seem to know that I was in the recent Martin Luther King march against segregation here. I cannot escape them. Suddenly, I know intuitively what to do. I cry out, "Elohim!" and sprout wings and fly above their heads. The sky is beautiful and I feel free of all anxieties, at peace, unreasonably hopeful about everything.

When I awoke, I was thinking of Chesterton's description of mystic experience as "absurd good news."

At the time of this dream, I was involved with Chicago friends in propagating the John Dillinger Died For You Society, a parody of Fundamentalist religions which, like all good jokes, had its serious side. I was fascinated by the way that certain outlaws like Dillinger (or Jesse James, or Robin Hood) were virtually forced to live to the full the archetypal myth of Osiris, Dionysus, Adonis, Christ and Dracula.

I also meditated much on the way in which outlaws who did not even approximately "live" the myth subsequently had their lives rewritten in folk-imagination to conform to it. The first part of the dream-record confronts me with the dark side of the archetype, and reminds me that real gangsters are not the mythic figures imposed on them by Poetic Imagination but nasty and frightening sociopaths.

In the second part of the dream, I enter into the Underground Initiation. Although using symbols from my own life (the subway), I find myself retracing the steps of Ishtar in the land of the dead, Odysseus sailing to Hades for wisdom, Jesus and Dante descending to Hell, etc. In alchemy this was called **negrito**, which Jung compares to the initial stages of psychotherapy.

In a sense, the Underworld Journey appears the reciprocal of, and preparation for, the Achievement of Flight.

Dante had to walk through Hell before climbing Mount Purgatory and soaring above the clouds to Heaven. In retrospect, I am especially delighted with the Freudian wit of the unconscious in using modern "Underworld" figures (gangsters) to represent the mythic Underworld.

In the third part of the dream, the traditional Wrathful Demons attack me, personified by the citizens of Al Capone's home town, Cicero, perhaps because the people out there always reminded me of Wrathful Demons whenever I had to associate with them. I escape by crying out a name from the Hebrew Bible, whereupon I am able to fly, like Dante or Daedalus, from the Pit to the Stars.

What I find most curious about these dream fragments is that, when I experienced them in 1968, I knew nothing about Cabala. I was puzzled on awakening about the name Elohim and the way I magically used it in the dream. All I knew about that name in those days was that it appears in the first chapter of Genesis and that there is a dispute between philologists and theologians about whether it means "God" or "the gods" — i.e., whether the first chapter of the Bible is or isn't a fragment left over from a polytheistic phase of Judaism.

It was over two years after this very Jungian dream that I became interested in Cabala and eventually learned that Elohim is therein considered a great Name of Power — used in e.g., the Middle Pillar Ritual, which every Cabalist in training is expected to do at least once a day. The function of Cabalistic ritual in general, and this ritual in particular, was once defined by Crowley as "to raise the mind of the student perpendicularly to Infinity" — beyond all limits.

This is symbolized in my dream, as in many dreams and myths, by the imagery of flight and the conquest of gravity. The 1968 dream seems to contain precognition of Cabalistic work I would be doing very seriously c. 1971-75.

Of course, if one dares to suggest that a dream contains precognition, the Rationalist immediately declares the connection between the dream image and later waking events "is" "mere coincidence." Those with a psychological block against recognizing electricity would probably say, similarly, that when you flick the switch and the light goes on that "is" also "mere coincidence."

At the time I had this dream or set of dreams in 1968, I was suffering from a moderately severe depression and the general symptoms of what we now call "mid-life crisis." I had a very good job at Playboy magazine, with an excellent salary for the 1960's, but I was approaching 40 and wanted to write full-time. (Three years later, after beginning Cabalistic work, I quit my job and have been writing full-time ever since. Although I have experienced the usual share of shocks, disappointments and bereavements, I have not suffered clinical depression again.)

The reader might find it illuminating to compare this record with a dream recounted in Joseph Campbell's *The Hero With a Thousand Faces*. In this case, the dreamer saw a winged horse with one wing broken, struggling to fly and falling continually back to Earth. Campbell does not even bother interpreting this symbolism, merely informing us that the dreamer was a poet forced to work at a menial job to support his family; one understands immediately.

In a sense, we have all had our "wings" broken; it remains the major function of such "hallowed institutions" as organized religion and Free Compulsory Education to see that our "wings" do get broken, or at least clipped, before we reach adulthood. How else will society have the insectoid units it needs to fill the cubicles in its hive economy?

But what if we begin to regrow healthy organs of Poetic Imagination and flight? What if we "put on the wings and arouse the coiled splendor within" as *Liber Al* urges? Is it not predictable that society will react with the fury described by Wayne Saalman in *The Dream Illuminati*? (Think of the careers of Dr. Wilhelm Reich and Dr. Timothy Leary . . .) Joyce did not name his emblematic Artist merely Daedalus but Stephen Daedalus — after St. Stephen the Protomartyr, who reported a Vision and was stoned to death for it.

And does it not appear ultimately beneficial, in evolutionary perspective, that society should react in that manner? Those of us who have no avocation for martyrdom must learn, when we realize how much neophobia remains built into the contraptions of "society" and "the State," the art of surviving in spite of them. In a word, we must "**get wise**" in both the Socratic meaning of that phrase and in the most hardboiled street meaning.

Neophobia functions as an Evolutionary Driver, forcing the neophiliac to get very smart very fast.

This theme is inexhaustible, but my space and time are not. As a final bit of hermetic wisdom, I offer you Proposition 12 of Aleister Crowley's masterwork, *Magick*:

> Man is ignorant of the nature of his own being and powers. Even his idea of his limitation is based on experience of the past, and every step in his progress extends his empire. There is therefore no reason to assign theoretical limits to what he may be, or to what he may do.

Old Man On A Balcony:
Views Of Monterey Bay #10

TWO FOR BISHOP BERKELEY

Clouds (visible) float

above hills (invisible);

Are the hills still there?

At this hour of night

I see more "dolphins" than at

Any other time.

THOUGHTS TO PONDER

We have found a strange foot-print on the shores of
the unknown. We have devised profound theories, one
after another, to account for its origin. At last, we have
succeeded in reconstructing the creature that made the
footprint. And Lo! It is our own!

— Sir Arthur Eddington

God's Morals

What amateurs we all are compared to Him.

— Hannibal Lecter, MD.

I saw the hon. rev. Jerry Falwell on CNN this morning and found him as amusing as ever. According to rev. Falwell, his god joined Al Qaeda — or at least aided and conspired with them — on 9/11, because the World Trade Center and Pentagon employed large numbers of Gays and persons affiliated with the American Civil Liberties Union.

This confirmed my low opinion of the morals (and intelligence) of Falwell's god. After all, even by Falwell's standards, many "innocent" people — folks who are neither Gay nor associated in any way with the ACLU — also died in that atrocity.

But I wonder: Does anybody have any statistics on how many Gays and civil libertarians worked at those places compared to the national average? Was it a condition of employment at either venue to be Gay or liberty-oriented?

Or has the rev. merely invented a sparkling new defense for shooting Gays and constitutionalists — "I only wanted to prevent more terrorist attacks"?

THOUGHTS TO PONDER

And the sun high over horizon hidden in cloud bank
lit saffron the88
cloud ridge
dove sta memora

— Ezra Pound, *Canto 76*

A-Gnosis

Whenever you stop and reflect, "Maybe I just think or act that way because I'm a Cosmic Schmuck," you become — for a moment — a bit less of a Cosmic Schmuck.

The more often you have such suspicions, the less of a Cosmic Schmuck you will become. Continue relentlessly and you will make yourself ineligible for political office. Tsarists will call you a flip-flopper.

On the other hoof, if you NEVER suspect that you might think or act like a Cosmic Schmuck, you will remain a Cosmic Schmuck forever. Continue on that path and you will accumulate so much power that nobody will dare tell you how enormous a Cosmic Schmuck you have become. You might even end your days in the Oval Office.

Or that's what I suspect.

Old Man On A Balcony:
Views Of Monterey Bay #11

The cat licks its paws:

I watch, three floors above: it

Looks up straight at me

THOUGHTS TO PONDER

We have certain preconceived ideas about location in
space and time which have come down to us from ape —
like ancestors.

— Sir Arthur Eddington

dove sta memora

You have not snared her,
Scarecrow Death:
She's in my pulse,
My heart, my breath.

Eye sees only
Local hardware;
Brain conceives
Nonlocal software;

Brain knows more
Than eye can see:
Brain can scan
Eternity.

Part II

ADVANCED HEAD TRIPS

Wilson describes himself as a "guerrilla ontologist," signifying his intent to **attack** language and knowledge the way terrorists **attack** their targets: to jump out from the shadows for an unprovoked **attack**, then **slink** back and hide behind a hearty belly-laugh."
— Robert Sheaffer, *Skeptical Inquirer*, Summer 1990

[Wilson "is"] a male feminist...a **simpering** pussy-whipped wimp.
— Lou Rollins, *Lucifer's Lexicon*

Joyce & Daoism

*I wrote this sometime in 1958, and it appeared in the **James Joyce Review** the following summer...which surprises me because I didn't try LSD until 1962 . . . Sure sounds like an Acid Head wrote it, doesn't it?*

Maybe I never needed all that acid after all. With James Joyce and Lao-Dzu as guides I might have ended up among the Terminally Bewildered anyway.

By the way, I learned the standard pre-Mao spellings of Chinese words about 40 year ago. In this book I attempt to use the current post-Mao spellings. Any blunders result from the clumsiness of an old dog trying to learn new tricks.

To Whatever Abysses

Throughout the long day of *Ulysses*, the thoughts of Stephen Dedalus and Mr. Bloom repeatedly return to the East; and this is not without reason. *Ulysses* is so profoundly Oriental in mood and conception that Carl Jung has recommended it as a new Bible for the white race. Molly Bloom's fervent "Yes" mirrors the author's acceptance of life in its entirety — an acceptance that transcends the dualisms of light and dark, good and evil, beautiful and sordid.

But every sensitive reader of *Ulysses* knows that this "acceptance" involved only part of the author's sensibility. The agony, the misanthropy, the (at times) Swiftian satire, all testify to Joyce's incomplete realization of what his instincts were trying to tell him. Only in *Finnegans Wake* does the true Oriental note sing uninterruptedly from beginning to end. The morbid rebel against the most morbid Church in Christendom had to go the long way round to reach the shortest way home. The affirmation of *Ulysses* seems forced (not "insincere" any more than the neurotic's desire to be cured is "insincere"); the affirmation of the *Wake* engages every level of the author's sensibility, from cortex to *cojones* — the whole man affirms, as in Nietzsche's *Zarathustra*.

The purpose of this present brief essay is to show that the Chinese philosophy of the Dao contributed largely to the shape of Joyce's affirmation. "Laotsey taotsey" (p. 242) or Lao-Dzu's doctrine of the Dao, explains a great many things about *Finnegans Wake*: the river-woman symbol, the Shem-Shaun dualism, the special quality of Joyce's humor, the "process" philosophy underlying its form.

Chapter 6 of the *Dao De Jing* says:

> Valley spirit never dies
> I call it Eternal Female.

Some Sinologists trace this "Eternal Female" back to a Chinese "Urmutter" myth of pre-Chou times, but Lao-Dzu was far beyond primitive mythology. He was using this myth as a pointer, to indicate the values that must have been in the society which created the myth. The distinction between Patrist and Matrist cultures made in such books as Ian Suttie's *The Origins of Love and Hate* and G. Rattray Taylor's *Sex in History* (not to mention Robert Graves' *The White Goddess* and Dr. Reich's *The Mass Psychology of Fascism*) places the Taoists as representatives of a Matrist social-ethical system living in Confucian Patrist China. The "Golden Age" of the Taoists did actually exist, whether or not it deserves to be called Golden: it was the Matriarchal, pre-Feudal China destroyed by the Chou State and official Confucian philosophy. Chapter 28 of the *Dao De Jing* defines the psychology and ethics of Daoism:

> He who knows the male, yet clings to the female,
> Becomes like a valley, receiving all things under heaven.

The "female" qualities of receptivity, acceptance, passivity, etc. are preferred to the "masculine" ethical rigor of Confucianism. Kuan Dzu explains this in its simplest terms:

> The sage follows after things, therefore he can control them.

Every married man knows how typically feminine — and how effective — this is. What is not so obvious is that this is, really, the philosophy of modern science. Bacon says: "We cannot command nature except by obeying her." (Cf. the Marxian "freedom as the recognition of necessity.") A letter by — of all people — Thomas Henry Huxley drives home the point, showing the innate connection between religious humility and scientific method.

> Science seems to me to teach in the highest and strongest manner the great truth which is embodied in the Christian conception of entire surrender to the will of God. Sit down before fact as a little child, be prepared to give up every preconceived notion, follow humbly wherever and to whatever abysses Nature leads, or you shall learn nothing.

The Daoists saw this attitude represented most clearly by women and by water, and made these the chief symbols of their religion. Orthodox Christians can understand why this approach is valuable to the scientist, but that it is the highest form of religion also, is certainly difficult for anyone conditioned to dogmatisms to accept. The Daoists put "open acceptance" where the West puts "dogmatic faith."

The female also stands, in Daoist thought, for those two forces regarded with most suspicion in Patrist societies: sex and love. The orthodox Freudians have said enough to familiarize us all with the neurotic illness that has come into Western culture with the triumph of anti-sex religions; what is not so obvious is how love, also, is under a pall in our society — see the chapter on "The Taboo on Tenderness" in Ian Suttie's *The Origins of Love and Hate*.*

~•~

* To date (2004), porn movies have explored every aspect of human sexuality except tenderness.

~•~

Water is, as we have said, the second great symbol of Daoism. It is, of course, the receptivity and yieldingness of water that recommends it to Lao-Dzu and Juang Jou. The philosophy of Judo (a Taoist invention) has come out of the observation of water, it is said. Judo co-operates with the attacking force, as water molds itself to its environment. Water and the Judo student bend and survive where bamboo and the ordinary man stand firm and break.

The values that Daoism sees in woman and water are their harmony with the Dao. I have not translated this key term, and I do not intend to; but Ezra Pound's translation — "the process" — seems to me more adequate than "the Way," "the Path" and most of the other attempts.*

~•~

* Daniel Coyle, Ph.D. has told me that "process" might fit the ideogram even better than "the process." I suspect "processing" would work in some contexts.

~•~

Students of General Semantics might understand if I say that the "Dao" comes very close to meaning what they mean when they say "the process-world." The Dao is the flux, the constant change, amid which we live and in the nature of which we partake; or it is the "law" of this change. (But, of course, the "law" and the "change" itself are not different in reality, only in our grammar and philosophy.)

A Zen master, asked how to get in harmony with the Dao, replied, "Walk on!"

Water and woman represent adjustment to the Law of Change, which "man, proud man, dressed in his little brief authority," and his abstract dogmas, tries to resist.

Anna Livia Plurabelle (ALP), the water woman, represents the values of the Dao in *Finnegans Wake*. The very first word of the book, "riverrun" — not the river and the running of the river, but "riverrun" — places us firmly in the "process-world" of modern physics, which is the world of the Dao. As Molly Bloom does in *Ulysses*, Anna gets the last word in *Finnegans Wake*, and it is a word that transcends the dualisms (Bloom and Stephen, Shem and Shaun, Mookse and Gripes) and affirms the unity behind them.

The parable of the Mookse and the Gripes expresses this

characteristic Daoist attitude with a quite characteristic Daoist humorous exaggeration. Adrian, the Papal Mookse, takes his stand on space, dogma and Aristotelian logic; the mystic Gripes verbally affirms time, relativity and the flux; but both are equally enmeshed in abstractions and both wither away in futile opposition to each other. Both, in short, are captives of the dualistic System they have themselves created. Nuvoletta, the avatar of ALP in this episode, is the Daoist female, unimpressed by the "dogmad", behaviour of the male. With Molly Bloom's resignation, she says:

> I see . . . there are menner.

It is important to grasp the distinction between the Gripes and Nuvoletta. Seemingly, they represent affirmation of the same cluster of things: time, the river, flux, mysticism, relativity, sex, love, the earth, Nature.

Actually, the Gripes' affirmation is verbal only, whereas Nuvoletta's affirmation is anything but verbal. None of Joyce's great Earth-Mother figures are given to philosophizing about "affirmation of Nature," etc. — they just do it. This is a crucial difference. As Lao-Dzu says:

> Those who speak do not know;
> Those who know do not speak.

Shem is a "sham and a low sham" because he is a "forger." Stephen Dedalus wanted to "forge in the smithy of my soul the uncreated conscience of my race"; but Shem merely seeks "to utter an epochal forged cheque on the public." Shem is one of those who speak but do not know; that his career is a satire on Joyce's own is the kind of irony implied in Christ's "Why callest thou me good? None is good but the Father," or the Sixth Patriarch's "I do not understand Buddhism." Probably everyone who ever gains any experience with the Dao begins by faking a little; it is really so much easier to verbalize about this affirmation than to live it. Joyce's portrait of the artist as a young forger is a self-confession that does penance for the whole race:

"you and I are in him."

ALP, the river-woman, does not have any such confession to make. Like the hen Belinda in Chapter Four, who "just feels she was kind of born to lay and love eggs" (p. 112), ALP lives in the Dao without question and without making a fuss about it (**wu-shih**). Her polar opposite is that figure whom Joyce describes as "Delude of Israel," "Gun, the Farther," or "Swiney Tod, ye Demon Barber" — the "phallic-destructive" Hangman God whose "criminal thumbprint" on the rock hangs over *Ulysses* and makes one realize that Molly Bloom's affirmation was something Joyce had not yet quite experienced when he wrote that saturnine masterpiece. In *Finnegans Wake* the Hangman God is securely put in his place, and from the first word, "riverrun," to the last dying murmur "a way a lone a last a loved a long the," the female figure of affirmation dominates the book.

Such Me

Putting the Hangman God in his places does not mean abolishing him; it means transcending him, in sweat and blood, rising above the dualistic delusion that makes Him seem credible. Nietzsche's "I write in blood, I will be read in blood," is testimony as to the superhuman effort required for an Occidental to make this transcendence.

Earwicker, as typical a product of Western dualism in its advanced stages as was Melville's Ahab, is, like Ahab, split down the middle by his own dualistic thinking. Joyce does not symbolize this as Melville did — by the scar from crown to toe that disfigures Ahab — but by projecting the two sides of Earwicker as Shem and Shaun, the Mookse and the Gripes, Mutt and Jute, Mercius and Justius, Glugg and Chuff, Muta and Juva, Butt and Taff, the Ondt and the Gracehoper. The Daoist orientation of Joyce's treatment of these dualities is indicated, on page 246, by the distortion of "Shem and Shaun" to "Yem and Yan."

Yin and Yang are the Taoist terms for the paired opposites

whose innate connectedness generates the entire world — process. Yin is feminine, dark, intuitive, etc.; Yang is masculine, light, rationalistic, etc. Neither can exist without the other, and both are parts of the Dao, and hence parts of each other.

The identity of the opposites, a central theme of Daoist thought, is indicated early in *Finnegans Wake*. The very first appearance of Shem and Shaun is as "the Hindoo, Shimar Shin," (p. 10) a single figure. Through the rest of the book they are split into two figures, but they are constantly changing roles and merging into each other (For instance, in the "School Lesson" chapter, where the Shem-type notes, left side of the page, leap suddenly to the right side, and the Shaun-type notes leap from right to left) Again, in the Mercius and Justius dispute, Shem and Shaun are picked up at the end and carried off together by ALP. "Sonnies had a scrap," she says with feminine equanimity.

The two philosophers most frequently mentioned in the Wake, Nicholas of Cusa and Bruno of Nola, taught a dialectic of resolution of opposites. Joseph Needham, in his monumental *Science and Civilization in China*, repeatedly mentions both Bruno and Nicholas as the only two Occidental philosophers before Liebnitz to have a basically Daoist outlook.

Every sensitive reader has noted the difference between the humor of *Ulysses* and the humor of *Finnegans Wake*. In writing *Ulysses*, Joyce's intention seems to have still contained a large element of the motive expressed to his publisher when describing *Dubliners*: "to show Ireland its own ugly face in a mirror." The humor in *Ulysses* is mostly satiric and negative, Swiftian; the joyous, Rabelaisian element is comparatively small. But in *Finnegans Wake* the humor is not only Rabelaisian, but Carrollian: it has that element of nonsense and childishness which only the well-integrated can sustain for long.

But this humor is also Daoistic. It is now suspected by scholars that the chapter of the Confucian "Analects" (**Lun Yu**) which contains a description of the Daoists as a band of madmen was interpolated by a Daoist writer! The rudely cheerful, very unselfconscious parody of Joyce himself in the "Shem the Penman" chapter has the same type of humor. Probably only an Irishman could understand that text about making oneself a fool for Christ's sake as a Daoist would understand it. Joyce, bending his incredible genius to the concoction of place names like "Wazwollenzie Haven"* and "Havva-ban-Annah" (not to mention "the bridge called Tilt-Ass") is exemplifying something that exists outside the *Wake* only in Lewis Carroll, Edward Lear and the Sacred Scriptures of the Daoists.

~•~

* German "Was wollen sie haben?" — What do you want?

~•~

("The Dao is in the dung-heap," said Juang Jou.)

To the Daoists, humor was what paradox is to Chesterton: a manifestation of divinity. Dao fa tsu-ran "The process just happens." (The entire passage reads:

> Ren fa di,
> di fa tien,
> tien fa Dao,
> Dao fa tzu-ran.

"Man molded by earth, earth molded by universe, universe molded by process, process just happens." Or — "process organizes itself") In short, determinism on one level results from chance on another level, as in thermodynamics.

Whether you call this Organicism and wax as self-consciously profound as Whitehead, or call it Materialism and get as self-righteously priggish as the American Association for the Advancement of Atheism, you still miss the point. That the Dao just happens, that it has no purpose or goal, no regard for man's self-importance ("Heaven treats us like straw dogs," Lao-Dzu says) — this is not a gloomy philosophy at all. When one understands this fully, on all levels of one's being, the only possible response is to have a good laugh. Daoist humor results from realization that the recognition of the most joyous truth of all seems to the egocentric man (you and me) frightening and gloomy.

Joyce is nowhere more thoroughly Daoist than when he

answers all the paradoxes and tragedies of life with the brief, koan-ish "Such me." Genial bewilderment ("Search me!") and calm acceptance ("Such I am") meet here as they meet nowhere else but in Daoism, and its intellectual heirs, Zen and Shinshu Buddhism and the neo-Confucianism of Chu Hsi. We cannot understand; neither can we escape — "Such me." (p. 597)

It is this attitude — which women seem to be able to grasp much more easily than men — that gives *Finnegans Wake* its air of goofy impartiality. The Buddhist (outside of the Zen school) labors strenuously to rise over the opposites; the Daoist dissolves them into a good horse-laugh. Joyce's method is Daoistic.

"Sonnies had a scrap;" "Now a muss was the little face;" "You were only dreamond, dear" — the tolerant, existentialist female voice, vastly unimpressed by masculine abstractions and ideologies, breaks in at every point where a Big Question is being debated. The Zen Patriarch who said, when he was asked for religious instruction, "When you finish your meal, wash your plates," had this attitude.

The Keys To

Wyndham Lewis saw in *Ulysses* an implicit acceptance of Bergson's time-philosophy and denounced Joyce, in his *Time and Western Man*, for contributing to what he called "the Time Cult" (other members: Einstein, Ezra Pound, Picasso, Whitehead, the Futurist painters, Gertrude Stein). Lewis, a classicist, set up the dualism of space philosophies (Aristotelian, rational, conservative, masculine, etc.) against time philosophies (oriental, intuitive, radical, feminine, etc.) Joyce wrote the *Wake* from "the Haunted Inkbottle, no number, Brimstone Walk, Asia in Ireland" (p. 182) placidly, even eagerly, accepting the non-Aristotelian position Lewis had attributed to him.

As is well known, the events of the *Wake* occur "at no spatial time" and cannot be sharply defined because "every parson, place and thing in the chaosmos anywhere at all connected with it was moving and changing all the time" (p. 118). In short, we are within the Einsteinian universe; and Joyce realizes, as did

Alfred Korzybski, that the Aristotelian "laws of thought" cannot hold in such a universe: "The sword of certainty which would identified the body never falls" (p. 51). The Law of Identity, that is, cannot hold in a process-world "where," as the mathematical physicist says, "every electron has a date and is not identical to itself from one second to another."

The Daoists were familiar with these relativistic considerations long before Einstein.

Juang Jou writes:

> There is nothing under the canopy of heaven greater than the tip of an autumn spikelet. A vast mountain is a small thing. Neither is there any age greater than that of a small child cut off in infancy. Bung Tzu* himself died young. The universe and I came into being together; and I, and everything therein, are one.

~•~

* Chinese isomorph of Methuselah.

~•~

A better description anywhere of the "inner logic" of *Finnegans Wake* can hardly be found. To ask what "is really happening" on any page is like asking a physicist whether light "is really" waves or particles. Jaun's sermon to the leap-year girls "is" a confession of Earwicker's incestuous desires; "is" a barrel rolling down the Liffey river; "is" a postman making his rounds; "is" Jesus saying farewell to the Daughters of Jerusalem; etc . . . Anna Livia Plurabelle "is" a woman, and she "is" also a river. Earwicker "is" a man, a mountain, an insect, the current Pope, the *Urvater* of Freudian theory, Finn MacCool, and he is also both Shem and Shaun. He is, as a matter of fact, every person, place and thing in the *Wake* — just as every man "is" the sum total of his own perceptions and evaluations. Earwicker is finally able to accept and affirm his world, Joyce is finally able to accept and affirm his world, because they recognize that "I, and everything therein, are one." "Such me."

Physics, psychology, semantics and several other sciences have entirely rejected the view which sees the universe as a collection of block-like entities.

We now think in terms of relations and functions: iron rod A has no absolute "length," but only $length_1$, $length_2$, $length_3$, etc., as it moves through the space-time continuum. $Smith_n$ has no absolute "self" but only a succession of roles in a succession of socio-psychological fields. A world of such inter-related processes is a seamless unity, and every perceiver "is" that unity at every second. That is why Emerson could write — and Joyce could demonstrate — that "The sphinx must solve his own riddle. All of history is in one man."

To the space-consciousness of a Wyndham Lewis, a chair is a static "thing" out there, apart from the observer; given, concrete, identifiable. To the time-mind of Joyce, the chair becomes a process, a joint phenomenon of observer and observed, a stage in the transmutation of energy: "My cold cher's gone ashley," he writes, (p. 213) seeing the future ashes in the present object. (Cf. Hiu Shih's paradox, "An egg has feathers")

Zen Buddhist teachers make this point, somewhat obliquely, by pointing to a picture of Bodhidharma (who was bearded), and asking the puzzled student, "Why doesn't that fellow have a beard?"

The answer of the witty Gracehoper to the conservative Ondt (p. 419):

> Your genus is worldwide, your spacest sublime,
> But Holy Saltmartin, why can't you beat time?

is Joyce's answer to Wyndham Lewis and the entire Western Tradition back to Aristotle which backs him up.

The Gracehoper had "jingled through a jungle of life in debts and jumbled through a jingle of love in doubts" but, as the rhythm and vocabulary suggest, he had vastly enjoyed himself doing so. Time, which strikes him down, will eventually strike down the "anal-acquisitive" Ondt also. All the abstractions man invents to give himself control over events and stave off doubt, all the preparations man makes to stay out of debt, are as nothing before the inscrutable workings-out of the Dao; the search for security, Alan Watts has frequently observed, is the main cause of insecurity. As Nuvoletta says, "Ise so silly to be flowing, but I no canna stay" (p. 159). The "secret" of Daoism, the secret of *Finnegans Wake*, is very simply expressed in Poe's "Descent Into the Maelstrom," whose hero saved himself by "studying the action of the whirlpool and co-operating with it."

This is the trick that explains Judo. It also explains Anna Livia Plurabelle's calm acceptance of her own end as she flows out to sea:

> The keys to. Given. Lps. A way a lone a last a loved a long the

The only word that can possibly complete that sentence is the "riverrun" at the beginning. We can find ourselves only by losing ourselves, all mystics testify. Anna loses herself into the ocean, but what she becomes is the true self she has always been: "riverrun," the process.

THOUGHTS TO PONDER

In short, philosophers, ancient and modern, appear to me as mad as Hindoos, Mahomatons and Christians.
— John Adams to Thomas Jefferson, 16 July 1814

Movie Haiku

For a while there [circa 1999 — 2001] I got into writing haiku about all the movies I really liked. Here's some I decided to preserve.

HANNIBAL

Lecter, too, grows old

But remains quite amusing,

Quite terrifying

TEQUILA SUNRISE

A major coke deal—

Treachery in sun-bright places—

One friendship survives

KING KONG

Can't blame the big ape:

I, too, went a bit goofy

Over Fay Wray once

HONKY TONK MAN

Addictions killed him,

Too much booze and cigarettes.

They still sing his songs.

AND THEN THERE WERE NONE

Unpleasantness and

Rash Actions: Even servants

Get drunk and murdered.

WHITE HUNTER, BLACK HEART

Arlen said it best:

"He had a good heart, really—

just too much Ego."

ON A CLEAR DAY YOU CAN SEE FOREVER

"Witchcraft" not spoken

But still the best film ever

About Wise Women

UNFORGIVEN

Drunk sociopath

Kills "guilty" and "innocent."

Seemed like Justice, then.

LADY FROM SHANGHAI

A yacht called Circe:

Trial: Chinese drama:

Crazy house: Hall of mirrors:

STARDUST MEMORIES

Woody's rage breaks loose:

A comedy of terrors.

The girl goes nuts, too.

MIDNIGHT IN THE GARDEN
OF GOOD AND EVIL

Courtrooms and Voodoo

Both leave us undecided—

"There ain't no answers!"

INTOLERANCE

Those who would do good

Often do the worst evil—

If they have True Faith . . .

BIRD

Did the junk ruin him

Or was it Whitey's racism?

Don't know. Bird is dead.

THE OUTLAW JOSEY WALES

The killing must stop—

And, guess what? this time it does:

No final shoot-out.

THE GHOST AND THE DARKNESS

The whites see lions—

The blacks see devils from Hell—

You'll wonder a bit . . .

THE MALTESE FALCON

Seventeen long years

And God-knows-how-many murders

Chasing a lead dream

BUS STOP

You can't discount it.

You can't forget it. It has

M*a*r*i*l*y*n M*o*n*r*o*e.

CHIMES AT MIDNIGHT

Winter: Wind, snow, chill:

Merrie England's dead and gone.

Falstaff, too, must die.

THE EIGER SANCTION

Three times the Eiger

Tried to kill him: And he looked

Into the abyss.

THOUGHTS TO PONDER

I don't think anybody ever really matures. Adults are just children who owe money.

— Kenneth Branagh

He Who Thunders From On High

Theotopology & Theometeorology

I've recently noticed "as if for the first time" that when people pray they always look "upward" — i.e., perpendicular to whatever place they're standing — or kneeling or groveling. I deduce that they conceive of their "god" as topologically isomorphic to a huge donut, about a thousand miles wider than Earth.*

~•~

* Or maybe they still think of the Earth as flat?

~•~

(Of course, if people ever pray at the north or south poles, this would have to change; then "god" would become isomorphic to a hollow sphere.)

When I raised this issue in a blog recently, Paul Krassner asked "Does this mean that the pledge of allegiance should be changed to 'one nation inside god'?"

Not necessarily. Although the Bible and Koran always speak of their god as "above," Christians, Jews and Moslems can either accept what their rituals imply — a donut god — or return to a flat Earth . . .

Giambattista Vico, "the father of sociology," suggested in *The New Science* that Thunder historically underlies the "god" idea; the Noisy Thing roaring in the sky, seemingly in rage, had to be appeased.

Sometimes lightning came from that roaring monster, and sometimes lightning killed somebody.

Hence *Zeus bronnton* (Zeus the thunderer)*; Jupiter, another thunder god; Thor, Donner, whose very name means thunder; etc . . . and Yahweh . . . and Allah . . .

~•~

* Zeus, to Arlen, sounded like rain, and bronnton like thunder...

~•~

Joyce uses this god = thunder equation repeatedly in *Finnegans Wake* (which drove me to read Vico . . .).

I have also observed that thunder on the sound-track — signaling on-coming tragedy or horror — appears in films as diverse as those of Orson Welles, James Whale, Howard Hawks, Wes Craven, Monty Python, etc., etc . . . Listen for it and note how bloody often it pops up...especially in thrillers . . .

The monotheistic idea implies a cruel and grumpy old electric donut surrounding Earth and ever threatening it.

I think this explains the "structural unconscious" or inarticulate neurosemantics of Bozo, Ariel Sharon and Osama bin Laden equally. They're all heaping up human sacrifices, as at Stonehenge, to Him Who Thunders From On High.

THOUGHTS TO PONDER

The sum total of all minds is one.

— Erwin Schrödinger

Get Your New York Garbage Online

http://www.nycgarbage.com

This guy sells beautifully boxed New York City garbage online.

I just saw him on CNN; he sez he started this er um enterprise to prove that Americans will buy fookin' ANYthing if it comes in an attractive package.

He also sez he's sold 500 boxes so far. I wonder how many got remailed to Bozo @ the White House?

Becoming What We "Are"

If you stroll through a large art museum, you will notice that Van Gogh does not paint the same world as Rembrandt, Picasso does not see things the way Goya did, Georgia O'Keefe doesn't much resemble Rivera, Salvador Dali looks like nobody but himself, and, in general, no world-class artist became a "classic" by doing what somebody else had already done or even what everybody else in his/her own era did.

And in science, the names of Einstein, Dirac, the Curies, Bohr, Heisenberg, Schrödinger, John Bell, etc. live on because none of them took Newton as Holy Gospel: they all made unique and unpredictable innovations in basic theory.

And, in case you think this applies only to "arts and sciences," consider the most successful people in industry. Henry Ford did not get rich copying Fulton's steamboat; he made a car so cheap that anybody could afford one. Howard Hughes produced movies that nobody else would have dared to attempt, and then went on to revolutionize the airline industry. Buckminster Fuller did not copy the cubical form of previous architects, but invented the geodesic dome; at last count, over 300,000 of his buildings existed, making him the most visibly successful architect in history. Steve Wozniak did not copy the computers of his day, but invented one that even a "bloody eejit" (like me) could use (and even enjoy!) Bill Gates created new kinds of software. Etc.

We all need constant reiteration of these truisms because we live in a world where a multitude of very powerful forces have worked upon us, from birth through school to jobs, attempting to suppress our individuality, our creativity and, above all, our curiosity — in short, to destroy everything that encourages us to think for ourselves.

Our parents wanted us to act like the other darling children in our neighborhood; they emphatically did not want a boy or girl who seemed "weird" or "different" or (Heaven forfend) "too damned clever by far."

Then we enter grade school, a fate worse than Death and Hell combined. Whether we land in a public school or a private religious school, we learn two basic lessons: [1] There exists one correct answer for every question; and [2] education consists of memorizing the one correct answer and regurgitating it on an "examination."

The same tactics continue through high school and, except in a few sciences, even to the university.

All through this "education" we find ourselves bombarded by organized religion. Most religions, in this part of the world also teach us "one correct answer," which we should accept with blind faith; worse, they attempt to terrorize us with threats of post-mortem roasting, toasting, boiling, broiling, charbroiling and freedomfrying if we ever dare to think at all, at all.

After 18 to 30+ years of all this, we enter the job market, and learn to become, or try to become, almost deaf, dumb and blind. We must always tell our "superiors" what they want to hear, what suits their prejudices and/or their wishful fantasies. If we notice something they don't want to know about, we learn to keep our mouths shut. If we don't—

"One more word, Bumstead, and I'll fire you!"

As my *mahatmaguru* J .R. "Bob" Dobbs says, "You know how dumb the average guy is? Well, mathematically, by definition, half of them are even dumber than that."

"Bob" may have the average confused with the median, but otherwise he hit a bull's eye. Half of the people you meet do indeed seem dumber than a box of turds; but they did not start out that way. Parents, peers, schools, churches, advertisers and jobs made them that way. Every baby at birth has a relentlessly curious and experimental temperament. It takes the first third of our lives to destroy that curiosity and experimentalism; but in most cases, we become placid parts of a docile herd.

This human herd all started out as potential geniuses, before the tacit conspiracy of social conformity blighted their brains. All of them can redeem that lost freedom, if they work at it hard enough.

I've worked at it for 50+ years now, and still find parts of me acting like a robot or a zombie on occasion. Learning "how to become what you are" (in Nietzsche's phrase) takes a lifetime, but it still seems the best game in town.

THOUGHTS TO PONDER

To the States or any one of them, or any city of the States,
  RESIST MUCH, OBEY LITTLE,
Once unquestioning obedience, once fully enslaved;
Once fully enslaved, no nation, state, city of this Earth,
ever afterward resumes its liberty.

— Walt Whitman

Old Man On A Balcony:
Views of Monterey Bay #12

Brother Raven, you

ain't no song-bird. You wusser

than the kiss of death

LSD, Dogs & Me

Greetings to Dr. Albert Hofmann 0n the 60th birthday of his "problem child!" And greetings to the Free World in general from the occupied U.S.A.!

Two major factors have rendered me incapable of believing in the dominant mechanistic-materialist model of mind and the universe: [1] dogs, all of my life, and [2] LSD, since 1962.

About dogs I will write elsewhere; here I will say only that no matter how much mechanistic biology I read, no dog who ever lived as a guest in my house ever seemed like a machine to me. They all seemed like four-legged people.

Every LSD voyager has his or her own unique reports to offer; here I offer only my own recollections of my own experiences, expressed in my own favorite metaphors.

After my first LSD voyage, dogs not only seemed even less like machines than before, but so did bugs and trees and birds and the starry sky itself. After my 100th trip, even I seemed less like a machine.

I have not embraced pantheism or even panpsychism as a philosophy; rather, I have given up on philosophies entirely. I live amid wonders. which I file under the law of general semantics which states that no map can ever show "all" the territory. In fact, I think we should ban the word "all" from ordinary speech and restrict it solely to pure mathematics.

Let me explain that a bit. Consider any large city you know well — Zurich, Berlin, Amsterdam, Los Angeles, whatever. For the sake of illustration, let me write "Dublin" and you may think of any other city you prefer. Do you think any map of Dublin can show the locations and directions of all the mice in that city? Even if you regard this absurdity as theoretically possible, this *maus* map still would not include the flowers, fleas, microbes, *und so weiter*; nor would it depict the emotions, joys, sufferings *u.s.w.* of the people (or the dogs) — *and it would remain relatively accurate for only seconds. (It could not remain totally accurate for even a nanosecond.)*

Now consider our other kinds of "maps" — our beliefs, our arts, our sciences. Does quantum mechanics tell "all" or even most of the reasons Bozo wants to kill lots and lots of people? Does Freudian theory, Marxism, postmodernism, bile samples, or oil prices — alone or combined into a mega-model — tell "all" about that?

Does Van Gogh tell more or less about vegetation than Beethoven's Sixth, Darwin's *Origin of Species*, or the latest papers on botany? Which geometry reveals "all" the truth about the starry sky above Dublin — Euclid, Gauss, Lobachevsky, Buckminster Fuller?

To fully grasp what I mean here, try the following simple experiment: try to say "all" about the page (or computer screen) on which you see these words. Assuming you have it in hard copy, try to write down all you know about the chemical composition of the ink and the paper; if you don't know enough, do some research.

Try to learn "all" about how it got from me to you, even if that requires six months of study of computer science and electronic theory. Who asked me to write this? Find out "all" you can about her or him. Don't neglect the others involved in the production of this page — their salaries, their worries, their religions if any, their politics, their sex-lives *u.s.w.*

And don't forget me: why did somebody ask **me** to write about LSD and why did I agree? Try to investigate "all" about me.

(Hint: in doing this exercise, I discovered that among the infinite reasons I became a writer I could not omit the Danes over-fishing the North Sea 15 centuries ago.)*

~•~

* My paternal grandmother had the name O'Lachlann, which means "son of the Dane" in Gaelic. The Danes took to invasion and conquest, of Ireland and elsewhere, after the fish problem arose . . .

~•~

If you continue this search for "allness" reasonably long enough (about two years minimum), the page may have yellowed and the ink might have faded, which will require more investigation into chemistry and even political history — e.g. the paper would last longer if made of hemp; why did the publisher use wood pulp instead?

Now imagine these gigabytes of information entering your brain not in two years, but in two nanoseconds, and radiating not just from this page but from the fruit on the table, the wall paint, the pencil, the cars passing in the street . . . and the furthest stars.

That's why LSD has altered the world for so many of us in the last 60 years. Like English poet William Blake, we have found "infinity in a grain of sand" and the deeper we look, the deeper the abyss grows. And like Nietzsche, we often suspect that as we gaze into the abyss, the abyss also gazes into us . . .

LSD seems to suspend the imprinted and conditioned brain circuits that normally control perception/emotion/thought, allowing a flood — an ocean — of new information to break through.

The experience will seem either very frightening or exhilaratingly educational, depending on how rigidly you previously believed your current map contained "all" the universe. Since I learned that no model equals the totality of experience long before I tried LSD, I never had a bad trip; but I have seen enough anxiety attacks and downright wig-outs in cases of the naive and dogmatic that I have never favored or advocated LSD's promiscuous use by the general population.

While splashing about and trying not to drown in this ocean of new *information*, you generally experience a second LSD surprise: an explosion of newfound *energy* within your own body. Whether you call this kundalini or bio-electricity or orgone or libido or Life Force, it can trigger muscle spasms, unbridled Eros or just "warm and melting" sensations — or all three in succession, or all three almost simultaneously — usually followed by something loosely called "near-death experience" or "out of body experience."

Again, this can seem either psychotically terrifying or "religiously" ecstatic, and can imprint short- or long-term tendencies toward paranoia (*"everything* wants to destroy me") or metanoia (*"everything* wants to help me"). In either case, one tends to retain a heightened awareness of those peculiar coincidences that Jung called synchronicities and Christian conspiracy buffs attribute to hostile occult forces.

In my case, after a few years I found myself seemingly forced to choose, not between paranoia and metanoia — both by then appeared pitiful oversimplifications — but between mysticism and agnosticism. I solved that problem, for myself anyway, by choosing agnostic mysticism in the tradition of Lao-Dzu:

> Something unknown, unspeakable,
> before Earth or sky,
> before life or death,
> I do not know what to call it
> So I call it Dao

What do I think we should do with Dr. Hoffman's "problem child"? Well, **no commodity becomes safer when its manufacture, sale and distribution all fall into the hands of professional criminals**; and prohibition, of alcohol and all other drugs, inevitably has that effect, followed by police corruption and public cynicism. Maybe governments should leave this arena entirely and let professional scientists, medical and otherwise, write the guidelines?

Old Man On A Balcony:
Views Of Monterey Bay #13

The orange cloudbank:

One bright touch in the grey sky

Above a grey bay

Keep Our Troops In Iraq!

I swear to God and/or Goddess I saw this and heard it, on CNN around 4 p.m. PST 14 April 2004:

> US Soldier in Iraq tells interviewer he doesn't mind three extra months but resents his current duty "guarding property." Sez he should be doing what he was sent there to do.
> "What's that?" prompts interviewer.
> "Kickin' in doors and killin' people," he says, as honest and innocent as Dr. Lecter announcing his gourmet preferences . . .

As criminologists know, the group most likely to commit all violent crimes — brawls, sports riots, drunk'n'disorderly, rape, mayhem, torture, murder, even suicide — consists of males between 16 and 24. In imperialist/repressive society, I think MOST of us go whacko in less "colorful," (i.e., less criminal) ways for at least a few years in there. See Reich, *Mass Psychology of Fascism*.

Maybe Dubya knows the crime statistics even if he don't know from this Reich guy . . .

My god, do you really want those galoots back here roaming OUR streets?

THOUGHTS TO PONDER

BELINDA: Ay, but you know we must return good for evil.
LADY BRUTE: That may be a mistake in the translation.

— Sir John Vanbrugh, The Provoked Wife

How to Win an Argument

The Swift Boat Veterans for Truth convinces me — as does the behavior of CSICOP — that the oldest and most cynical view of politics remains true: if you throw enough shit at the Enemy, some of it will stick, and he will stink.

At least in the minds of those who don't pay close attention.

Old Man on A Balcony:
Views Of Monterey Boy #14

ANOTHER MIDNIGHT HAIKU

Dark, dark: no waves splash,

no barking dogs, no wind. Just

the sound of no sound

Mary, Mary, Quite Contrary

Say the magic word and the duck will come down and
pay you $100.

— Marx

In the small and otherwise little-known town of
Rennes-le-Chateau in Southern France, near the Spanish border,
stands a decidedly odd cathedral which has become a center of
controversy, conspiracy theories and occult speculation for over
a century. Although it belongs to the Roman Catholic church,
and looks superficially orthodox from a distance, you don't
even have to go inside to begin suspecting you have found the
weirdest goddamn church in the entire Christian world, because
over the entrance stand the ominous words

THIS PLACE IS CURSED

If nameless awe and Lovecraftian fears of cosmic horror do not
drive you back, you will proceed, and discover that this temple
is dedicated to Mary Magdalene, the most poorly recorded,
yet ill-reputed, of the disciples of Jesus. In the Bible itself, she
appears as a name and only a name. According to long-held
legend, she was a common whore; and even after she reformed,
she remains a bit of an embarrassment to the more puritanical
Christians; i.e., most of them.

An "accursed" church named after the Monica Lewinsky of
the New Testament does present a puzzle, but the real mindfucks
appear inside, on the Stations of the Cross. One station seems to
show shadowy figures smuggling Jesus's body out of the grave
in the middle of the night (as if to fake the Resurrection?) and
another, even more unorthodox when you think it over, shows
a Scotchman in kilts amid the crowd at the Crucifixion (as if to
validate the secret tradition of Scotch Rite freemasonry . . . ?).

Lest you think all this the work of the Monty Python crew, the

Church of Mary Magdalene was built in the 1890's by the local parish priest, Father Beranger Sauniere, but where he got the money for the construction seems even more problematic than the eldritch edifice itself. Rennes-le-Chateau, a small town, could barely afford a priest, and Father Sauniere in his early days often survived on free meals from his congregation, yet he suddenly became rich. In addition to the church, he built a Tower, also dedicated to Mary Magdalene, and a bridge, and other public works, but nobody knows where he got the money.

Some legends soon grew in the village, claiming that Father Sauniere had found the lost treasure of the Knights Templar (who had a castle in the area) or that he had rediscovered the secret of alchemy. In *L'Or de Rennes-le-Chateau (The Treasure of Rennes-le-Chateau)*, an odd bloke named Gerard de Sede claimed that Sauniere had discovered some old parchments containing a "priceless" historical and occult revelation. He even reproduces the alleged parchments, which consist only of two pages from the New Testament, in Latin.

Three other researchers named Lincoln, Baigent and Leigh later discovered that some of the letters in these parchments do not follow the alignment of the rest of the text, but hang above it, like exponents in mathematics. These letters formed words, not in Latin but in French — but the words create a new mystery of their own. Slightly condensed, they say:

THIS TREASURE BELONGS TO DAGOBERT II KING AND HE IS THERE DEAD SHEPHERDESS NO TEMPTATION THAT POUSSIN TENIERS HOLD THE KEY PEACE 681 BY THE CROSS AND THE HORSE OF GOD I COMPLETE THIS DEMON GUARDIAN AT NOON BLUE APPLES

We shall return to this dazzling revelation, or surrealist hoax, but first we will examine Father Sauniere a bit more deeply. This simple country priest often visited Paris and evidently mingled with the occult lodges there, including some of those associated with Aleister Crowley (a hint?). Before he died, Sauniere made a final confession, as a good Catholic should; but the priest who heard the confession found it so terrible that he denied the last rites and refused to grant absolution. According to Catholic dogma, Sauniere immediately went to Hell — for an accursed church, a Scotchman at the Crucifixion, noon blue apples, and some aeon-old horror that allegedly makes sense of all this . . .

Wait. It gets even weirder.

Gerard de Sede, whom I have already dared to call an odd bloke, produced another book, *La Race fabuleuse (The Fabulous Race)*, which deals with Stenay, a town far from Rennes-le-Chatteau, which happens to have the head of Satan on its Coat of Arms. Although de Sede prominently mentions (but never does explain) this blasphemy, he does have a lot of interesting things to say. Frogs often fall out of the sky onto Stenay, an annoyance to orthodox science, which cannot explain them.

Charles Fort and the Fortean Society have catalogs of inexplicable frogfalls. And fishfalls. And some falls of strange metal objects. I hope that helps you, here in the murk.

The Merovingian kings, a dark age dynasty (c. 400-700 e.v.), had a falling frog on their Coat of Arms. (Less sinister than Satan, but more perplexing?) The church in Stenay is built so that on midsummer day you can stand at the altar, look through the arched doors and see Sirius rising behind the sun. And Dagobert II, a Merovingian king, was murdered by persons unknown in the Ardennes Forest on 23 December, 679 c.e.

THIS TREASURE BELONGS TO DAGOBERT II KING AND HE IS THERE DEAD . . .

Hey, maybe some of this makes sense?

De Sede finally offers us a revelation, or part of one, thanks to one Marquis de B. (All the best conspiracy books have sources who cannot be identified. Even Woodward and Bernstein had "Deep Throat.") The Marquis, himself descended from Dagobert, tells de Sede that the spooky Merovingians resulted from matings between certain ancient Israelites of the Tribe of Benjamin and extraterrestrials from Sirius. They have lived in hiding and obscurity for many centuries, because a certain powerful conspiracy has tried to murder them all, just like it murdered poor old Dagobert. Although neither de Sede nor de B. name this conspiracy, the evidence seems arranged so as to point a strong finger of suspicion at the Vatican.

Although the Marquis promised further revelations, he never got to provide them. Like Dagobert II, he was murdered on 23 December (in 1972) in the Ardennes forest. Or so de Sede claims.

Another part of the puzzle emerges from a Swiss source — journalist Mathieu Paoli, who, in a book titled *Les Dessous (Undercurrents)* exposed what he considered a conspiracy to restore monarchy in France, under the guise of two groups called respectively [a] the Committee to Protect the Rights and Privileges of Low-Cost Housing and [b] the Priory of Sion. His evidence actually seems to indicate that both groups act as fronts for something even older and more esoteric.

Both of these secretive organizations had links with the Grand Loge Alpina in Switzerland and the Committee for Public Safety, an office of the de Gaulle government in Paris.

The Grand Loge Alpina ranks as the richest freemasonic lodge in the world, since most of its members belong to the elite Swiss banking families that British Prime Minister Harold Wilson once claimed had more power than all the governments of Europe combined. He even called them "the Gnomes of Zurich." Timothy Leary also used to say that the Cold War came to an end when the Americans and Russians discovered that the Swiss own the whole world already.

The Committee for Public Safety seemed to consist of only Andre Malraux, Nobel Laureate in literature, and Pierre Plantard de Saint Clair, a fabulously rich occultist. Both men had served heroically in the Resistance, during the Nazi occupation, and had long personal friendships with de Gaulle. Yet Paoli's evidence seemed to implicate them in a plot to replace de Gaulle's democratic (if right-wing) government with a restored monarchy.

It does not compute, as Robby the Robot would say.

But dig this: Paoli reproduces the front page of one issue of Circuit, the official journal of the Committee to Protect the Rights and Privileges of Low-Cost Housing and/or the Priory of Sion: it shows a map of France with a Star of David superimposed on it and a conventional "flying saucer" hovering above.

What was it de Sede claimed about ancient Israelites who mated with extraterrestrials from Sirius? Hmmm . . . ?

After publication of *Les Dessous*, Paoli went to Israel, where the government arrested him for spying, convicted him, and shot him dead by firing squad, he then quickly dying of natural causes as a result. Unless we want to let this stuff really weird us out, we better regard that as a mere coincidence. Even considering it a synchronicity might get us into deep and murky waters, especially if we're a little bit stoned.

La Race fabuleuse and *Les Dessous* both appeared in 1973. On 23 July that year, I had the first of a series of experiences which seemed like communications from Sirius, although, grown older and wiser, or at least more cautious, I now tend to attribute them to Too Much Acid. (See my *Cosmic Trigger* trilogy.) Early the next year, sci-fi supergenius Philip K. Dick had a set of similar experiences, which he at times attributed to communications from Sirius — although he also thought they might actually emanate from his dead friend, Bishop James Pike, or from a Gnostic disciple of Jesus named Thomas.

In 1976 appeared *The Sirius Mystery* by Robert KG. Temple, a fellow of the Royal Astronomical Society, who evidently had felt the Sirius Vibe in his own academic way. His book argues that ancient intercourse between Earth and Sirius had occurred about 4500 years ago in the mid-East, but unlike de Sede he does not suggest sexual intercourse, merely the intellectual variety, and he locates the contact point in Sumeria, not Israel . . . but still . . .

Things heated up in 1982 with the publication of *Holy Blood, Holy Grail* by the aforementioned Baigent, Lincoln and Leigh.

It had no references to Sirius, but among other things, it tried to prove that de Sede belonged to the Priory of Sion (the real brains behind the Committee to Protect the Rights and Privileges of Low-Cost Housing); that the Priory had existed since the 14th Century and carried on the secret inner traditions of the Knights Templar, the warrior-monks systematically exterminated by the

Inquisition 1300-1307 on charges of heresy; that Pierre Plantard de Saint Clair acts as the current Grand Master of the Priory; and that the Priory serves to protect the Merovingians and their descendants from a murderous vendetta by the Vatican (a thesis only hinted at by de Sede).

Baigent, Lincoln and Leigh even obtained an interview with Priory Grand Master Plantard de Saint Clair, who evaded most of their questions, but did admit that Father Sauniere found a "treasure," adding hermetically that the treasure was not material but "spiritual," that it belonged to Israel, and that it would be forwarded thereto "at the proper time." Well, that sure helps a lot, doesn't it?

The real bombshell falls at the end, when the authors offer their own solution to these enigmas. Jesus, they claim, married Mary Magdalene and they had a son. After the Crucifixion, the widow and the widow's son fled to France, and he became the progenitor of the Merovingians. They even produce a photo of the sepulcher of the widow's son, which is quite near Rennes-le-Chateau, and point out its strong resemblance to a similar tomb in the painting, *Shepherds of Arcadia*, by Nicholas Poussin.

SHEPHERDESS NO TEMPTATION THAT POUSSIN
TENIERS HOLD THE KEY PEACE 681

This painting shows three shepherds looking in awe at the tomb, and the tomb bears the inscription, *Et in Arcadia ego . . .* ("And in Arcadia, I . . .") Baigent *et al.* point out that if you permute the letters of this fragment, you can obtain I TEGO AR-CANA DEI ("I conceal the secrets of God.") I surmise that with further ingenuity you could obtain "Noon Blue Apples" again, perhaps in Lithuanian.

De Sede had already mentioned this cryptic painting, in *La Race fabuleuse*, hinting that it was linked to the Merovingians and Father Sauniere. He also claimed that it once belonged to Louis XVI, who kept it in an isolated room where visitors to the palace could not see it.

But to return to the late Redeemer and his alleged paramour, Ms. Magdalene, *if* one accepts them as the ancestors of the Merovingians, as Baigent *et al.* would have it, and *if* one accepts the divinity of Jesus, as most Christians do, then the medieval doctrine of "the divine right of kings" suddenly makes sense. The Merovingians seem to have intermarried with every other royal family in Europe — royals only marry royals, you know — so almost every king and queen of Europe from the middle ages onward has carried some of the holy "blood" of Jesus by way of the holy grail of Mary's uterus. If you translate "blood" as genes, this makes sense, sort of.

Maybe we should give up all the democratic heresy of the last 200 years and accept the genepool of Jesus and Mary Christ as our God-given rulers?

Well, not if you think de Sede has a more plausible argument for the extraterrestrial/Hebraic origin of the Merovingians.

Or you can skeptically regard all this as a complicated joke perpetrated by an odd consortium of aristocrats with too much time on their hands.

But then, why did the Swiss bankers get involved? They definitely do not have too much time on their hands. And where the hell did Sauniere get his sudden wealth and why did he use part of it to build a church for an allegedly reformed alleged hooker?

Baigent and his associates also produce a heap of genealogical charts showing who, in the modern world, belongs to the "divine" Merovingian genetic pool, together with an alleged list of Grand Masters of the Priory of Sion. Some interesting names appear:

Prince Bernhard of the Netherlands. He's related to the Merovingians and, although this does not appear in the Baigent genealogy, he founded the Bilderbergers, a mysterious group of rich white males who appear in dozens of conspiracy theories by both Leftwing and Rightwing opponents of the current power structure. Although never convicted of any real crime in any real court, the Bilderbergers do indeed look conspiratorial to a lot of writers not rich enough, white enough or male enough to gain admittance; and they act with extreme secrecy. According to Lawrence Wilmot, writers for both the London Economist and the French TV news admitted to him that they have orders not to mention the Bilderbergers, and other journalists responded with "ironic laughter" when asked why they never touched on this subject.

(A few known American members of the Bilderbergers: George Bush Sr., Bill Clinton, David Rockefeller.)

Dr. Otto von Hapsburg, heir of the longtime rulers of the Austro-Hungarian Empire, descendent of the Merovingians and another Bilderberger. According to Baigent & Co., the von Hapsburg family financed Father Sauniere and the building of the Church of Mary Magdalene in the last century. According to Maynard Solomon's very scholarly and non-conspiracy-oriented biography, *Beethoven*, the Emperor Joseph von Hapsburg, in the 18th Century, appeared as a hero, an "Enlightened Monarch," to the Bavarian Illuminati, who commissioned Ludwig to immortalize him in the *Emperor Joseph Cantata*, where he is hailed as "foe of darkness and bringer of light." Dr. Otto himself still carries the mysterious title, King of Jerusalem, which always belongs to the eldest male von Hapsburg of every generation. (Because they are descended from King Jesus? Or from those Jewish Extraterrestrials?)

Jean Cocteau, 23rd Grand Master of the Priory of Sion and a major figure in modernist art, having done notable work in painting, film, drama, poetry, ballet, etc. A Gay opium addict, related to much of the French aristocracy, Cocteau had friendships with Ezra Pound, Dali, Picasso, Orson Welles, and almost everybody important in High culture, and helped create the surrealist movement. That may explain the Noon Blue Apples — if Sauniere didn't really find those parchments and Somebody forged them later . . .

And other revelations and/or hoaxes have surfaced . . .

In *The Messianic Legacy* [1987] Baigent, Lincoln and Leigh spend half the book proving links between the Priory of Sion and modern banking, implicating banks in England, Canada and the U.S. as well as the Usual Suspects in Switzerland. The other half of the book concerns the equality of men and women in early

Christianity, placing the Papist all-male priesthood as the first "heresy."

Pierre Plantard de Saint Clair also appears again, for a brief interview, in which he announces that he has resigned as Grand Master of the Priory, refuses to name his successor, and drops dark hints that the whole megillah has secretly come under the control of the Knights of Malta, a rightwing Catholic organization often accused elsewhere of plotting a revival of Fascism.

An undated pamphlet, *Scandals of the Priory of Sion*, signed "Cornelius," has circulated among conspiracy buffs for some time. It links the Priory to the Mafia and the P2 conspiracy in Italy.

You've heard of the Mafia. P2, better known in Europe than over here, grew out of the CIA's Project Gladio, created by James Jesus Angleton, Chief of Counter Intelligence — a man who appears in more conspiracy theories than anyone since Adam Weishaupt. Gladio, intended to influence Italian elections, had an Italian organizer named Licio Gelli, who had previously worked for both the Gestapo and the Communist Underground during World War II, convincing each side that he was betraying the other. As soon as Angleton hired Gelli, Gelli repeated his previous achievement and got on the payroll of the KGB, too, again convincing each side that he was really loyal to them and betraying the other guys. Gelli also belonged to the Knights of Malta, by the way.

Once he had funding from both the CIA and the KGB, Gelli formed P2, a secret society recruited entirely from 30 members of the Grand Orient Lodge of Egyptian Freemasonry. P2 then became the "secret government" of Italy, infiltrating over 900 members into the official government, laundering drug money through the Vatican Bank and Banco Ambrosiano, and assassinating everybody who seriously pissed them off. Murders charged to P2 include many leftwing labor leaders; Prime Minister Aldo Moro; Mino Pecorelli (the first journalist to expose their machinations); Roberto Calvi (president of Banco Ambrosiano, who after being indicted, seemed inclined to turn state witness); Michele "The Shar" Sindona (president of Franklin National Bank, who also seemed inclined to turn informer after being convicted of murdering a bank examiner); and, probably, the previous Pope. Calvi and Sindona also belonged to the Knights of Malta — and so does Dr. Otto von Hapsburg (see above).

According to "Cornelius," P2 was a tool, a front, for the Priory of Sion; James Jesus Angleton only *thought* he ran the show from CIA headquarters in Langley. (However, according to Larry Gurwin of the *Institutional Investor*, Italian investigators believe the real control came from a still-unidentified Puppet Master in Monte Carlo.) Cornelius also claims the Priory of Sion murdered Giorgio Ambrosoli, the bank examiner whose death the courts had blamed on Michele "The Shark" Sindona of P2; and that Cardinal Jean Danielou also belonged to the Priory.

Cardinal Danielou had literary friendships with Jean Cocteau, of the Priory of Sion, and Nobel laureate Andre Malroux of de Gaulle's Committee for Public Safety and the esoteric Committee for the Rights and Privileges of Low Cost Housing and/or the Priory of Sion.

The Cardinal himself died, somewhat oddly, in the apartment of a striptease dancer, in 1974.

In 1985 David Wood produced *GENISIS* — not a misprint, but a Joycean pun. (Gen-ISIS — get it?) Based on the English science, or art, or group madness, called ley hunting, this book seeks a mystic secret in the geographical arrangements of the sites important in the Priory/Magdalene mystery. You do this by connecting all the key points with straight lines, and if nothing significant emerges, you may try curved lines if they are arcs of a circle. If that doesn't work, try a smaller map and a thicker pencil. Using the right map and pencil, plus a few circles, Wood emerges with a design he calls the Vagina of Nuit.

Although it doesn't look like any human vagina I ever saw outside of a Picasso painting, the Vagina of Nuit does yield some interesting geometrical proportions — numbers significant in mystic tradition. From these, Wood deduces that Mary Magdalene never existed as a person; she is the Egyptian sky-goddess Nuit in disguise. Furthermore, the Merovingians came from Atlantis, not the stars, but the whole human race was genetically engineered by a group of extraterrestrial scientists from Sirius.

I *knew* that Sirius would creep back into the story eventually.

Wood also asserts that members of the Priory of Sion must all amputate their penises to obtain initiation, as a sacrifice to Nuit, or Isis, or (if we must use current mythology) Mary Magdalene.

Sounds less attractive even than Heaven's Gate, which only wanted you to cut off your balls.

But, at this point, I cannot resist inserting the fact that several quite intelligent scientists have offered evolutionary theories as far out as Wood's. Sir Francis Crick, Nobel laureate and co-discoverer of the DNA molecule, has long argued that the DNA contains too much information to have happened by means of any finite series of "lucky accidents." Since the word "God" remains taboo in scientific circles, Crick claims the designer of DNA, and hence of all life on Earth, must be an advanced extraterrestrial race. Similar ideas have come forth from the distinguished astronomer, Sir Fred Hoyle, and from Dr. Timothy Leary, among others.

Inside the "Men's Club": Secrets of the Patriarchy, by "Hawthorne Abendsen" (no date: A-Albionic Research, Ferndale, Michigan) offers yet another perspective on all this weirdity. The Priory of Sion, Abendsen claims, controls all the other all-male secret societies you ever heard of, and thus all of our civilization. It worships *Al-Shaddai* (Lord of Battles), the god who appeared to Abraham, and it has created all later, gentler images of divinity (e.g., the God of Love) as deceptions to fool the masses. You might say Hannibal Lecter, MD. is their High Priest.

Worship of Al-Shaddai consists of making wars, as a God of Battles would wish, and also of periodic animal and human sacrifices of the sort Fundamentalist Christians attribute to Satanists. Satan has nothing to do with it, according to Abendsen: blood sacrifice, in or out of warfare, remains the central ritual of the Judaic-Christian-Moslem system, and anything else you've heard is just part of the cover-up, to conceal why our rulers do the murderous things they do.

Although this yarn sounds a lot like put-on or parody, Abendsen has a certain family resemblance to a great many serious thinkers of recent decades. Radical Feminists all consider our culture Patriarchal; Dr. Wilhelm Reich called it Authoritarian-Patriarchal; Dr. James De Meo calls it Armored Patrist; etc. The latest cuss word for it, logophallocentrist, contributed by the postmodernists, means that we have a social system based on belief in the special magic power of words and penises. Dr. Leonard Shlain, in *The Alphabet Versus the Goddess*, blames it all on the invention of the alphabet, an argument that out-McLuhans McLuhan.

"Hawthorne Abendsen," by the way, seems to have gotten borrowed or stolen from Philip K. Dick, who used it as the name of the author of the book-within-the-book, in his sci-fi classic, *The Man in the High Castle*.

Yes: the same Phillip K. Dick who later decided he was receiving messages from Sirius . . .

As the French themselves say, it must make one furious to think and to jump up and down. And in Rennes-le-Chateau, the accursed church of Mary Magdalene still stands, or lurks, still announcing its accursedness. A friend of mine, Fred Lehrman of Nomad University, recently visited the site and tells me he met an intrepid researcher there, who had discovered that one of the statues contained a sliding panel with a German newspaper from 1904 hidden inside. Since some of the words in the paper had underlining in pen, this investigator hopes to find a code revealing Everything.

I wish him luck; but I fear he will find something like "*Stately plump Buck Mulligan has never wept nor dashed a thousand kim JFK Dallas 1963 midnight purple bananas . . .*"

Old Man On A Balcony:
Views Of Monterey Bay #15

The stone Buddha sits

Still as the Eiger: silent . . .

The waves crash and splash

Left and Right:
A Non-Euclidean Perspective

I have been invited to contribute an article on whether my politics are "left" or "right," evidently because some flatlanders insist on classifying me as Leftist; and others, equally Euclidean, argue that I "am" obviously some variety of Rightist.

Naturally, this debate intrigues me. The Poet prayed that some power would "the giftie gie us /to see ourselves as ithers see us"; but every published writer has that dubious privilege. I have been called a "sexist"(by Arlene Meyers) and a "male feminist . . . a simpering pussy-whipped wimp" (by LA. Rollins), "one of the major thinkers of the modern age" (by Barbara Marx Hubbard) and "stupid" (by Andrea Chaflin Antonoff), a "genius" (by *SOUNDS*, London) and "mentally deranged" (by Charles Platt), a "mystic" and "charlatan" (by the Bay Area Skeptics), and a "materialist" (by an anonymous gent in Seattle who also hit me with a pie); I am also frequently called a "Satanist" in some amusing, illiterate and usually anonymous crank letters from Protestant Fundamentalists.

I can only conclude that I am indeed like a visitor from non-Euclidean dimensions whose outlines are perplexing to the Euclidean inhabitants of various dogmatic Flatlands. Or else, Lichtenberg was right when he said a book "is a mirror. When a monkey looks in, no philosopher looks out."

Of course, we live in curved space (as noted by Einstein); that should warn us that Euclidean metaphors may prove misleading. Science has also discovered that the Universe can count above two, which should make us leery of either/or choices. There are eight — count 'em, eight — theories or models in quantum mechanics, all of which use the same equations but have radically different philosophical meanings; physicists have accepted the multi-model approach (or "model agnosticism") for over 80 years now.

In modern mathematics and logic, in addition to the two-valued (yes/no) logic of Aristotle and Boole, there are several three-valued logics (e.g., the yes, no and maybe Quantum Logic of von Neumann; the yes, no and po of psychologist Edward de Bono; etc.); at least one four-valued logic (the true, false, indeterminate and meaningless of Rapoport); and an infinite-valued logic (Korzybski). I myself have presented a multi-valued logic in my neuroscience seminars; the bare bones of this system can be found in my book, *Quantum Psychology*.

Two-valued Euclidean choices — left or right of an imaginary line — do not seem very "real" to me, in comparison to the versatility of modern science and mathematics.

Actually, it was once easy to classify me in simple Euclidean topology. To paraphrase a recent article by the brilliant Michael Hoy [Critique #19/20], I had a Correct Answer Machine installed in my brain when I was quite young. It was a right-wing Correct Answer Machine in general and Roman Catholic in particular. It was installed by nuns who were very good at creating such machines and implanting them in helpless children. By the time I got out of grammar school, in 1945, I had the Correct Answer for everything, and it was the Correct Answer that you will nowadays still hear from, say, William Buckley, Jr.

When I moved on to Brooklyn Technical High School, I encountered many bright, likable kids who were not Catholics and not at all right-wing in any respect. They naturally angered me at first. (That is the function of Correct Answer Machines: to make you have an adrenaline rush, instead of a new thought, when confronted with different opinions.) But these bright, non-Catholic kids — Protestants, Jews, agnostics, even atheists fascinated me in some ways. The result was that I started reading all the authors the nuns had warned me against — especially Darwin, Tom Paine, Ingersoll, Mencken and Nietzsche.

I found myself floating in a void of incertitude, a sensation that was unfamiliar and therefore uncomfortable. I retreated back to robotism by electing to install a new Correct Answer Machine in my brain. This happened to be a Trotskyist Correct Answer Machine, provided by the International Socialist Youth Party. I picked this Machine, I think, because, the alternative Correct Answer Machines then available were less "Papist" (authoritarian) and therefore less comfortable to my adolescent mind, still bent out of shape by the good nuns.

(Why was I immune to Stalinism — an equally Papist secular religion? Because of my youth, probably. The only Stalinists left in the U.S. by the late 1940's were all middle-aged and "crystallized" as Gurdjieff would say. Those of us who were younger could clearly see that Stalinism was not much different from Hitlerism. The Trotskyist alternative allowed me to feel "radical" and modern, without becoming an idiot by denying the totalitarianism of the U.S.S.R., and it let me have a martyred redeemer again as I had in my Catholic childhood.)

After about a year, the Trotskyist Correct Answer Machine began to seem a nuisance. I started to suspect that the Trotskyists were some secular clone of the Vatican, whether they knew it or not, and that the dogma of Papal infallibility was no whit more absurd than the Trotskyist submission to the Central Committee. I decided that I had left one dogmatic Church and joined another. I even suspected that if Trotsky had managed to hold on to power, he might have been as dictatorial as Stalin.

Actually, what irritated me most about the Trots (and now seems most amusing) is that I already had some tendency toward individualism, or crankiness, or Heresy; I sometimes disputed the Party Line. This always resulted in my being denounced for "bourgeoisie tendencies." That was irritating then and amusing now because I was actually the only member of that Trot cell who did not come from a middle-class background. I came from a working class family and was the only genuine "proletarian" in the whole Marxist *kaffeeklatsch*.

At the age of 18, then, I returned to the void of incertitude. It began to seem almost comfortable there, and I began to rejoice in my agnosticism. It made me feel superior to the dogmatists of all types, and adolescents love to feel superior to everybody (especially their parents — or have you noticed that?) Around the same time as my Trotskyist period, I began to read the first Revisionist historians, whom I had been warned about by my high school social science teachers, in grave and awful tones, as if these men had killed a bat in the sacristy. My teachers were too Liberal to tell me I would go to Hell for reading such books (as the nuns had told me about Darwin, for instance), but they made it clear that the Revisionists were Evil, Awful, Unspeakable and probably some form of Pawns of the Devil.

I recognized the technique of thought control again, so I read all the Revisionists I could find. They convinced me that the New Deal Liberals had deliberately lied and manipulated the U.S. into World War II and were still lying about what they did after the war was over. (In fact, they are still lying about it today.)

The Revisionist who impressed me most was Harry Elmer Barnes, a classic Liberal who was a bit of a Marxist (in methodology — i.e., in his way of looking for economic factors behind political actions). I was amused and disgusted by the attempt of the New Deal gang to smear Professor Barnes as a right-wing reactionary. Barnes, in fact, was an advocate of progressive ideas in education, economics, politics, criminology, sociology and anthropology all his life.

Charles Beard, another great historian of classic Liberal principles, agreed that Roosevelt deliberately lied to us in World War II, and was smeared in the same way as Professor Barnes. This did not encourage me to have Faith in any Party Line, even if it called itself the "modern, liberal, enlightened" Party Line.

(I have never been convinced by the Holocaust Revisionists, however, simply because I have met a great many Holocaust eyewitnesses, or alleged eyewitnesses, in the past 40 years. Most of these people I seemingly met by accident, in both Europe and America. A conspiracy that has that many liars planted in that many places — or has always paid such special attention to me that it placed these liars where I would meet them — is a conspiracy too omnipotent and omnipresent, and therefore too metaphysical, for me to take seriously. A conspiracy so Godlike in its powers could, in principle, deceive us about anything and everything, and I wonder why the Holocaust Revisionists still believe that World War II itself occurred, or that any of past history ever happened.)

I reached 20 and became an employee (i.e., a robot) in the McCarthy Era and the Eisenhower years; my agnosticism became more total and so did my suspicion that politics consists of a carnival of buncombe (as Mencken once said). It seemed obvious to me that, while Senator Joe was a liar of stellar magnitude, a lot of the Liberals were lying their heads off, too, in attempts to hide their previous fondness for Stalinism. That was something I, as a former Trotskyist, knew about by experience. In *bon ton* East Coast intellectual circles, before McCarthy, Stalinism was much more "permissible" than Trotskyism; it was almost chic.

If I still regard the McCarthy witch-hunt of the 1950's as abominable, I also remember that some of the victims had engaged in similar witch-hunts against the Trotskyists in the early 1940's.

It is probably impossible for a social mammal to be totally "apolitical." Even if I was allergic to Correct Answer Machines, my mind kept searching for some general social ideas that I could take more or less seriously. For a while I dropped in and out of colleges and in and out of jobs and searched earnestly for some pragmatic mock-up of "truth" without a Correct Answer Machine attached. And yet both Left and Right continued to appear intellectually bankrupt to me.

Coming from a working class family, I could never have much sympathy for the kind of Conservatism you find in America in this century. (I do have a deep respect for the classic Libertarian Conservatives of the 18th Century, especially Edmund Burke and John Adams.) *

~•~

* This respect does not extend to our current [2004] neo-conservatives, who have junked both Adams and Burke, along with Coke, Blackstone and Magna Carta, to peddle Tsarism in red, white and blue.

~•~

After I married and had children to support, the abominations of the Capitalist system and the wormlike ignominy of the employee role began to seem like prisons to me; I was a poor candidate for the Conservative cause. On the other hand, the FDR Liberals, I was convinced, had lied about World War II; they first smeared and then blacklisted the historians who told the truth; and they had jumped on the Cold War bandwagon with ghoulish glee.

I seem anti-war by "temperament" (whatever that means — early imprints or conditioning? Genes? I don't know the exact cause of such a deep-seated and life-long bias). Marxist dogma seemed as stupid to me as Catholic dogma and as murderous as Hitlerism. I now thought of myself as an agnostic on principle. I was not going to join any more "churches" or submit to anybody's damned Party Line.

My agnosticism was also intensified by such influences as further reading of Nietzsche, existentialism, phenomenology, General Semantics, and operational logic. They have remained major influences on me and I want to say a few words about each.

Nietzsche's philosophy of the Superman did not turn me on in youth; coming from the proletariat, I could not see myself as one of his aristocratic *Uebermenschen*. On the other hand, his criticism of language, and of the metaphysical implications within languages, made a powerful impression on me; I still re-read one or two of his books every year, and get new semantic insights from them. He is, as he bragged, a hard nut to digest all at once.

Existentialism did not convert me back to Marxism (as it did to Sartre); it merely magnified my Nietzschean distrust of capitalized nouns and other abstractions, and strengthened my preferences for sensory-sensual ("existential") modes of perception/conception. The phenomenologists — especially Husserl and the wild man of the bunch, Charles Fort — encouraged my tendency to suspect all general theories (religious, philosophical, even scientific), and to regard human sense experience as the primary datum.

My polemics against Materialist Fundamentalism in *The New Inquisition* and the Aristotelian mystique of "natural law" (shared by Thomists and some Libertarians) in my *Natural Law; or, Don't Put a Rubber On Your Willy* are both based on this existentialist-phenomenologist choice that I will "believe" in — or gamble on — human experience, with all its muddle and uncertainty, more than I will ever "believe" in capitalized Abstractions and "general principles."

General Semantics, as formulated by Korzybski, increased

this anti-metaphysical bias in me. Korzybski also stressed that the best sensory data (as revealed by instruments that refine the senses) indicates that we live in a non-Aristotelian, non-Euclidean and non-Newtonian continuum. I have practiced for 30 years the exercises Korzybski recommends to break down Aristotelian-Euclidean-Newtonian ideas buried in our daily speech, and retrain myself to perceive in ways compatible with what our instruments indicate about actuality.

Due to Korzybski's neurolinguistic training devices, it now feels "natural" for me to think beyond either/or logic, to perceive the unity of observer/observed, and to regard "objects" as human inventions abstracted from a holistic continuum.

Many physicists think I have studied more physics than I actually have; I merely neurologically *internalized* the physics that I do know.

Operational logic (as formulated by the American physicist Percy Bridgman and recreated by the Danish physicist Niels Bohr as the Copenhagen Interpretation of science) seemed the approach to modern science that appealed to me in the context of the above working principles. The Bridgman-Bohr meta-model rejects as "meaningless" any statements that do not refer to concrete experiences of human beings. (Bridgman was influenced by Pragmatism, Bohr by Existentialism.) Operationalism also regards all proposed "laws" only as maps or models that are useful for a certain time. Thus, Operationalism seems the one "philosophy of science" that warns us, like Nietzsche and Husserl, only to use models where they're useful and never to elevate them into Idols or dogmas.

Although I dislike labels, if I had to label my attitude I would accordingly settle for existentialist-phenomenologist-opera-tionalist, as long as no one of those three terms is given more prominence than the other two.

In the late 1950's, I began to read widely in economic "science" (or speculation) again, a subject that had bored the bejesus out of me since I overthrew the Marxist Machine in my brain ten years earlier. I became fascinated with a number of alternatives — or "excluded middles" — that transcend the hackneyed debate between monopoly Capitalism and totalitarian

Socialism. My favorite among these alternatives was, and to some extent still is, the individualist-mutualist anarchism of Proudhon, Josiah Warren, S.P. Andrews, Lysander Spooner and Benjamin Tucker.

I do not have a real Faith that this system would work out as well in practice as it sounds in theory, but as theory it still seems to me one of the best ideas I ever encountered.

This form of anarchism is called "individualist" because it regards the absolute liberty of the individual as a supreme goal to be attained; it is called "mutualist" because it believes such liberty can only be achieved by a system of mutual consent, each agreeing to defend the liberty of all. Tucker defined this as a non-invasion compact; the hippie version says "Nobody gets on nobody's back." In this Utopia, free competition and free cooperation are both encouraged; it is assumed that persons and groups will decide to compete or to cooperate based on the concrete specifics of each case. (This appeals to my "existentialism" again, you see.)

Land monopolies are discouraged in individualist — mutualist anarchism by abolishing State laws granting ownership to those who neither occupy nor use the land; "ownership," it is predicted, will then only be contractually recognized where the "owner" actually occupies and uses the land, but not where he charges "rent" to "allow" others to occupy or use it.

The monopoly on currency, granted by the State, is also abolished, and any commune, group, syndicate, etc., can issue its own competing currency; it is claimed that this will drive interest down to approximately zero. With rent at zero and interest near zero, it is argued that the alleged goal of socialism (abolition of exploitation) will be achieved by free contract, without coercion or totalitarian Statism. That is, the individualist-mutualist model argues that the land and money monopolies are the "bugger factors" that prevent Free Enterprise from producing the marvelous results expected by Adam Smith. With land and money monopolies abolished, it is predicted that competition (where there is no existential motive for cooperation) and cooperation (where this is recognized as being to the advantage of all) will prevent other monopolies from arising.

Since monopolized police forces are notoriously graft-ridden and underlie the power of the state to bully and coerce, competing protection systems will be available in an individualist-mutualist system. You won't have to pay "taxes" to support a Protection Racket that is actually oppressing rather than protecting you. You will only pay dues, where you think it prudent, to protection agencies that actually perform a service you want and need. In general, every commune or syndicate will make its own rules of the game, but the mutualist-individualist tradition holds that, by experience, most communes will choose the systems that maximize liberty and minimize coercion.

Being wary of Correct Answer Machines, I also studied and have given much serious consideration to other "Utopian" socio-economic theories.

I am still fond of the system of Henry George (in which no rent is allowed, but free enterprise is otherwise preserved); but I also like the ideas of Silvio Gesell (who would also abolish rent and all taxes but one — a demurrage tax on currency, which should theoretically abolish interest by a different gimmick than the competing currencies of the mutualists).

I also see possible merit in the economics of C.H. Douglas, who invented the National Dividend — lately re-emergent, somewhat mutated, or maybe mutilated, as Theobold's Guaranteed Annual Wage and/or Nobel laureate Milton Friedman's Negative Income Tax. And I am intrigued by the proposal of Pope Leo XIII that workers should own the majority of stock in their companies.

Most interesting of recent Utopias to me is that of Buckminster Fuller in which money is abolished, and computers manage the economy, programmed with a prime directive to *advantage all without disadvantaging any* — the same goal sought by the mutualist system of basing society entirely on negotiated contract.

Since I don't have the Correct Answer, I don't know which of these systems would work best in practice. I would like to see them all tried in different places, just to see what would happen.

(This multiple Utopia system was also suggested by Silvio Gesell, who was not convinced he had a Correct Answer

Machine; that's another reason I like Gesell.)

My own bias or hope or prejudice is that individualist-mutualist anarchism with some help from Bucky Fuller's computers would work best of all, but I still lack the Faith to proclaim that as dogma.

There is one principle (or prejudice) which makes anarchist and libertarian alternatives attractive to me where State Socialism is totally repugnant to my genes-or-imprints. I am committed to the maximization of the freedom of the individual and the minimization of coercion. I do not claim this goal is demanded by some ghostly or metaphysical "Natural Law," but merely that it is the goal that I, personally, have *chosen* — in the Existentialist sense of choice. (In more occult language, such a goal is my True Will.) Everything I write, in one way or another, is intended to undermine the metaphysical and linguistic systems which seem to justify some Authorities in limiting the freedom of the human mind or in initiating coercion against the non-coercive.

. . . and then came what Charles Slack calls "the madness of the sixties." I was an early, and enthusiastic, experimenter with LSD, peyote, magic mushrooms and any other compound that mutated consciousness. The result was that I became even more agnostic but less superior about it.

What psychedelics taught me was that, just as theories and ideologies (maps and models) are human creations, not divine revelations, every perceptual grid or existential reality-tunnel is also a human creation — a work of art, consciously or unconsciously edited and organized by the individual brain.

I began serious study of other consciousness-altering systems, including techniques of yoga, Zen, Sufism and Cabala. I, alas, became a "mystic" of some sort, although still within the framework of existentialism-phenomenology-operationalism. But, then, Buddhism — the organized mystic movement I find least objectionable — is also existentialist, phenomenologist and operationalist . . .

Nietzsche's concept of the Superhuman has at last become meaningful for me, although not in the elitist form in which he left it. I now think evolution still continues and even accelerates:

the human brain seems likely to evolve to a state that seems Superhuman compared to our previous history of domesticated primatehood. My favorite science is neuroscience, and I am endlessly fascinated by every new tool or technique that breaks down robot circuits in our brains (Correct Answer Machines) and spurs creativity, higher intelligence, expanded consciousness, and, above all, broader compassion.

I see no reason to believe that only an elite is capable of this evolutionary leap forward, especially as the new tools and training techniques are becoming more simple. In neuroscience, as in all technology, we seem to follow Bucky Fuller's rule that each breakthrough allows us to do more work with less effort and to create more wealth out of less raw matter.

Once I broke loose from the employee role and became self-supporting as a writer, the "horrors of capitalism" seemed less ghoulish to me, since I no longer had to face them every day. (As Shakespeare said, we can all bear a toothache philosophically, except the pore bloke wot's got it.) I prefer to live in Europe rather than pay taxes to build more of Mr. Reagan's goddam nuclear missiles, but I enjoy visiting the U.S. regularly for intellectual stimulation.

I agree passionately with Maurice Nicoll (a physician who mastered both Jungian and Gurdjieffian systems) when he wrote that the major purpose of "work on consciousness" is to "decrease the amount of violence in the world." The main difference between our world and Swift's is that while we have stopped killing each other over religious differences (outside the Near East and Northern Ireland), we have developed an insane passion for killing each other over ideological differences. I regard Organized Ideology with the same horror that Voltaire had for Organized Religion.*

~•~

* Especially now that they're back in bed together, on both sides of the Terrorwar.

~•~

Concretely, I am indeed a Male Feminist, as L.A. Rollins claimed (although seeing myself often on TV, I deny that I simper; I don't even swish); like all libertarians, I oppose victimless crime laws, all drug control laws, and all forms of censorship (whether by outright reactionaries, or Revolutionary Committees of Radical Feminists).

I passionately hate violence, but am not a Dogmatic Pacifist, since I don't have Joan Baez' Correct Answer Machine in my head. I know I would kill an armed aggressor, in a concrete crisis situation where that was the only defense of the specific lives of specific individuals I love, although I would never kill a person or employ even minor violence, or physical coercion, on behalf of capitalized Abstractions or Governments (who are all damned liars). All these are matters of Existential Choice on my part, and not dogmas revealed to me by some god or some philosopher-priest of Natural Law.

I prefer the various Utopian systems I have mentioned to the Conservative position that humanity is incorrigible, and I also think that if none of these Utopian scenarios are workable, some system will eventually arrive better than any we have ever known. I share the Jeffersonian ("Liberal"?) vision that the human mind can exceed all previous limits in a society where freedom of thought is the norm rather than a rare exception.

Does all of this make me a Leftist or a Rightist? I leave that for the Euclideans to decide.

La Belle Dame Sans Merci

The four weirdest and scariest drug stories I know all involve belladonna, a chemical for which I now have the same sincere respect as I have for hungry tigers, earthquakes, floods, wildfires, the IRS and Dr. Hannibal Lecter.

The first story I'll tell comes from a younger friend, then a 1960's drop-out hippie freak but now, in 2004, a Ph.D. in sociology. He tried belladonna around 1965 under the impression that it had much the same effects as LSD. When he immediately went into toxic convulsions, friends rushed him to a hospital where the ER staff pumped out his stomach — probably saving his life, but a bit too late to save him from delirium, since the belladonna had already entered his bloodstream.

When he returned to what seemed normal consciousness, he found himself in a hospital bed, surrounded by people in other beds with different ailments. Then a Beautiful Blonde Nurse with Great Big Hooters entered the ward, accompanied by an olde style New Orleans jazz band.

As my friend watched entranced, the nurse proceeded to perform a classic Strip Tease dance with plenty of tantalizing tease but eventual total nudity followed by even more bumps and grinds. The music seemed louder and raunchier than any jazz he had ever heard, and came to a wild Dionysian climax when the naked nurse crawled into bed with a delighted patient and proceeded to make love to him, loudly and frequently and more ways than a dozen porn stars.

My friend never once suspected that this might be a hallucination. Nor did it seem an unusually innovative medical procedure. You don't ask philosophic or ontological questions during a belladonna journey the way you usually do on real psychedelics. He only began to wonder if any of that sex stuff really happened the following morning.

. . . and that's this whole story. Belladonna erases a great deal of your memory of what you saw during the trip. He might have had dozens of other visions that night but all he ever remembered was the nurse from Mitchell Brothers Clinic for the Horrendously Horny. I guess I would have remembered her, too.

The second, more perplexing yarn comes from another 1960's veteran, but I lost touch with him and have no idea how his life worked out. He told me he took the belladonna in his dorm room at the college he attended and then waited for psychedelic fireworks and transcendental experiences.

Nothing happened for a while.

Then his friend Joe entered the room and asked what he was doing. He told Joe about the belladonna and said he was waiting to feel an effect. Joe asked him something but he didn't quite hear it.

Then his friend Joe entered the room and asked what he was doing. He told Joe about the belladonna and said he was waiting to feel an effect. Joe asked him something but he got distracted by having two Joes in the room. He tried to explain about the two Joes but then one of them vanished. He tried to tell Joe "Hey, you came in before you came in," but his tongue seemed unable to function and he thought he was merely grunting like a hog.

Then his friend Joe entered the room, and this time he got The Fear. He fled the room and the dorm and hopped on his motorcycle to Get Away, speeding across the campus and down the nearest highway as fast as he could gun her.

He didn't even own a motorcycle. I often wonder what the other people on campus and on the highway thought they saw when he went racing past them on his phantom bike . . . ?

Medieval witches used belladonna in their brews, and some scholars think that's why they believed they could fly through the sky on broomsticks. Modern witches — at least the ones I've known — prudently substitute the kinder, gentler cannabis.

The next morning my friend returned to "consensus reality" and found himself in a ditch several miles from campus. He had no bumps or bruises — and nobody else's motorcycle either — but his right shoe and right sock had disappeared. He never did find them and never remembered anymore of that night either.

My longest yarn involves my own experience with belladonna, in 1962. What can I say about why I did it? I hadn't heard the above stories yet, I was young, I was a damned eejit, and the guy who gave it to me said it was "just like peyote."

Let me explain that this happened on a farm in the deep woods.

A few minutes after I took the stuff — drank it as a tea, actually — my wife Arlen developed a severe case of Fangs and quickly turned into a beautiful, sexy, red-headed vampire with malice in her eyes. I immediately rushed to the kitchen sink, stuck a finger down my throat and forced several painful fits of vomiting. When I could vomit no more I told her — she looked normal again for a moment: beautiful, sexy, red-headed but friendly, not vampirish — "This is a Bad Trip, but I'll find my way back to you, I promise."

Those were the last sane words I spoke for the next 12 hours.

I remember taking a long walk through a forest of magic green jewels with the Tin Woodsman of Oz. Later, the next day, it became clear that this was Jeff, a friend Arlen had phoned to help me through the Emergency. He was walking me around our cabin, thinking fresh air might help.

I remember some dwarfs in Nazi uniforms trying to shove me into a furnace literally "as hot as Hell." I have never felt more terror in my life.

Blank space: memory loss.

I remember thinking the worst was over and trying to tell Arlen and Jeff that some parts of it were quite good, really. I was lighting one cigarette after another, chain-smoking I thought. Jeff and Arlen saw me striking the lighter repeatedly but I never did have a cigarette in my mouth.

I remember trying to explain something I had discovered Out There. Arlen wrote it down. The note said, "The literary critics will all have to be shot because of the Kennedy administration in Outer Space of the Nuremberg pickle that exploded."

Not quite as good as the last words of Dutch Schultz, I'd say, but a bit better than what William James brought back from his nitrous oxide adventure: "Over all, there is a smell of fried onions."

Around dawn, I had to go to the outhouse. Jeff accompanied me to make sure I didn't wander off into the Pink Dimension or get lost amid the buzzing and whistling things in the Realm of Thud.

I opened the outhouse door and found Jeff already in there. I closed the door and told him, "I can't go in. You're already in there."

He persuaded me reasonably that he wasn't in there, but outside with me, so I opened the door again, found nobody inside and took a healthy crap.

I felt even closer to "normal" when I came out, but then I noticed King Kong peeking at me over the top of the trees. He seemed whimsical and unthreatening, and when I looked again he turned into just another tree.

The next day I moved slowly back into the ordinary world, and by evening I felt well enough to go to a movie, Kurasawa's *The Seven Samurai*. I enjoyed the first half, especially the innovative technique of alternating between black-and-white and color, but in the second half Toshiro Mifune's nose started growing like Pinocchio's and I knew I was hallucinating again, which vexed me a bit.

No more flashbacks occurred for about a month and then one day all the people in the supermarket turned into iguanas. That only lasted a few seconds, and it was the last of the trip. I never tried this nefarious chemical again, and I hope to gawd you won't either.

My last story I heard from novelist William S. Burroughs, who bought some "morphine" once that some wiseacre had cut with belladonna. He never remembered anything of the experience, but a friend did: he said that at one point William walked to the window, opened it and stuck a leg out.

"What the fuck you doing?" the friend asked.

"Going down for some cigarettes," William replied. The friend grabbed him and dragged him back into the room, which was on the third floor.

"Bella donna," by the way, means *beautiful lady* in Italian. Go figure.

THOUGHTS TO PONDER

The State — all it has, it has stolen!
It even bites with stolen teeth!

— F.W. Nietzsche

The Relativity of "Reality"

1. From the viewpoint of semantics, "reality" is a multi-ordinal concept, having different meanings on different levels of abstraction. On the lowest level of abstraction "reality" refers to immediate sensory consistency. "Is there really a kangaroo in that chair?" can be answered by obtaining the consensus of the group; or, if everybody is stoned, by bringing in some objective observers with objective instruments, etc. On the highest level of abstraction, "reality" refers to logical consistency with a body of established scientific fact and theory. "Is entropy real?" can be answered by consulting a reliable textbook on thermodynamics. Between the level of kangaroo and the level of entropy, there are many other levels of abstraction and, hence, many kinds of "reality."

For instance, "Is the Gross National Product real?" is a question on a certain level of abstraction; and if equally intelligent people can, and do, argue about this, it is because they are talking on different levels of abstraction and are not aware of the fact that there are different levels of abstraction and different kinds of "reality."

I call this the semantic relativity of "reality."

2. Every tribe has its own "reality — map," or worldview, or *weltanschauung*. What is "real" to the Eskimo is not what is "real" to the Zuni Indian or the Congolese or the Japanese Buddhist or the German businessman or the Russian commissar, etc. If you travel around the world with the naive assumption that everybody is living in the same "reality," you will make numerous embarrassing mistakes, insult countless people unintentionally, make a splendid ass of yourself and generally contribute to the worldwide belief that tourists are a Curse of God sent to punish people for their sins. To recognize that every culture, and sub-culture, has its own "reality" is the prerequisite of sophistication, tact, and true tolerance. Otherwise you come

on like the Englishman who claimed all Chinese understand English if you just shout loud enough.

I call this the anthropological, or cultural, relativism of "reality."

3. Every nervous system creates its own "reality." Out of the billions, or billions of billions, of energies intersecting the room in which you read this, your brain, performing 100,000,000 processes per minute (almost all of them unconscious to those circuits called the ego and recognized as "me") arranges a few hundred or thousand into the Gestalt which you experience as the "reality" of the room. To demonstrate this, in my Info-Psychology classes, I will have the students describe the hall outside the lecture room; no two will describe exactly the same hall.

Or, I will have everybody write down what they hear in the room during a minute of clock-time; no two lists of these sounds will be identical. A variety of chemicals introduced into the nervous system, or direct brain stimulation with electrical impulses, or yoga, etc., will create an entirely different neurological "reality" while you are still sitting in the "same" room.

I call this neurological relativism, or the relativity of perceived "reality."

4. Two scientists moving at different accelerations can measure the same phenomenon with equally accurate instruments and obtain totally different readings of its extensions in the space and time dimensions. (Einstein, *Special Relativity*.) On the quantum level, a variety of different philosophical reality-maps, or "models," describe equally well both the experimental data and the mathematical equations that are known to "fit" the data. Any attempt to get around this by adding more sophisticated instruments leads to adding still more sophisticated instruments to monitor the first set, and so on, forever. (Von Neumann's "catastrophe of the infinite regress.")

I call this physical Relativity, or the relativity of instrumental "reality."

In conclusion, "reality" is a concept borrowed from the theologians who, being bankrupt, are in no position to loan anything to anybody. We would do better to restrict ourselves to questions that can be answered. Such questions take the form, "At this date, with the knowledge presently possessed by humanity, which model best accords with the facts?"

When it turns out, as it usually does these days, that several models work equally well, we might then ask: which models are most amusing? most optimistic? most worthy of our time and energy? most elegant and esthetic? And we can keep in mind, too, biologist J.B.S. Haldane's warning, "The universe may be not only stranger than we think, but stranger than we *can* think."

Old Man On A Balcony:
Views Of Monterey Bay #16

Some waves cry "Terror!"

Hitting the beach like boulders:

Dark night: darker thoughts.

Committee for Surrealist Investigation of Claims of the Normal (CSICON)

I wrote this baby somewhere around 2000 for some website that no longer exists.

Dublin, 1986. I had given a talk to the Irish Science-Fiction Society and the question period began.

"Do you believe in UFOs?" somebody asked.

"Yes, of course," I answered.

The questioner, who looked quite young, then burst into a long speech, "proving" at least to his own satisfaction that all UFOs "really are" sun-dogs or heat inversions. When he finally ran down I simply replied, "Well, we both agree that UFOs exist. Our only difference is that you think you know what they are and I'm still puzzled."

An elderly gentleman with blonde-white hair and a florid complexion cried out in great enthusiasm, "By God, sir, you're right. I myself am still puzzled about everything!"

And thus I met Timothy F.X. Finnegan, Dean of the Royal Sir Myles nu gCopaleen Astro-Anomalistic Society, Dalkey, sometime lecturer at Trinity College, Dublin, and founder of the Committee for Surrealist Investigation of Claims of the Normal.

In fact, Prof. Finnegan signed me up as a member of CSICON that very night, in the Plough and Stars pub over our ninth or tenth pint of Ireland's most glorious product, *linn dubh*, known as Guinness to the ungodly.

Now I hear that Prof. Finnegan has died, or at least they took the liberty of burying him, and I feel that the world has lost a great man.

CSICON, however, lives on and deserves more attention than it has received hitherto. Prof. Finnegan always asserted that the idea for CSICON derived from a remark passed by an old Dalkey character named Sean Murphy, in the Goat and Compasses pub shortly before closing time on 23 July 1973.

Actually, it started with two old codgers named O'Brian and Nolan discussing the weather. "Terrible rain and wind for this time of year," O'Brian ventured.

"Ah, faith," Nolan replied, "I do not believe it is this time of year at all, at all."

At this, Murphy spoke up. "Ah, Jaysus," he said, "I've never seen a boogerin' normal day." He paused to set down his pint, then added thoughtfully, "And I never met a fookin' average man neither."

(About Sean Murphy nothing else appears in the record except a remark gleaned by Prof. LaPuta from one Nora Dolan, a housewife of the vicinity: "Sure, that Murphy lad never did any hard work except for getting up off the floor and navigating himself back onto the barstool, after he fell off, and he only did that twice a night.")

But Murphy's simple words lit a fire in the subtle and intricate brain of Timothy F.X. Finnegan, who had just finished his own fourteenth pint (de Selby says his fifteenth pint). The next day the aging Finnegan wrote the first two-page outline of the new science he called 'patapsychology, a term coined in salute to Alfred Jarry's invention of 'pataphysics.

Finnegan's paper began with the electrifying sentence, "The average Canadian has one testicle, just like Adolf Hitler — or, more precisely, the average Canadian has 0.96 testicles, an even sadder plight than Hitler's, if the average Anything actually existed." He then went on to demonstrate that the normal or average human lives in substandard housing in Asia, has 1.04 vaginas, cannot read or write, suffers from malnutrition and never heard of Silken Thomas Fitzgerald or Brian Boru. "The normal," he concluded "consists of a null set which nobody and nothing really fits."

Thus began the science of 'patapsychology, Prof. Finnegan's most enduring, and endearing, contribution to the world — aside from the computer-enhanced photos of the Face on Mars with which he endeavored to prove the Face depicted Moishe

Horwitz, his lifelong mentor and idol. This, of course, remains highly controversial, especially among disciples of Richard Hoagland, who believe the Face looks more like the Sphinx, those who insist it looks like Elvis to them, and the dullards who only see it as a bunch of rocks.

Nobody should confuse 'patapsychology with parapsychology, although this precise misunderstanding evidently inspired the long and venomous diatribes against Finnegan by Prof. Sheissenhosen of Heidelberg.

(We need not credit the allegations of Herr Doktor Hamburger that Sheissenhosen also dispatched the three separate letter-bombs sent to Finnegan in 1982, 1983 and 1987. Even in the most heated academic debate some limits of decorum should remain, one would hope.)

Sheissenhosen evidently believed that "parapsychology" represented an unprovoked attack on his language and thought, and that Finnegan often leaped from shadows; he even suspected the Dalkey sage of slinking and of hiding behind a belly laugh, although the latter seems physiologically impossible. (I tried it once and found it made me more visible, not less.) In fact, Sheissenhosen never did correct his original error of misreading 'patapsychology as parapsychology. You will find more about the Sheissenhosen-Finnegan — LaPuta-Hamburger controversy in deSelby's *Finnegan: Enigma of the Occident, Tourneur's Finnegan: Homme ou Dieu?* and/or Sheissenhosen's own *Finneganismus und Dummheit*, 6 volumes.

'Patapsychology begins from Murphy's Law, as Finnegan called the First Axiom, adopted from Sean Murphy. This says, and I quote, "The normal does not exist. The average does not exist. We know only a very large but probably finite phalanx of discrete space-time events encountered and endured." In less technical language the Board of the College of 'Patapsychology offers one million Irish punds (around $1,400,000 American) to any "normalist" who can exhibit "a normal sunset, an average Beethoven sonata, an ordinary Playmate of the Month, or any thing or event in space-time that qualifies as normal, average or ordinary."

In a world where no two fingerprints appear identical, and no two brains appear identical, and an electron does not even seem identical to itself from one nanosecond to another, 'patapsychology seems on safe ground here.

No normalist has yet produced even a totally normal dog, an average cat, or even an ordinary Chickadee.

Attempts to find an average Bird of Paradise, an ordinary haiku or even a normal cardiologist have floundered pathetically. The normal, the average, the ordinary, even the typical, exist only in statistics; i.e., the human mathematical mindscape. They never appear in external space-time, which consists only and always non-normal events in non-normal series.

Thus, unless you're an illiterate and malnourished Asian with exactly 1.04 vaginas and 0.96 testicles, living in substandard housing, you do not qualify as normal but as abnormal, subnormal, supernormal, paranormal or some variety of non-normal.

The canny will detect here the usual Celtic impulse to make hash out of everything that seems obvious and incontrovertible to Saxons, grocers and other Fundamentalist Materialists.

In the patapsychological model, the normal having vanished, most generalizations, especially about nonmathematical groups, disappear along with it. The monorchoid Mr. Hitler, for instance, could not generalize about "the Jews" within the patapsychological model, because first he would have to find a normal or average Jew, which appears as intractable to demonstration as exhibiting the Ideal Platonic Jew (or the Ideal Platonic Chicken Farm complete with Ideal Platonic Chickenshit).

As Korzybski the semanticist said, all we can ever find in space-time consists of Jew-1, Jew-2, Jew-3, etc. to Jew-n. (For the nonmathematical, that means a list comprising Abraham, Sarah, Moses, Ruth, Jesus, Woody Allen, Richard Bandler, Felix Mendelssohn, Sigmund Freud, Paulette Goddard, Betty Grable, Noam Chomsky, Bernard Baruch, Paul Newman, the Virgin Mary, Albert Einstein, Lillian Hellman, Baron Rothschild, Ayn Rand, Max Epstein, Emma Goldman, Saul Bellow, etc. etc. etc. to the final enumeration of all Jews alive or dead.)

Each of these, on inspection, will have different fingerprints, different brains, different neuro-immunological systems, different eyes, ears, noses, etc.; different life histories, different conditioning and learning, etc.; and different personalities, hobbies, passions, etc . . . and none will serve as a norm or Ideal Form for all the others.

To say it otherwise, world Jewish population stood at about 10 million when Hitler formed his generalizations.

He could not possibly have known more than at maximum about 500 of them well enough to generalize about them; considering his early prejudices, he probably knew a lot fewer than that. But taking 500 as a high estimate, we find he generalized about 10 million individual persons on the basis of knowledge limited to around 1/20,000 or 0.00005% of them.

It seems, then, that Nazism could not have existed if Hitler knew the difference between norms or averages (internal estimates, subject to error due to incomplete research or personal prejudice) and the phalanx of discrete non-normal events and things (including persons) that we find in the sensory space-time continuum outside.

Similarly, the male human population currently stands at 3 billion 3 million 129 thousand, more or less (3,004,129,976, the last time I checked the World Game Website a while ago). Of these 3 billion+ discrete individuals, Robin Morgan, Andrea Dworkin and other Radical Feminists probably have not known more than about 500 to generalize from. This means that Rad Fem dogma consists of propositions about 3 billion critters based on examination of less than 0.00000001 percent of them. This amounts to a much more reckless use of generalization than Hitler's thoughts on Judaism. You can no more find the male norm from Gandhi, Bozo, Gen. George Custer, Buddha, Bill Clinton, Louis Pasteur, Osama bin Laden, Kung Fu Dzu, Bruno, Father Damien, Michelangelo, Mozart, Ted Bundy, etc. than you can find the Jewish norm from Emma Goldman, Harpo Marx, Felix Mendelssohn, Spinoza, Barbra Streisand, Nathaniel Branden, Emma Lazarus, Jerry Seinfeld, etc.

Now you know how the word "feminazi" got into the language. The two ideologies have a strong isomorphism. They both confuse the theoretical norm with a vast array of different individuals — and they both have no idea how to create even a tolerably scientific norm (which will still differ in many respects from the actual series of individuals the norm allegedly covers).

CSICON applies the same Deconstructive logic all across the board.

For instance, to return to our starting point, whatever your idea of the "normal" UFO — whether you consider it a spaceship, a secret U.S. government weapon, a hoax, or a hallucination, etc. — such a general idea will render you incapable of forming a truly objective view of the next UFO that comes along. The only way to cancel such pre-judgment lies in 'patapsychology (and in general semantics). You must remember the difference between the individual and unpredictable event that gets called a UFO and your past generalizations about "the UFO" or the "normal UFO."

Otherwise you will only note how this UFO fits your Ideal UFO and will unconsciously ignore how it differs therefrom. This mechanical reflex will please your ego, if you like to feel you know more than most people, but it will prove hazardous to your ability to observe and think carefully.

People who think they know all about Jews or males or UFOs never see a real Jew or male or UFO. They see the generalized norm that exists only in their own brains. We never know "all" — we only know what I dub sombunall — **some-but-not-all**. This applies also to dogs (the 'patapsychologist will not say "I love them," "I hate them," "I fear them," etc.), and to plumbers, bosses, right-wingers, left-wingers, cats, lizards, sitcoms, houses, nails, Senators, waterfalls, ostriches and all other miscellaneous sets or groups.

Personally, I see two or three UFOs every week. This does not astonish me, or convince me of the spaceship theory, because I also see about 2 or 3 UNFOs every week — Unidentified Non-Flying Objects. These remain unidentified (by me) because they go by too fast or look so weird that I never know whether to classify them as hedgehogs, hobgoblins or helicopters — or as stars or satellites or spaceships — or as pookahs or pizza — trucks or probability waves. Of course, I also see things that I feel fairly safe in identifying as hedgehogs or stars or pizza trucks, but the world contains more and more events that I cannot identify fully and dogmatically with any norm or generalization. I live in a spectrum of probabilities, uncertainties and wonderments.

Perhaps I got this way by studying Finnegan's work. Or maybe I just drank too much *linn dubh* during my years in Ireland.

O *rare*, Tim Finnegan!

THOUGHTS TO PONDER

If we knew what it was we were doing, it would not be
called research, would it?

— Albert Einstein

Part III

IN DEFENSE OF THE DAMNED

Secrecy — the first refuge of incompetents — must be at a bare minimum in a democratic society . . .
— House Committee on Government Operations, 1960

Everybody knows that corruption thrives in secret places . . . it is a fair presumption that secrecy means impropriety.
— Woodrow Wilson

[The Bush] administration is . . . even more secretive than the Nixon administration.
— Larry Klayman, Judicial Watch

George W. Bush and Richard B. Cheney have created the most secretive presidency of my lifetime. Their secrecy is far worse than during Watergate, and it bodes even more serious consequences.
— John W. Dean, former counsel to Richard Nixon

Old Man on a Balcony:
Views of Monterey Bay #17

New bud on the vine:

But three thousand miles due East

Wall Street still smoulders.

Guns & Dope Party

This has passed through several drafts c. 2000-2004 and in 2002 I actually ran for Governor of California on more or less this platform . . . Currently, I support Everybody for President; **vide infra, dig?**

A free people ought not only to be armed and disciplined, but they should have sufficient arms and ammunition to maintain a status of independence from any who might attempt to abuse them, which would include their own government.

— George Washington

Must we always choose the lesser of two Bonesmen?

EVERYBODY FOR PRESIDENT

Well, at least everybody who feels ready for the responsibility of self-government. Those who still need a Big Daddy or a Big Momma to discipline and dominate them should vote for whatever fuehrer or saviour they like best.

If you want self-government don't vote for the Two Lying Bastards of the Democan and Republicrat parties . . . or for any minority party that also wants to govern you.

WRITE IN YOUR OWN NAME

The Guns and Dope Party advocates:

[1] guns for those who want them, no guns forced on those who don't want them (pacifists, Quakers, etc.)

[2] drugs for those who want them; no drugs forced on those who don't want them (Christian Scientists, Natural Hygienists, etc.)

[3] an end to Tsarism and a return to constitutional democracy

[4] equal rights for ostriches

I'm as mad as Hell, and I'm not going to take this anymore!

— Howard Beale

DON'T TREAD ON ME

Position Paper #5

The official flag: the Gadsden flag — the oldest American flag of all.

Official motto: "Like what you like, enjoy what you enjoy — and don't take crap from anybody!"

First order of business on assuming office: Fire 33% of the Congress (names selected at random), and replace them with full-grown adult ostriches, whose mysterious and awesome dignity will elevate the suidaen barbarity long established there.

33% Ostriches in Congress!

GUNS & DOPE PARTY

Both the gun owners and the dopers (medical, religious and/or recreational) feel like minorities, and the TSOG (*Ts*arist *O*ccupation *G*overnment) agrees with this estimate of their weakness.

Our contention holds that in the Western States both groups working together make a MAJORITY.

Ergo, they have much to gain and nothing to lose in combining forces. We have NO Ideology, NO "theory" and NO arguments in favor of guns-n-dope people joining together — except this:

TOGETHER WE CAN WIN

Each side only has to realize this and agree: "We'll tolerate their hobbies if they'll tolerate ours" and we can drive the Tsarists back to Russia!

I'll tolerate your hobbies
if you'll tolerate mine.
Guns and Dope Party

The Guns and Dope Pledge

We will never, never, NEVER vote for any candidate who advocates destroying the Second Amendment;

We will never, never, NEVER vote for any candidate who advocates destroying the Tenth Amendment;

We will never, never, NEVER cease or rest in our efforts to abolish Tsarism and restore constitutional democracy in general and especially the First Amendment.

If you agree with this, why not print a few copies and send them to "your" representatives in Congress

Position Paper #23

Little Tony was sitting on a park bench munching on one candy bar after another.

After the 6th candy bar, a man on the bench across from him said, "Son, you know eating all that candy isn't good for you. It will give you acne, rot your teeth, and make you fat."

Little Tony replied, "My grandfather lived to be 107 years old." The man asked, "Did your grandfather eat 6 candy bars at a time?" Little Tony answered, "No, he minded his own fucking business."

FREETOPIA!

Every Man, Woman and Ostrich is a Tsar!

A Maybe Map of the Future
Position Paper 23e

The goal of the Guns and Dope Party — return to constitutional democracy — will probably remain unacceptable to many in this country (the Terminally Gullible).

Especially in the middle of the continent, a majority seems to prefer the tyranny of TSOG and its associated "faith-based organizations." Thus, Western Secession must remain on our agenda, at least as a distinct "maybe."

After we all vote to take the responsibility of self-government upon ourselves, we will end all "faith-based" bans on scientific and medical freedom, including the *verbots* against orgonomic medicine, LSD, cloning, stem-cell research, medical marijuana, alternative medicine, etc.

Every citizen will choose the type of health care he or she wants, just as they did in the old U.S. before the Tsarist take-over.

Every scientist will research whatever she or he finds most interesting.

In short, we will become full members of the "civilized" world again, and ostriches will have the respect they deserve.

Position on Prostitution

If fucking is legal,
and selling is legal,
then selling fucking should be legal.
— paraphrased from the philosopher Carlin

Also Sprach RAW

If I announce (as I've considered) that God supports the Guns & Dope Party, how many of you will consider that claim

1. schizo or delusional

2. genuine Divine intervention

3. a con game

4. a hoax, satire, jape, etc.

How do you rank the similar claims of Bozo, Jerry Falwell, Son of Sam, the Tsars of Russia, the Tsars of USA, Osama bin Laden, the popes of Rome, etc.?

Anyway, God has personally endorsed the GUNS AND DOPE PARTY and cursed Tsardom.

He told me so, speaking through an ostrich named Olga who co-starred with Orson Welles in a thriller called *Southern Star*.

Olga spoke in Orson's most sonorous and resonant voice, the one he used for Father Mapple in *Moby Dick*. (Orson, in another second-rate villain role, spoke in a lispy, squeaky, very Gay, upper-class English voice, which made the character, a bandit chief, a lot more interesting.)

At the climax, Olga said, looking through the camera — at me! "I am the Lord God. Do you believe that?"

I giggled and said, "No . . . I think I just took too much pain medicine . . ."

"Good," said Olga/Orson/Father Mapple.

"I'm sick and tired of gullible fools like Bozo and Son of Sam. Just keep an open mind, old chum, and watch me rear back and work some Miracles for the Guns and Dope Party. Damn those pesky Tsarists!! By the way, don't forget your promise to include 33% ostriches in your government."

Governments lie.
— I.F. Stone

When I asked Olga how to contribute most to the coming unity of all critterkind, instilling respect for "all life however small" as it says in the *Upanishads*, she suggested appointing ostriches as 1/3 of the legislature. Of course, some left-wing aardvarks have complained about this (they call it "bipedal chauvinism") but I trust Olga.

Most humans haven't gotten to the level of realizing the personhood of other races yet, you know. Bipedalism represents a great leap forward toward universal critterkind, and you have to take these things one step at a time. The six-legged majority still inspire fear and loathing in backward societies.

If Olga doesn't talk to you, you need more pain medicine, and frankly I don't understand how you've survived three years of Bozo without it.

Maybe you should try the Bible or the Koran or Chinese fortune cookies.

LIVE

NEXT▶ **VOLUNTARY TAX?**
DEPUTY DIRECTOR
GUNS AND DOPE PARTY   12:10p PT
JROUS EXHALATION CONGLOBED IN A CLOUD BY THE CIRCUN

Taxes

Question: Would the Guns and Dope Party attempt to eliminate all taxes?

Answer: We'd follow Lysander Spooner's voluntary tax plan combined with the lightspeed of Internet. Every citizen would receive a semi-annual Republic budget, telling what the Republic of Freetopia wanted to do for them or to them, and each would send in their share of the fee for whatever projects seemed sensible and useful to them. Nobody would pay a penny for anything that seemed pointless, useless, invasive, tyrannical or even annoying to them. If nobody paid for a project, it would get dumped for lack of funding.

As Spooner wrote earlier:

Constitutions are utterly worthless to restrain the

tyranny of governments, unless it be understood that the people will by force compel the government to remain within constitutional limits. Practically speaking, no government knows any limits to its power except the endurance of the people.

Voluntary taxation expresses the endurance of the people directly and immediately, "before the horse gets out of the stable."

A GOVERNMENT WHICH TAKES YOUR MONEY BY FORCE LIKE A COMMON THIEF WILL USE THIS STOLEN MONEY TO FURTHER ENSLAVE YOU AND TO PREVENT ANY REBELLION ON YOUR PART.

— Olga Struthio

God and Tsardom

Tsarism represents an intermediate form between
European monarchism and Asian despotism, being,
possibly, closer to the latter of these two.

— Leon Trotsky,
Russia's Social Development and Tsarism

"THEY'LL TAKE AWAY MY MEDICINE
WHEN THEY PRY MY COLD DEAD FINGERS
FROM THE PILL BOTTLE"

GUNS & DOPE PARTY

The Guns & Dope Party primarily wants to abolish Tsarism and restore constitutional democracy in the California Republic. If our example inspires the other 49 states, so much the better.

Why do we oppose Tsarism? How does the U.S. drug Tsar function?

Allegedly, this Omniscient Official knows what drugs, herbs, compounds, etc. you should use for your medical problems better than your doctor knows!!!!!!

Even more magically, the Tsar "knows" this without doing any physical examination of you, — blood pressure readings, other scientific tests, etc. that your doctor does — and often from a distance of 3000 miles — and the Tsar does it without even looking at you, or talking to you!

The Tsar doesn't even know if you have hangnail or cancer, AIDS or flu, belong to the senior set or haven't even reached voting age yet. He can't even classify you as male, female or undecided.

In short, the Tsar knows nothing about you or your medical problems, by ordinary data, but he still know more about your medical care than your doctor knows, by some supernatural means unknown to mere mortals.

This makes sense if and only if we have a devout faith that our Tsar, like the Russian Tsars "of olde," receives guidance directly from "God." No other, less spooky explanation fits the claims made by Tsardom.

The government accordingly spends more and more of our tax money financing "faith-based organizations." Without faith we might relapse into scientific or rational thinking, which leads by a "slippery slope" toward constitutional democracy.

A NATION WITH ONLY
ONE TSAR = TYRANNY

GUNS & DOPE PARTY
Every man and every woman is a tsar!

It is not only the juror's right, but his duty, to find
the verdict according to his own best understanding,
judgment and conscience, though in direct opposition
to the directions of the court.

— John Adams

Do not annoy people at home. Do not pester them at
work. Leave them alone, or they will curse you.

— Lao-Dzu

Every Ostrich is a Tsar!

GUNS & DOPE PARTY

Why Olga Remains Essential

Olga remains essential to the serious, scientific and sincerely surrealist aspects of the Guns and Dope Party. Personal liberty, scientific and medical freedom, the rights of Imagination: all these appear dead or dying under the tyranny of Tsarism, and we all need to fight back "by any means necessary."

After all, this may become the last — the very last — battle for individual rights in this moribund Republic, before rampant medievalism closes down the democratic age.

NONETHELESS, we all need Olga also. Without her, we might take ourselves — and featherless biped politics in general — too damned seriously, following the usual "slippery slope" downward from Ideology to Idiocy. We need the perspectives of our feathered cousins, no matter how weird they may sound at times.

Thus, while we stand beside the Gun Owners of America (www.gunowners.org) in strict adherence to the Second Amendment we oppose what Jimmy Breslin called "poor usage of a revolver."

We also oppose poor usage of napalm, bazookas, shrapnel, automatic rifles, nukes, etc. Common Errors in Usage of all of these seem rampant in the Tsarist States, not only by the Goober government there, but increasingly by the baffled and maddened citizens, which explains why we feel secession may become necessary.

As the philosopher William Claude Dukenfield [1889-1945] noted: "Sooner or later we must take the bull by the tail and look the facts in the face."

WHEN A GOVERNMENT FIRST TAKES YOUR MONEY BY FORCE AND THEN DISARMS YOU, IT DOES NOT HAVE YOUR BEST INTEREST AT HEART.
— "Bob"

Recommended URLs

Political philosophy in depth:
www.lysanderspooner.org

Our philosophical advisor:
www.rawilson.com

Deeper philosophy: www.madsci.org/~lynn/juju/surr/ paranoia/CP.html

Deeper than deep:
www.kbuxton.com/discordia

Medical rights:
www.wamm.org

Self-defense:
www.gunowners.org

Monetary policy: www.questionsquestions.net/docs04/ declaration.html

THOUGHTS TO PONDER

The State is the coldest of all cold monsters and coldly it tells lies, and this lie oozes from its lips: "I, the State, am the people."

— F.W. Nietzsche

"Like what you like,
enjoy what you enjoy, and
don't take crap from anybody."

GUNS & DOPE PARTY

Damnation by Definition

These fragments come from a book I started in 1964 called **Authority and Submission**. *When five publishers in a row rejected it, I gave up attempting books for six full years and only wrote shorter pieces. I still had a lot of pessimism and masochism in those days.*

Parts of **Authority and Submission** *eventually got rewritten and incorporated into* **Illuminatus!** *and* **Prometheus Rising.**

The most thoroughly and relentlessly Damned, banned, excluded, condemned, forbidden, ostracized, ignored, suppressed, repressed, robbed, brutalized and defamed of all Damned Things is the individual human being. The social engineers, statisticians, psychologists, sociologists, market researchers, landlords, bureaucrats, captains of industry, bankers, governors, commissars, kings, presidents, etc. are perpetually forcing this Damned Thing into carefully prepared blueprints and perpetually irritated that the Damned Thing will not fit into the slot assigned it. The theologians call it a sinner and try to "reform" it. The governor calls it a criminal and tries to "punish" it. The psychologist calls it a neurotic and tries to "cure" it. Still, the Damned Thing will not fit into their slots.

I once overheard two botanists arguing over a Damned Thing that had blasphemously sprouted in a college yard. One claimed that the Damned Thing "was" a tree and the other claimed that it "was" a shrub. They each had good scholarly arguments, and they were still debating when I left them.

The world is forever spawning Damned Things — things that are neither tree nor shrub, fish nor fowl, black nor white — and the categorical thinker can only regard the spiky and buzzing world of sensory fact as a profound insult to his card-index system of classifications. Worst of all are the facts which violate "common sense," that dreary bog of Stone Age prejudice and muddy inertia. The whole history of science is the odyssey of a pixilated card-indexer perpetually sailing between such Damned Things and desperately juggling his classifications to fit them in, just as the history of politics is the futile epic of a long series of attempts to line up the Damned Things and cajole them to march in regiment.

Every ideology is a mental murder, a reduction of dynamic living processes to static classifications, and every classification is a Damnation, just as every inclusion is an exclusion. In a busy, buzzing universe where no two snow flakes are identical, and no two trees are identical, and no two people are identical — and, indeed, the smallest sub-atomic particle, we are assured, is not even identical with itself from one microsecond to the next — every card-index system is a delusion. "Or, to put it more charitably," as Nietzsche says, "we are all better artists than we realize."

It is easy to see that the label "Jew" was a Damnation in Nazi Germany, but actually the label "Jew" is a Damnation anywhere, even where anti-Semitism does not exist. "He is a Jew," "She is a doctor," and "He is a poet" mean, to the card indexing centre of the cortex, that my experience with him or her will be like my experience with other Jews, other doctors, and other poets. Thus, individuality is ignored when identity is asserted.

At a party, or any place where strangers meet, watch this mechanism in action. Behind the friendly overtures there is wariness as each person fishes for the label that will identify and Damn the other. Finally, it is revealed: "Oh, she's an advertising copywriter"; "Oh, he's an engine lathe operator." Both parties relax, for now they know how to behave, what roles to play in the game. Ninety-nine percent of each has been Damned; the other is reacting to the one percent that has been labeled by the card-index machine.

Certain Damnations are socially and intellectually necessary, of course.

A custard pie thrown in a comedian's face is Damned by the physicist who analyzes it according to the Newtonian laws of motion. These equations tell us we want to know about the impact of the pie on the face, but nothing about the human meaning of pie-throwing.

A cultural anthropologist, analyzing the social function of the comedian as shaman, court jester, and king's surrogate, explains the pie-throwing as a survival of the Feast of Fools and the killing of the king's double. This Damns the subject in another way.

A psychoanalyst, finding an Oedipal castration ritual here, has performed a third Damnation, and the Marxist, seeing an outlet for the worker's repressed rage against the bosses, performs a fourth.

Each Damnation has its values and uses, but is nonetheless a Damnation unless we recognize its partial and arbitrary nature. The poet, who compares the pie in the comedian's face with Decline of the West or his own lost love, commits a fifth Damnation, but in this case the game element and the whimsicality of the symbolism are safely obvious. At least, one would hope so; reading the New Critics occasionally raises doubts on this point.

Human society can be structured either according to the principle of authority or according to the principle of liberty.

Authority demands a static social configuration in which people act as superiors and inferiors: a sado-masochistic relationship.

Liberty represents a dynamic social configuration in which people act as equals: an erotic relationship.

In every interaction between people, either Authority or Liberty becomes the dominant factor. Families, churches, lodges, clubs and corporations all seem either more authoritarian than libertarian or more libertarian than authoritarian.

It becomes obvious as we proceed that the most pugnacious and intolerant form of authority is the State, which even today dares to assume absolutism which the Church itself has long ago surrendered and to enforce obedience with the Church's old and shameful Inquisition. Every form of authoritarianism "is," or at least acts like, a small "State," even if it has a membership of only two. Freud's remark to the effect that the delusion of one person is mental illness and the delusion of many persons is religion can be generalized: The authoritarianism of one man is crime and the authoritarianism of many is State. Benjamin Tucker wrote quite accurately:

Aggression is simply another name for government. Aggression, invasion, government are interchangeable terms. The essence of government is control, or the attempt to control. He who attempts to control another is a governor, an aggressor, an invader; and the nature of such invasion is not changed, whether it be made by one man upon another man, after the manner of the ordinary criminal, or by one man upon all other men, after the manner of an absolute monarch, or by all other men upon one man, after the manner of a modern democracy.

Tucker's use of the word "invasion" is remarkably precise, considering that he wrote more than fifty years before the basic discovery of ethology.

Every act of authority is, in fact, an invasion of the psychic and physical territory of another.

Every fact of science was once Damned. Every invention was considered impossible. Every discovery was a nervous shock to some orthodoxy.

Every artistic innovation was denounced as fraud and folly. The entire web of culture and "progress," everything on earth that is human-made and not given to us by nature, is the concrete manifestation of some person's refusal to bow to Authority. We would own no more, know no more, and be no more than the first apelike hominids if it were not for the rebellious, the recalcitrant, and the intransigent. As Oscar Wilde truly said, "Disobedience was man's Original Virtue."

The human brain, which loves to read descriptions of itself as the universe's most marvelous organ of perception, is an even more marvelous organ of rejection. The naked facts of our economic game are easily discoverable and undeniable once stated, but conservatives — who are usually individuals who profit every day of their lives from these facts — manage to remain oblivious to them or to see them through a very rose-tinted lens.

(Similarly, the revolutionary ignores the total testimony of history about the natural course of revolution, through violence, to chaos, back to the starting point, in the form of a new tyranny.)

We must remember that "thought" means *abstraction*. In Einstein's metaphor, the relationship between a sensory or instrumental fact and our mental reception of that fact is not like the relationship between beef and beef-broth, a simple extraction and condensation; rather, as Einstein goes on, it is like the relationship between our overcoat and the ticket given us when we check our overcoat. In other words, *human perception involves coding even more than crude sensing.*

The mesh of language, or of mathematics, or of a school of art, or of any system of human abstracting, gives to our mental constructs the structure, not of the original fact, but of the symbol system into which it is coded, just as a mapmaker colors a nation purple not because it "is" purple but because his code demands it. But every code excludes certain things, blurs other things, and overemphasizes still other things.

Nijinski's celebrated leap through the window at the climax of *Le Spectre de la Rose* is best coded in the ballet notation system used by choreographers; verbal language falters badly in attempting to convey it; painting or sculpture could capture totally the magic of one instant, but one instant only, of it; the physicist's equation, Force = Mass x Acceleration, highlights one aspect of it missed by all these other codes, but loses everything else about it. Every perception is influenced, formed, and structured by habitual coding habits-neurosemantic game habits — of the perceiver.

All authority is a function of coding, of game rules. Men have arisen again and again armed with pitchforks to fight armies with cannon; men have also submitted docilely to the weakest and most tottery oppressors. It all depends on the extent to which coding distorts perception and conditions the physical (and "mental") reflexes.

It seems at first glance that authority could not exist at all if all men were cowards or if no men were cowards, but flourishes as it does because most men are cowards and some men are thieves. Actually, nowadays, the inner dynamics of cowardice and submission on the one hand and of heroism and rebellion on the other are seldom consciously realized either by the ruling class or the servile class.

Submission is identified not with cowardice but with virtue, rebellion not with heroism but with evil. To the Roman slave-owners, Spartacus was not a hero and the obedient slaves were not cowards; Spartacus was a villain and the obedient slaves were virtuous. The obedient slaves believed this also. The obedient always think of themselves as virtuous rather than cowardly.

If authority implies submission, liberation implies equality; authority exists when some persons obey others, and liberty exists when people do not obey other mere humans. Thus, to say that authority exists is to say that class and caste exist, that submission and inequality exist.

To say that liberty exists is to say that classlessness exists, to say that brotherhood and equality exist. Authority, by dividing people into classes, creates dichotomy, disruption, hostility, fear, disunion. Liberty, by placing us all on an equal footing, creates association, amalgamation, union, security. When the relationships between people are based on authority and coercion, they are driven apart; when based on liberty and non-aggression, they are drawn together. The facts are self-evident and axiomatic. If authoritarianism did not possess the in-built, preprogrammed double-bind structure of a Game Without End we would long ago have rejected it and embraced libertarianism.

The usual pacifist complaint about war, that young men are led to death by old men who sit at home manning bureaucrats' desks and taking no risks themselves, misses the point entirely. Demands that the old should be drafted to fight their own wars, or that the leaders of the warring nations should be sent to the front lines on the first day of battle, etc., are aimed at an assumed "sense of justice" that simply does not exist.

To the typical submissive citizen of authoritarian society, it is normal, obvious and "natural" that he should obey older and more dominant males, even at the risk of his life, even against his own kindred, and even in causes that are unjust or flagrantly absurd.

The mechanism by which authority and submission are implanted in the human mind is coding of perception. That which fits into the code is accepted; all else is Damned to being ignored, brushed aside, unnoticed, and — if these fail — it is Damned to being forgotten. A worse form of Damnation is reserved for those things which cannot be ignored. These are daubed with the brain's projected prejudices until, encrusted beyond recognition, they are capable of being fitted into the system, classified, card-indexed, buried. This is what happens to every Damned Thing which is too prickly and sticky to be excommunicated entirely. As Josiah Warren remarked, "It is dangerous to understand new things too quickly." Almost always, we have not understood them. We have murdered them and mummified their corpses.

A monopoly on the means of communication may define a ruling elite more precisely than the celebrated Marxian formula of "monopoly in the means of production." Since humans extend their nervous systems though channels of communication like the written word, the telephone, radio, TV, Internet, etc., whoever controls these media controls part of the nervous system of every member of society. The contents of these media become part of the contents of every individual's brain.

Thus, in preliterate societies, taboos on spoken word are more numerous and more Draconic than at any more complex level of social organization.

With the invention of written speech — hieroglyphic, ideographic, or alphabetical — the taboos are shifted to this medium; there is less concern with what people say and more concern with what people write. (Some of the first societies to achieve literacy, such as Egypt and the Mayan culture of ancient Mexico, evidently kept a knowledge of hieroglyphs a religious secret which only the higher orders of the priestly and royal families were allowed to share.)

The same process repeats endlessly: Each step forward in the technology of communication is more heavily tabooed than the earlier steps.

Thus, in America today (post-Lenny Bruce), one seldom hears of convictions for spoken blasphemy or obscenity; prosecution of books still continues, but higher courts increasingly interpret the laws in a liberal fashion, and most writers feel fairly confident that they can publish virtually anything; movies are growing almost as decentralized as books, although the fight is still heated in this area; television, the newest medium, remains encased in neolithic taboo. (When the TV pundits committed *lese majeste* after an address by the then Dominant Male, a certain Richard Nixon, one of his lieutenants quickly informed them they had overstepped, and the whole tribe — except for the dissident minority — cheered for the reassertion of tradition.) When a more efficient medium [Internet?] arrives, the taboos on television will decrease.

Old Man on a Balcony:
Views of Monterey Bay #18

Grey and pastel pink —

A water-color painting —

This light before dawn.

CyberRevolution Montage

written in Los Angeles 1989

1954: Bard College, Annandale-on-Hudson, NY . . . It was the first time I ever heard Buckminster Fuller speak. He said that by the late 1980's we would all be living in a "one-town world." In 1988, I have been ostensibly "living" in Los Angeles, but in these twelve months I have visited or re-visited Maui, San Jose (2 times), Berkeley, San Diego, Vancouver, Seattle (3 times), Phoenix, Boulder, Dallas (2 times), Philadelphia, Wilmington, New York (2 times), Boston, and — overseas — Dublin, Berlin, Hamburg, Heidelberg, Frankfurt, Munich, Berne and Vienna.

I don't suppose this travel log will impress many readers of *Mondo 2000*. Still, reliving 1954 in memory, I am astounded at the mutation that has occurred. Though many people still use the word "jet-setter" to mean some kind of millionaire, most of the folks who are hopping around the globe are not rich at all. They have simply redefined travel.

Throughout evolution, the average mammal has never traveled more than ten miles from the place it was born. Throughout human history, the average person has never traveled more than ten miles from the place she or he was born . . . [Source: *Sociobiology*, Edward O. Wilson]

Since 1900, the speed of travel has increased by a factor of 100; known energy resources by 1000; explosive power of weaponry by 1,000,000; and speed of communication by 10,000,000. [Source: J.R. Platt, Michigan State University]

Americans have also eaten 1.8x10,000,000,000 McDonald's hamburgers . . .

Deforestation . . .

According to *Popular Mechanics*, February 1938, a new invention would soon make it possible to end the cutting of trees to produce paper for our books, offices and newspapers. *Popular Mechanics* was so enthusiastic about this invention that they predicted farmers would earn billions of dollars a year making paper this way and would never cut down another tree.

As you look around at our devastated forestlands, you might ask yourself, what the hell happened in the past 50 years? Where did the wonderful invention go?

Well, kiddies, the wonderful invention was a device that made it possible to harvest hemp more cheaply than ever before. Hemp was the chief ingredient in paper throughout most of history (our Declaration of Independence was written on it, for instance) and paper made of hemp lasted a good long time compared to paper made of wood pulp. Ever notice how 19th or 18th century books or even 17th century books like the original folio of Shakespeare's plays, printed on hemp, are still around, while modern books printed on wood pulp fall apart in only decades?

Our books continue to rot away quickly, and our forests continue to be destroyed because the U.S. Government declared war on hemp. They had found out that some people smoke it and get happy.

Puritanism, to quote H.L. Mencken, is "the haunting fear that somebody, somewhere, might be having a good time."

Piss Wars

George H.W. Bush volunteered to be one of the first Americans to take a urine test for drugs. During the Iran-Contra investigations, however, Bush refused to take a lie detector test. As Paul Krassner astutely commented, it appears Bush doesn't want us to know whether he's telling the truth or lying, but he wants us to be sure he's not stoned while doing it.

Neurologically, Piss Wars opens awesome possibilities. The most widely used urine test in the country detects traces of marijuana and cocaine but does not detect LSD. The corporate structure of the short-term future will therefore thin out the ranks of pot smokers and coke freaks while the acid heads climb merrily upward in the hierarchy. This would suggest that the sensuality of grass and the wired aggression of coke will dwindle in Power Centers but the morphogenetic/futuristic evolutionary visions of LSD will play an ever-larger role in shaping policy.

Think about it.

One Ton a Day?

On the other hand, a friend of mine in Silicon Gulch recently told me there is a ton of grass smoked every day in that area — where most of the software of *Star Wars* is being produced.

I couldn't believe it at first, but he worked it out on his computer and showed me. The population is 4 million. Assuming only half of them smoke grass and they smoke only one joint a day — reasonably conservative estimates, I think — one comes out with a ton of weed, and a heavy log of cannabis vapor circulating "in the belly of the beast" (as SDS used to say).

Most of the companies in the Gulch are unwilling to institute Piss Wars. They know if they did, they'd lose their most talented, diligent and inspired software experts immediately.

The modern "barbarians" — the Cyberpunks — are not only within the gates, but have penetrated the Citadel itself.

THOUGHTS TO PONDER

The rise of the Net and the Web represents a victory for
the counterculture and the subculture. The next generation,
raised on the Net as their primary medium, won't even
know what consensus reality is.

— R.U. Sirius

Old Man on a Balcony:
Views of Monterey Bay #19

"Sweet! Sweet!" sings a bird —

Old Ez in Virginia

Heard one cry "Tulip!"

The Horror on Howth Hill

It was the rains, I swear — the interminable, unspeakable Irish rains— that drove us over the edge. My old Gothic castle, located high atop the hill of Howth facing Dublin Bay, was not only damp, dank and dark (due to the omnipresent clouds), but rapidly becoming eldritch, noisome and foetid. In fact, it looked like the set for a Bela Lugosi film — an appropriate scene, I thought later, for the terrible encounter of Professor Timothy Finnegan and J. R. "Bob" Dobbs.

The rain had gone on for two months this time, bringing a clammy, enervating muskiness to everything. In the library, even the pages of my prized German translation of the banned and forbidden *Necronomicon* (*Dos Verichteraraberbuch*, von Juntz, 1848) and de Selby's disturbing and debatable *Teratologica Ontologicum* were sticking together.

Rancid, the butler, was falling-down drunk every day and I could hardly blame him. The maids — dark, sensuous Immaculata and blonde, buxom Concepcion — were not only dykes, as I suspected from the first, but speed freaks as well. They spent all day in their room, injecting and 69ing, injecting and 69ing. They totally neglected their duties and the entire castle had begun to look like the bottom of a box where the cat had kittens. Adam, my grand old gardener, had been tripping his brains out on LSD since the third week of the rains and the grounds had the ghoulish and nameless appearance of the swamps of Yuggoth redesigned by Salvador Dali. If the damnable downpour did not cease soon, I feared that we all should become mad. I think I myself would have been sunk in lethargy and existential despair if it were not for my mescaline and XTC stashes.

Worst of all, it was drawing near the aeon-cursed Walpurgis Night and Professor Finnegan had come to pay his annual visit again.*

~•~

* Finnegan was the most controversial Irish philosopher of the later twentieth century. For biographical details, see O'Brien, *Dalkey Archive*, Picador Books London, 1976, and/or Wilson, *The Widow's Son*, formerly with New Falcon Publications, 2004

Highlights of the Finnegan furor will be found in Conneghen, *The Finnegan Code*, Royal Sir Myles na gCopaleen Anthropological Society Preas, Dalkey, 1937; Flahive, *Teratological Evolution*, Royal Sir Myles na gCopaleen biochemical Institute Press, Dalkey, 1972; Vinkenoog, *Finnegan: De onbekende filosoof*, De Kosmos, Amsterdam, 1951; La Foumier, *Finnegan — l 'Enigme de l'Occident*, University of Paris, 1933; Han Tui Po, *Finnegan Du Jhing*, Univer- sity of Beijing, 1972; La Toumier (not to be confused with La Foumier), *Finnegan: Homme ou Dieu?*, Editions J'ai Lu, Paris, 1904; Sheissenhosen, *Finneganismus und Dummheit* (6 vols.), University of Heidelberg, 1942-52; La Puta, *La Estupidez de Sheissenhosen*, University of Madrid, 1975; Turn-und-Taxis, *Ist Finnegan eine Droge oder haben wir sie nur falsch verstanden?*, Sphinx Verlag, Basel, 1922; O'Broichnan, *A Chara, na caith tabac*, Royal Sir Myles na gCopaleen Zoological Institute Press, Dalkey, 1992.

~•~

Of course, I personally have always liked Finnegan, who is not at all a bad chap in his own weird way. But he lives always, not just in the turmoil of academic controversy, but in the epicenter of a veritable spider's web of clandestine operations: where Tim Finnegan walks, the CIA and KGB are sure to skulk close behind, and the IRA and even the PLO may be showing interest also, not to mention the Knights of Malta,* the Illuminati,* the Priory of Sion,* the Campus Crusade for Cthulhu* and the other secret societies and cults whose reputations are unsavory and whose goals remain inscrutable to ordinary wholesome men and women.

~•~

* **The Knights of Malta** — or, more properly, the Sovereign Military Order of Malta (abbreviated SMOM) — is the eight-hundred-year-old Vatican "secret police" or "dirty tricks

bureau." According to *Covert Action Information Bulletin #25*, Winter 1986, notable recent members of SMOM have included Dr. Otto vou Hapsburg (a prime organizer of the infamous "Bilderbergers"), Franz von Papen (the man who persuaded President von Hindenburg to resign and appoint Hitler chancellor of Germany), William Casey (the CIA chief who died mysteriously during the Iran-Contra hearings), Major General Reinhard Gehlen, General Alexander Haig, Roberto Calvi, Michele Sindona and Licio Gelli. Baigent, Lincoln and Leigh in *The Messianic Legacy* (Henry Holt, New York, 1987) have added to the list of SMOM members Alexandre de Marenches, former chief of French intelligence, and claim mysterious links between SMOM and the Priory of Sion. Gordon Thomas and Max Wittman in *The Year of Armageddon* (Corgi, London, 1984) claim that SMOM members act as couriers between the Vatican and the CIA. Most scholars dissent vehemently from von Hanfkopf's ill-documented charge that de Selby, Flahive, La Toumier, Finegan and the shadowy La Foumier are or were all members of SMOM.

* **The Illuminati**, founded in Bavaria in 1776, was (or is) a secret society within a secret society, since all members were first Freemasons before being invited into the Illuminati itself. See Nesta Webster, *World Revolution*, Christian Back and other secret societies and cults whose reputations are unsavory and whose goals remain inscrutable to ordinary wholesome men and women. Club of America, Hawthorne, California, n.d.; "Inquire Within," *The Trail of the Serpent*, Christian Book Club of America, Hawthorne, California, n.d.; and Wilson, *Cosmic Trigger*, Falcon Press, Santa Monica, 1987. The Illuminati technique of forming a secret society within another secret society was later imitated by the Molly Maguires, an Irish revolutionary group within the Ancient Order of Hibernians, and the P2 conspiracy which recruited within the Grand Orient Lodge of Egyptian Freemasonry in Italy — although secretly managed, as noted above, by three members of the Vatican secret service, SMOM. Professor Flahive was under great personal stress when he began his campaign to convince the learned community that von Hanfkopf was actually the ringleader of an Illuminati conspiracy against Finnegan.

* According to Paoli (*Les Dessous d'une ambition politique*,

Hurhaus Verlag, Basel, 1973), the **Priory of Sion** is a serious
political conspiracy of aristocratic French Freemasons who intend
to restore monarchy in France. According to de Sede (*La Race
fabuleuse*, Editions J'ai Lu, Paris, 1973), the Priory is descended:
from superhumans born of matings between ancient Hebrews and
extraterrestrials from Sirius. According to Baigent, Leigh and
Lincoln (*Holy Blood, Holy Grail,* Delacorte, 1982), the Priory
is descended from the royal line of Jesus and Mary Magdalene.
According to Michael Lame (*Jules Verne, initiate et initiateur*,
Editions J'ai Lu, Paris, 1985), the Priory is a front for the Illuminati
and Veme's "science fiction" novels are subtle Illuminati recruiting
manuals. Finnegan claims (*Omni qua sunt*, Royal Sir Myles
na gCopaleen Philosophical Society Press, Dalkey, 1957) that
the Illuminati/Priory axis is an attempt to spread electric light
everywhere, thereby banishing the "teratological molecules" which
move backwards in time and generate Chaos, but this must be
considered one of the more imaginative flights of the Dalkey sage.

* **The Campus Crusade for Cthulhu** has been alleged to
be responsible for the recent crop of child murders and cattle
mutilations elsewhere attributed to Satanists; see Rev. Jedidiah
Blather, *The Cthulhu Cult, Interstellar Bankers and Punk Rock*,
True Christian Book Club of America, Tulsa, 1987. Although few
credit this wild charge, the CCC is definitely responsible for the
bumper stickers that say things like IT FOUND ME; ABDUL
ALHAZRED WAS NOT MAD YOG SOTHOTH NEBLOD ZIN;
etc. Von Hanfkopf's attempts to link La Puta to the CCC are best
described as tenuous and (as Ferguson said) "clutching straws."
It was after Professor Ferguson uttered these views on the BBC
that the police of his hometown, Loch Pookah, received letters
claiming he, Ferguson, was the Yorkshire Ripper. These letters were
in clumsy English ("rather like that of the Katzenjammer Kids,"
according to Inspector MacAndrew, who handled the investigation)
and had Heidelberg postmarks.

~•~

Some of these types would be beyond the comprehension
of the Los Angeles Vice Squad or the specialists in abnormal
psychology at the Kinsey Institute, I swear.

As usual, Finnegan has a new obsession this year. He is

determined to discover the exact dimensions of the penis of a fictitious gorilla. Any ordinary scholar, however eccentric, might decide to write a paper on the dimensions of the wingwang of a real gorilla, dead or alive, but dear old Timothy wants to discover the magnitude of the Willy of a gorilla who never really existed at all — King Kong in the famous horror film of 1933. Naturally, being Finnegan, he has reasons for this which no normal person can understand.*

~•~

* The Finnegan/CSICON controversy originally erupted into political mania after Professor Sheissenhosen charged (see his *Werke*, vol. XXIII, pp. 506-666ff.) that some of the moneys embezzled from Banco Ambrosiano of Milan in the early 1980's (by the bank's president, Roberto Calvi, and his associates in the P2 conspiracy) had been "laundered" through a Dublin bank account which Finnegan allegedly used to finance IRA terrorism in Northern Ireland. Although this charge was unsubstantiated, Professor Flahive rebutted it at great length (*Proceedings of the Royal Sir Myles na gCopaleen Institute of International Relations,* vol. LVI, pp. 309-417) and it was after this that the Special Branch of the Gardia (the police of the Republic of Ireland) began receiving letters with a Heidelberg postmark charging (in broken English) that Flahive himself was involved in running guns for the IRA. This was immediately after the unfortunate and much-debated incident involving Professor Flahive and the fourteen-year-old Girl Scout from Sallynoggin, and the distressed savant, a devout Catholic and conservative, began making wild charges about "intentional plots" and "frame-ups" and, sadly, eventually degenerated to the same tactics as Sheissenhosen, claiming that the Heidelberg philosopher was formerly associated with the Gehlen *apparat* and the CIA's "Russian" branch — the group, under Major General Reinhard Gehlen, Knights of Malta and former head of army intelligence for Hitler, which conducts espionage within the Soviet Union itself. Of course, the crude (and ineffective) letter bomb sent to Professor Flahive at this point, although postmarked Langley, Virginia, could have been sent by anybody (and one assumes the CIA are at least hip enough not to mail such devices from a city universally known to be their international headquarters); but after Roberto Calvi, President of Banco Ambrosiano, was found

hanging from Blackfriars Bridge in London that same week, and his secretary, Ms. Graziella, fell or was pushed from a window of the Milan office of that bank, sheer paranoia descended upon all those involved in the Finnegan feud or even in the abstract mathematical arguments about Finnegan's "plenuminary time" and "teratalogical molecules." As La Puta has incisively remarked, "The entire Finnegan furor is degenerating into the worst academic schlemozzle since the Bacon-Shakespeare lunacy."

~•~

Finnegan says 1932 (when King Kong was being produced) was a pivot in evolution, in some mystic sense that only he comprehends.

"In 1932," he was telling me at breakfast this morning, "Alice Pleasance Liddell died, and so did John Stanislaus Joyce."

"Who the hell were they?" I asked irritably.

"Alice P. Liddell," he said somberly, "was the model for *Alice in Wonderland*. Charles Dodgson and/or Lewis Carroll — the world's most successful dual personality — loved her um ah er 'not wisely but too well.' Too well, at any rate, to avoid the speculations of Freudians. And John Stanislaus Joyce was the father of James Joyce. Do you see the connection?"

I admitted that the linkage evaded me.

"Alice Pleasance Liddell or APL," Finnegan said simply, "is one aspect of Anna Livia Plurabelle or ALP, the superwoman who contains all women, in Joyce's *Finnegans Wake*."

"Oh," I said. It seemed the only adequate comment.

"I have wondered," de Selby went on, "if one can equate APL with ALP on Cabalistic grounds, since both equal 111, what of PLA?*

~•~

* "PLA" is Dublin slang for Portlaois Lunatic Asylum, the institution which many of Finnegan's critics claimed would be his ultimate destination. As La Foumier wrote (*Finnegan; l'Enigme de la Occident*, p. 23), "While much about the sage of Dalkey remains in dispute, none have denied that he held a greater number of strikingly original ideas than any philosopher in history not known to have resided in a padded cell." Sheissenhosen's claim that Le

Foumier was a mask, a nonentity, a fiction, a stalking horse behind which Finnegan wrote commentaries on himself, in French no less, has not been conclusively verified, and La Puta claims to have refuted it entirely in his *La Estupidez, op. cit.* It was after this work was published that the Spanish police began receiving letters, with a Heidelberg postmark, alleging in bad Spanish that La Puta was the chief opium smuggler in Madrid and a KGB agent. Professor Hamburger's attempts to link La Puta to the Illuminati (*Proceedings of the London Musicological Society*, vol. XXIII, pp. 7-133) do, however, appear to be well documented and possess some merit, although Hamburger's argument that it was La Puta, not Finnegan, who laundered the cocaine money for the P2 conspiracy is far from convincing. As Penny Lernoux documents in her *In Banks We Trust* (Anchor Press/Doubleday, Garden City, New York, 1984), most of the cocaine money went through the World Finance Corporation in Miami and the Cisalpine Overseas Bank in the Bahamas, which was owned by the deceased Robert Calvi and Archbishop Marcinkus. The argument of Yallop (*In God's Name*, Bantam, New York, 1984) that Calvi and Marcinkus collaborated in the murder of Pope John Paul I is, of course, highly speculative.

~•~

But that is an irrelevance, I've decided. What is important is that in 1932 not only did Alice P. Liddell and John S. Joyce die, but the atom was split for the first time, and the 92nd chemical element was discovered — the last natural element, you see. For the first time in history, humanity had access to the energy of the stars and possessed a full catalog of the basic building blocks of the universe.

"And, of course, Roosevelt II was elected in America, and Hitler in Germany, that very same year, 1932, which incidentally adds numerologically to 15, the number of the Devil card in the Tarot. King Kong, you see, had to emerge from the collective unconscious at exactly that point, especially since Cary Grant was 28 years old on January 18 that year."

Professor Finnegan went on in that vein for quite a while, but I sort of lost the thread of his argument — something that often happens to readers of his books, as numerous critics have complained. All I could ever remember afterwards was that Cary Grant was 28 when I was born and 28 is a number connected with menstruation, the ancient Celtic moon goddess, Bridget, and the synchronous link from Lewis Carroll's obsession with premenstrual girls to Cary Grant's habit of avoiding the Academy Award dinners, staying home, taking LSD and watching the award ceremonies on TV while "laughing uncontrollably and jumping up and down on the bed," according to the testimony in his third divorce trial.

Eventually, we finished our leisurely breakfast. It was ten thirty and the pubs opened, so Timothy put on his brown mackintosh (he seems to have worn it since 1904, I think) and sallied forth in search of Irish Inspiration.

I went to the study and tried again to work on my new science-fiction novel, *Wigner's Friend*, which deals with a parallel universe where Moe Howard became Pope and Adolf Hitler migrated to the United States and became a popular writer of Western movies. As usual lately, my creativity was dampened by the depressing rain, the eldritch, unhallowed and Peter Lorre-like giggles of the gardener after his day's dose of LSD took effect and the strange, fetid and nameless fungi that have grown on the furniture since the maids got hooked on methamphetamines and stopped even pretending to clean up.

Rancid, the butler, lurched into the study, staggered, knocked over a Ming vase, puked into the potted fern, and asked if I needed anything. I sent him away with no rancor. He was too drunk to understand anything I said, anyway. I did wish, however, that he looked a little less like Boris Karloff as the alcoholic (and eventually homicidal) butler in *The Old Dark House*. The rain continued to fall and the sky remained overcast and gloomy, turning my thoughts to the most morbid subjects imaginable. I was actually happy when Finnegan returned, in a car driven by an American tourist he had met at the Royal Howth, a Mr. J.R. "Bob" Dobbs.

"Bob," Finnegan said grandly, "meet 'Bob.'" I could see that he had put away at least five or six pints of Guinness stout already, and I tried not to become uneasy or let my imagination run riot over the simple fact that "Bob" had a Campus Crusade for Cthulhu bumper sticker on his Toyota. Americans often have a strange sense of humor. Nonetheless, as we entered the castle, I looked back at the car and shuddered involuntarily at the other words on the bumper.

Have you hugged your shoggoth today?

We went to my study, where Finnegan, with his usual exuberant Celtic generosity, opened a bottle of my best Tullamore Dew and offered a healthy double shot to "Bob." I was pleased when he offered some to me, too.

"'Bob' has some real data on Kong's dong," Finnegan began at once, finishing the rest of the bottle in a gulp.

I raised an enquiring eyebrow, a trick I had learned from Basil Rathbone movies. "Bob" was busy relighting his Pipe for a moment but then he spoke in a mellow Texas drawl.

"The average man," he said, "stands between about five foot eight and about six foot, right? And the average human erection, at least according to my wife, 'Connie' — who is more of an expert on males in heat than I am — is between five and seven inches. The nine-inchers and twelve-inchers you see occasionally in porn movies are freaks of nature like Watusis or basketball players who can be seven or eight feet tall. Follow me? So the average human male, statistically, has about six inches. Kay? Now in the case of Kong, we have an anthropoid standing at least twenty-four feet tall, as you can judge by the scene in the theater. That means he would have about four times as much as a man of six feet.

Four times six is twenty-four, so Kong had twenty-four inches or two feet."

"No wonder Fay Wray did so much screaming," I said. "She'd be in the position of the young lady from Sidney in the poem by T.S. Eliot." Finnegan raised an enquiring eyebrow (he's seen a lot of Basil Rathbone movies, too) and courteously opened another bottle of my Tullamore Dew. To explain my remark, I recited the immortal lines from *Ash Wednesday*:

> There was a young lady from Sidney
> Who liked it right up to her kidney
> A man from Quebec
> Shoved it up to her neck
> He had a big one, didn't he?

Finnegan refilled our glasses all around and sat down in an easy chair. He looked troubled.

"Well," I said to him cheerfully. "Your mystery is solved. There's no prob with 'Bob.'"

"I don't know," the Sage of Dalkey replied thoughtfully. "We may be approaching this matter from the wrong angle entirely. 'Bob' is treating Kong as a creature in biology, which is emphatically what the Big Fellow is not at all, at all. Kong is a creature in mythology, in um ah er the collective unconscious."

"Why, sure," said "Bob" quickly. "Hellfire, boy, there ain't no twenty-four-foot gorillas in the real world. But if we grant that, for argument's sake, how in hell do we reason about Kong at all? What are the dimensions of a myth, a dream, a Special Effect? Tell me that." And he grabbed the Tullamore Dew and poured another hearty slug. I could see we were in for a day of heavy going.

"Well," Finnegan said, "we must take our clues from the records of the collective unconscious itself. Kong is a Nature Divinity, to say the least of it, and, considering his um concupiscence — that means horniness in American, 'Bob' — he's more specifically a Fertility God. We must approach this from the perspective of 'patapsychology."

"What are you getting at?" I asked uneasily. In the distance, a dog barked and, further off, there was an ominous rumble of thunder.

"Well," Finnegan said. "We know one thing about Fertility Gods. Anthropologists call them *ithyphallique* and not without reason. They make the studs in porn movies look puny by comparison. Osiris is portrayed in Egyptian art as having about three times as much Willy as one would expect in a man, or god, of his size. In Greece, Hermes was usually depicted with a tool almost the size of his body — why, statues of him look almost like a bureau with the middle drawer pulled all the way out. As for Finn Mac Cool, some of the most powerful verses in the Finn epic — the most beautiful lines of Gaelic in our tradition, although usually expunged in English translations — describe him as, well, virtually a pole-vaulter with a built-in pole."

"Why, hell's bells, son," said "Bob" chortling, "that's the most persistent of all legends. When I was young, everybody in the States believed Dillinger had twenty-three inches and it was preserved in alcohol at the Smithsonian after his death. Later on, the myth got attached to an actor named Errol Flynn. Long crullers, the kind you call Berliner over here, were called Errol Flynns."

"Say," I interrupted, smitten with whimsy, "when John Fitzgerald Kennedy went to Germany and said, *'Ich bin ein Berliner,'* was he jus being diplomatic, or was he bragging?"

They ignored me. "Dillinger and Mr. Flynn had become semi-divine in folklore," the professor said, pouring more Tullamore Dew, "and so naturally they were expected to have semi-divine prongs, two or three times the norm. Truly divine beings have much, much more. Considering Osiris and Hermes, I would say a divine being would have six times the norm, at least. As a fertility spirit, Kong must have, not the mere two feet that a biological twenty-four-foot gorilla would possess, but around twelve feet."

"That fits with the anthropological books I've read," I agreed. "The primitive theory is, the greater the Willy, the greater the divinity indwelling."

We paused to consider the 'patapsychological ramifications of our theorizing. Thunder rumbled closer to my castle and more dogs began howling in anxiety.

"You know, fellers," Dobbs said, filling his Pipe again — I had begun to recognize the aroma of what he was smoking and understood why he always had the same contented grin — "I come from Texas, where we got ourselves almost as many Catholics as here in Ireland. There's a big donnybrook going on in the Catholic church these days because some nuns have become Feminists and are demanding the right to say Mass. The Pope absolutely refuses to consider it. He says you absolutely have to have a Willy to perform the sacrament."

Finnegan had been hunting in my bar for more Tullamore, and, finding none, opened a bottle of my Jameson. "Why, of course a priest must have a Willy in Catholic theology," he said mildly. "The priest represents God, who has the biggest Willy of all — even bigger than Kong's."

"What was that?" I objected. "There was a quantum jump or something there. Run that by me again."

"You said it yourself," Finnegan drawled. "'The greater the Willy, the greater the divinity indwelling.' Yahweh, the Jewish God who became the Christian God, always claimed to be bigger and better than any of the other Near Eastern gods who competed with him. He would have to be endowed with a schlong that would make Osiris or Dionysus, say, look almost impotent by comparison."

"Just how big would it be?" I challenged. If Finnegan and "Bob," with only two bottles of malt in them, could deduce the size of King Kong's dong, I was sure that with another bottle they could do the same for YHVH.

"Well," de Selby said, "Yahweh himself isn't much bigger than Kong. He walks around Eden at twilight — without smashing down the trees or causing any notable wreckage of the sort Godzilla would leave in his wake. He shows his backside to Moses and nobody in Greece or even Babylon sees that cosmic spectacle.

"I would say he couldn't be more than forty or fifty feet tall. In biologic, he should have about four to five feet of johnson. In mytho-logic, if he were any ordinary fertility god like Hermes or Finn, he would have six times that or around twenty-four to thirty feet. As the Lord of Lords and King of Kings, etc., he would double our expectations at least. He should have around fifty feet. In passion, he would be symmetrical, fifty feet high and fifty wide in the middle, sort of like a giant F with the top stroke missing."

"I begin to feel the same sympathy for the Virgin Mary that I experienced earlier for Fay Wray," I said, finishing off my own shot of Jameson. But then another thought struck me. "Yahweh may have been about that size — probably was that size, I think — back in Biblical times. The scriptures are full of lots of other references that show him about the height of Finn Mac Cool or Zeus, say. But he has grown during the scientific epoch. Every new advance in astronomy has necessitated that the whole Judeo-Christian tradition has had to make him bigger and uh er more gaseous, as it were. By the time of Newton, he had to be at least millions of miles in circumference to create the known universe. Since we started finding other galaxies in the 1920's, he has swollen to billions and billions of light-years — at least."

"Yes," said "Bob" thoughtfully. "To be consistent with known cosmology, the Judeo-Christian God would have to be bodacious, to say the least of it. And the size of his john thomas — gol dang, the mind spins at the thought."

"And yet, if we accept Christianity in any sense, even as metaphor like Mr. T.S. Eliot," Finnegan muttered pensively, "the metaphor demands such a whang for its divinity. Billions of zillions of parsecs from foreskin to base. The only way out of that logic is the Feminist path. Neuter the divinity. He has no dong at all. He isn't a he anymore. A cosmic eunuch."

"Well, there's also the Radical Feminist-path," I suggested. "He's she."

"Lawdy, lawdy," said "Bob" dazedly, quickly gulping some more Jameson. "Now we have to try to visualize a vagina quadrillions of parsecs deep."*

~•~

* I have often thought, later, that it was this conversation which inspired Finnegan's most controversial essay, "Can Goddess Create a Stone So Heavy That She Herself Cannot Lift It?," which he optimistically submitted to several Radical Feminist journals in San Francisco. It was after this that WITCH (the Women's International Terrorist Conspiracy from Hell) began picketing Finnegan's home in Dalkey. It is unfortunate that Flahive, in his passion to defend Finnegan against all detractors, attempted to prove the WITCHes were a "front" for the Knights of Malta. If Flahive had not been himself a former CIA agent and coincidentally present, like Kerfooey, in Dealey Plaza on November 22, 1963, not even the intemperate Hamburger would have claimed evidence foul play in Flahive's subsequent tragic death in a hunting accident with Profesor La Puta.

~•~

It was at this point, alas, that the whiskey began to go to my head and I nodded off in my chair. Professor Finnegan and "Bob" politely did not try to arouse me, reasoning that I needed the rest, and went ahead helping themselves to my rare cognacs, now that the Jameson was exhausted. In that hypnopompic state midway between drunkenness and coma, I was half aware, or dreamed I was half aware, of the continuing conversation.

Somehow Finnegan and "Bob" wandered from the high theological contemplation of divine dongs back to the King himself, and were united in condemning the cheap remakes produced by some Japanese studio and the abominable caricatures of De Laurentiis. Still: They thought it was time for a "sincere" remake, and soon had sketched out a film which I, in my reverie, could see as clearly as if they had already shot it.

Ann Darrow, this time, would be played by Marilyn Chambers, on the grounds that *Behind the Green Door* was, psychoanalytically considered, already a part of the Kong mythos. Like Fay Wray in the original, Marilyn *in Green Door* is kidnapped and ordered as a mate to a divinely endowed Fertility Spirit. "Bob" and Finnegan agreed heartily that the black superstud in *Door*, with his gargantuan tool (and the "savage" bone in his nose) represented the same primitive generative force as Kong. "Pornography," I heard "Bob" say profoundly, "merely makes explicit what is implicit in folk art like Kong."

In the new *Kong*, Marilyn Chambers and a porno producer, played by Al Pacino, sail to Skull Island to make the ultimate wet-shot epic. Kong appears with his five-foot whang clearly visible in every shot. "No fig leaves!" said "Bob" emphatically. The giant dinosaurs and other monsters run amok, as in the original, creating ample mayhem for the S-M crowd, and Marilyn is rescued by a different crew member each time Kong or one of these reptiles menaces her; she expresses her gratitude in traditional Chambers fashion, for the voyeur majority.

At the climax, when Kong is running wild in New York, looking for his mate, Marilyn, his giant tool attracts the horrified notice of Andrea Dworkin, playing herself. She quickly rounds up a crew of five hundred fat ladies from circuses and they overrun and bring down the Big Fellow without any help from airplanes. They then emasculate him in gory detail, on wide screen with Technicolor.

The offensive organ is then weighed down with a lead block

and thrown in the East River so it will never rise again.

While Dworkin leads a horde of Radical Feminists in a victory celebration, the film cuts to a conference room at a university and switches to documentary style. Various leading spokescritters for the Committee for the Scientific Investigation of Claims of the Paranormal — e.g., Carl Sagan, Martin Gardner, James Randi and Professor Sheissenhosen — are then given equal time to persuade the audience that gorillas never grow to twenty-four feet tall and that the film just shown has been fantasy and therefore nefarious.

Sheissenhosen gets the microphone first, but his talk soon degenerates into incoherent ravings about cocaine abuse in Hollywood, CIA plots, the "Vatican-Mafia axis," etc., and he is gently persuaded to relinquish the podium. Randi begins denouncing everybody who disagrees with him about anything, saying they are all frauds, felons and child abusers.

Martin Gardner gets the microphone away from him and argues that all the wreckage in midtown Manhattan does not prove the existence of giant apes and can be "more economically and scientifically explained" by positing the crash of a giant meteor. Dr. Sagan then approaches the podium and urges everybody to beware of wild and fanciful ideas. He rambles off into lyrical exposition about "billions and billions" of galaxies with billions and billions of stars, and is about to proceed further in that vein when suddenly a huge black hand crashes through the floor and grabs him by the testicles.

At that point, I drifted into deeper sleep. In a while, however, I was either startled awake or fell into the worst nightmare of my life — I have never been sure which — but it seemed to me that Finnegan had returned to his original subject, the dimensions of divine dongs, and was arguing that Catholicism remains the last survivor of the ithyphallic cults of the ancient Mediterranean.

Not only must one have a Willy to be a priest, he was saying, but the Pope continues to insist on that because the inner order within the church — I think he meant the Knights of Malta — still holds the antediluvian credo about the biggest Willy containing the greatest Animal Magnetism, or magick, or indwelling divinity, or something like that. He proposed a totally new, and shocking, theory as to how Popes are selected by the College of Cardinals and why these proceedings are always hidden from the public behind locked doors and no details are ever revealed.

Evidently, he was seriously suggesting that, just as it requires a Willy to turn a piece of bread into the body of a dead Jew, it requires the biggest Willy on the planet to anoint others and pass on the power to perform this astounding alchemical transformation.

While I was grappling with this thought, imagining the secret conclaves of the Curia looking like the casting sessions for male lead in a porn epic, and wondering why Kong had not been appointed at least an Honorary Pope. Rancid the butler suddenly burst into the room, carrying a Thompson submachine gun.

"This has gone far enough!" he shouted, glassy-eyed and foaming a bit.

"Come, come, old man — " I began gently, as one must begin with drunks.

"Don't 'old man' me, you Unitarian pervert," he screamed hysterically. The tommy gun, aimed loosely at all of us before, now pointed directly at my gut. "I am no damned butler. I am Cardinal Luigi Mozzarella, of the Holy Office for the Doctrine of the Faith, and Grand Master of the Sovereign Military Order of Malta."

There was a "pregnant" or stifled or grisly silence, as we all took this in.

"We don't have the Maltese Falcon, honestly," said "Bob" weakly.

"Fuck that damned bird," Cardinal Mozzarella shouted. "We've wasted eight hundred years looking for it, and eight hundred years is more than enough on a losing project. I am one of the thirty-two agents assigned to monitor the heresiarch, Finnegan, and it is just as we feared. You have guessed the inner secrets of our Holy Order and you will have to be eliminated. All of you."

He raised the tommy gun and I felt that sinking sensation which Chandler, I believe, has defined as the acute consciousness that one is not bullet-proof.

"All right, Luigi, drop the gun!"

All of us spun about to stare at the door, where Adam, the grand old gardener, stood, no longer grand or old. He had removed his white wig and abandoned his crouched posture. He was a young and dangerous man, and he carried an automatic rifle.

Cardinal Mozzarella dropped his tommy gun, stunned. Finnegan darted forward and picked it up.

"Permit me to introduce myself," said the stranger who had once been my gardener. "I am Adam Weishaupt IX, primus illuminatus, and Grand Master of the Ordo Templi Orientus, the Scotch Rite, the York Rite, the Egyptian Rite and the Rite of Memphis and Mizraim. In short," he summed up, "I control every Freemasonic conspiracy on the planet. We have been watching and protecting you for a long time, Professor Finnegan, since we knew the Knights of Malta would eventually attempt to take your life."

Finnegan carefully placed the tommy gun on the writing desk, in the corner. I absently noticed that "Bob" wandered off in that direction and sat casually on the edge of the desk, relighting his Pipe. Just then the French windows smashed open and the maids, Immaculata and Concepcion, burst into the room, each carrying a bazooka. "Put down that rifle, Illuminati dog," cried Immaculata. "We are taking charge here."

"Who the hell are you?" Cardinal Mozzarella gasped, evidently unable to believe there could be so many conspiracies afoot in one Gothic castle.

"We are the High Priestesses of the Paratheo-Anametamystik-hood of Eris Esoteric, or POEE," Concepcion said. (POEE was pronounced "pooey," at least in her dialect.)

"Eris?" cried the primus illuminatus.

"Eris, goddess of chaos, discord, confusion, bureaucracy and international relations," Immaculata explained. "Our slogan is 'Disobedience was Woman's original virtue.' Too long has the world been run by male conspiracies. We are the first all-female conspiracy."

"Heresssssssssy," hissed the cardinal venomously.

"The inevitable yin balance to our yang energies," the Illuminatus muttered thoughtfully.

"Are you going to kill us?" I asked, being practical about the situation.

"No, of course not," Immaculata said. "Chaos is our Lady's natural metier. We came here to stop you from killing one another. We want you all alive, so you can go on spreading disputation and confusion and Chaos will always steadily increase. Hail Eris. All hail Discordia."

"So," Concepcion said, "we must ask all of you to move the guns — with your feet please — to the center of the room. And then you must leave by separate doors. Go forth in peace," she added piously, "and continue to preach false doctrines."

"Just a minute, ladies," said Finnegan. "I have a brief statement to make. Professor Finnegan died in his sleep, peacefully, over ten years ago. I have been impersonating him ever since. I am a time traveler, in your terms. I was originally born in Damascus over a thousand years ago. My name was Abdul Alhazred and I was the first to learn the art of positronic reincarnation. In lay terms, when one brain wears out with age, I simply move my quantum energy into another brain. I took over Finnegan as he was dying and simply continued the Great Work to which the Order of the Hashishim have been dedicated for a millennium — the return of the Great Old Ones, or GOO, as we call them."

"Goo?" Immaculata cried, stunned.

"Well, they are kind of slimy," Abdul admitted, "but they are stronger than your Eris, or the other gang's Yahweh, or any of these recent parvenu gods. And now that I have the leaders of all the other and hence lesser cults assembled in one place, I shall summon Great Cthulhu to eat your souls." And he began chanting in a nameless Elder Tongue:

"Ia, Shub-Niggurath! Cthulhu fthagn! Yog Sothoth neblod zin! Ia! Io! Nov shmoz ka pop! Ph'nglui mgIw'nafl nagcopaleen Baile atha Cliath wgah'nagl fthagn Tsog!"

As he chanted this blasphemous and nameless invocation, the mad Arab began to metamorphose before our very eyes, growing, swelling, becoming like unto a huge bowl of green yogurt, then changing into a jellyfish with a million bloodshot eyes, then becoming a pit bull with AIDS, then a Republican attorney general, a werewolf, every fearsome creature of nightmare and horror imaginable by a hashish-crazed brain, for all these horrific visions were, I now realized, individual aspects of the multiple monstrosity that was Cthulhu, the Interstellar Banker, source of all evil and conspiracy, inventor of punk rock, Eater of Souls — the Thing in the center of the Pentagon!!!

And then, "Bob," so drunk that he had lost track of who was in charge, tried to kick the tommy gun into the center of the room, as the Erisians had demanded, and the gun began to spray bullets in all directions. I dived for the window and rolled dizzily down the lawn, my brain temporarily unhinged by the terrible visions I had seen.

They tell me that neighbors found me wandering in the rain, gibbering incoherently. They called an ambulance. I have been in St. John of God's Hospital for alcohol abusers for two weeks now. They think the terrible things I was muttering when brought here indicate too much Irish whiskey, and I am willing to let them think that. I dare not tell the good nuns here how Popes are actually chosen, or why it requires a Willy to perform the transubstantiation of molecules in the eucharist . . . or that in the last mind-numbing moment before "Bob" accidentally set off the tommy gun I saw the face of Cthulhu, the master of this Death Universe, and recognized that it was my own . . . for now the positronic transformation is being accomplished again. Yes, Abdul Alhazred lives anew, for I am he, and I know now that I was wrong in my youth to believe that good was better than evil because it is generally nicer. Now I know, from one thousand years of memories of many lives, that evil is better than good because it always wins in the end . . . Ia! Shrug-Yrsh'ldrs! Notary sojac! Sinn fein amhain!

Sexual Alchemy

The Chariot of Antimony by Basil Valentine (1642) contains the following typical bit of Alchemical exposition:

> Let the Lion and Eagle duly prepare themselves as Prince and Princess of Alchemy — as they may be inspired. Let the Union of the Red Lion and the White Eagle be neither in cold nor in heat . . . Now then comes the time when the elixir is placed in the alembic retort to be subjected to the gentle warmth . . . If the Great Work be transubstantiation then the Red Lion may feed upon the flesh and blood of the God, and also let the Red Lion duly feed the White Eagle — yea, may the Mother Eagle give sustain-molt and guard the inner life.*

~•~

* See "The Triumphal Chariot of Antimony," reproduced in The Alchemical Tradition in the Late Twentieth Century, ed. Richard Grossinger, North Atlantic Books, Berkeley, 2nd edition 1983, pp. 34-47.

~•~

In general, the preceding passage is representative of the limpid clarity of exposition and crystalline lucidity of style to be found in alchemical literature We can already see why so many Rationalist historians have concluded that the alchemists simply went off their skulls from inhaling too many narcotic and/or toxic vapors and wrote hallucinogenic gibberish.

Occultists of various schools, of course, have other ideas. They all agree that alchemical literature was written in code — because "humanity is not ready to receive certain knowledge," say the esoteric, because any alchemist who wrote clearly would bring down the wrath of the Inquisition on his head, say the more pragmatic. Unfortunately, there are a few dozen theories about what the code means. What follows is the theory that I have found most satisfactory over the years, although I am not smart enough to be absolutely sure it is the one and only correct theory.

According to Louis T. Culling, Grandmaster of an occult lodge called the G.B.G. (short for Great Brotherhood of God), in his *Manual of Sex Magick*, the main terms in the code, and their translations, are as follows:

RED LION — the male Alchemist, or his penis.

WHITE EAGLE — the Alchemist's mate, or her vagina.

RETORT — the vagina and/or womb.

TRANSMUTATION — (or transubstantiation) an altered state of consciousness.

ELIXIR — the semen.*

~•~

* A Manual of Sex Magick, Louis T. Culling, Llwellyn Publications, St. Paul, Minnesota, 1971, p. 57.

~•~

Applying this key to Valentine's gnomic paragraph, we find that he is instructing the novice alchemist to find a suitable mate, and to take a "royal" or lofty attitude — i.e., he is a Prince, she a Princess, ergo they are no longer ordinary people. (cf. Tim Leary's 1960's slogan, "Every man a Priest, every woman a Priestess, every home a shrine.")

The union of the alchemical mates should be "neither in cold nor in heat — they must be passionate, not indifferent to each other or merely sensual, but they must not be too damned passionate. That is, they should not gallop toward Climax in the manner all too typical of our culture. The sexual communion, in short, should be tantric, leading to the "transubstantiation" — a higher state of consciousness.

The late Dr. Francis Israel Regardie, a remarkable chap who had two separate selves and careers — as Dr. Francis Regardie he was a neo-Reichian psychotherapist, while as Israel Regardie he wrote a series of books which have influenced contemporary American occultism more than the work of any other single author — also taught this interpretation of alchemy, but, unlike Culling, only in the traditional codes. For instance, in *The Tree of*

Life Regardie offers the following advice on how the Cabalistic Magician may add alchemy to his working armory:

Through the stimulus of warmth and spiritual Fire to the Athanor, there should be a transfer, an ascent of the Serpent from that instrument to the Cucurbite, used as a retort. The alchemical marriage or the mingling of the two streams of force in the retort causes at once the chemical corruption of the serpent in the menstruum of the Gluten, this being the *Solve* part of the alchemical formula of *Solve et coagula* . . . The operation should not take less than an hour.*

~•~

* *The Tree of Life*: A Study in Magic, Israel Regardie, Samuel Weiser, Ne York, 1975 edition, p. 251.

~•~

Dr. Regardie offers the further helpful hint that, complex as it sounds, the operation is "no harder than riding a bicycle." In correspondence, Dr. Regardie cheerfully acknowledged that I had decoded this correctly. Culling differs from Regardie chiefly in claiming that the ascent of the Serpent requires at least two hours.

If some readers still feel a bit in the dark about what is involved in the prolonged tantric act, consider the following broad hints from Thomas Vaughn, another 17th Century alchemist roughly contemporary with Basil Valentine:

The true furnace is a little simple shell . . . But I had almost forgot to tell thee that which is all in all, and is the greatest difficulty in all the art — namely the fire . . . The proportion and regimen of it is very scrupulous, but the best rule to know it by is that of the Synod: "Let not the bird fly before the fowler." Make it sit while you give fire and then you are sure of your prey. For a close I must tell thee that the philosophers call this fire their bath, but it is a bath of Nature, not an artificial one; for it is not of any kind of water . . . In a word, without this bath, nothing in the world is generated.*

~•~

* "Coelum Terrae," in *The Works of Thomas Vaughn*, ed., A.E. Waite, University Books, New Hyde Park, NY, 1968, pp. 219 — 221.

~•~

As Kenneth Rexroth noted in his introduction to *The Works of Thomas Vaughn*, Vaughn seems to have been less concerned with hiding the secret, like earlier alchemists, than with making it clear by progressively broader and broader hints. There is only one bath from which all creatures are generated and that is the bath of vaginal fluids, which is "not of any kind of water." The furnace that is also a shell is a nice poetic image of female anatomy, worthy of John Donne — whose poems sometimes suggest that he was in on the secret. Note especially Donne's "Love's Alchemy," with its "pregnant pot" and "The Ecstasy," with its clear tantric emphasis.

The "bird" (English slang for woman, but also a cross-reference to the traditional Eagle symbolism) must sit while the alchemist gives fire. This is, of course, the traditional tantric position, which slows down the sexual communion and creates maximum intimacy and tenderness. Similarly, the lovers in Donne's "The Ecstasy" sit and make "pictures" in each other's eyes, leading most commentators to think no sexual connection was involved, but the yabyum (sitting) position of Tantra also demands communion by eye contact.

John Donne and other Elizabethans who show signs of knowing this tradition — Sir Philip Sydney and Sir Walter Raleigh, especially, but try rereading Shakespeare's sonnets with this model in mind — probably came under the influence of Giordano Bruno of Nola, who was lecturing at Oxford while Donne was there. It was during those Oxford years that Bruno published his *Eroica Furioso*, which alternates love poems with prose passages on the union of the soul with God. It is usually assumed that the poems are allegories about the soul's pilgrimage, but they may just as well be keys to the yoga that produces the ultimate union and communion. (Incidentally, the historian Frances Yates believes that Bruno was the model for at least two of Shakespeare's characters — Berowne in *Love's Labour's Lost* and Prospero in *The Tempest*.)*

~•~

* *Giordano Bruno and the Hermetic Tradition*, Frances A. Yates, Univ. of Chicago Press, 1977, p. 357.

~•~

Bruno, of course, ultimately returned to Italy, where the Inquisition locked him in a dungeon for eight years and then burned him at the stake. Most historians note only that the Nolan (as he liked to call himself) was condemned for teaching the Copernican theory of astronomy, but actually he was charged with 18 offenses, including practicing Magick and organizing secret occult societies dedicated to overthrowing the Vatican. Francis Yates suspects that the latter might be true and finds a Bruno-esque influence in the first Rosicrucian manifestoes.*

~•~

* *The Rosicrucian Enlightenment*, Frances A. Yates, Routledge & Kegan Paul, Huston, 1974 ed., p. 216.

~•~

Certainly, *The Alchemical Marriage of Christian Rosycross* shows more than a tinge of Bruno's Tantrism, and "dark sayings" like "It is only on the Cross that the Rose may bloom" strongly suggest both Bruno's sex-magick and his love of paradox.*

~•~

* Reprinted in *Commentary on the Chymical Wedding*, Gareth Knight and Adam McLean, Magnum Opus Hermetic Sourceworks #18, Edinburgh, 1984.

~•~

(Two of the Nolan's favorite koans were "In filth, sublimity; in sublimity, filth" and "In joy, tears; in tears, joy.")

The question of how this tantric tradition got into Europe has no clear, unambiguous answer. Ezra Pound, in addition to his other achievements and infamies, was one of the leading scholars in the area of early French poetry, and in the revised 1916 edition of *The Spirit of Romance* included a chapter presenting evidence that a tantric cult existed in Provence at the time of the Troubadours and is referred to guardedly in much of their poetry. In addition to the data presented by Pound, I have noted that the characteristic verse-form of the Troubadours, seven stanzas, may refer to the seven "chakras" involved in tantric yoga. Certainly, there is nothing earlier in European literature (but much in

Tantra) to foreshadow Pierre Vidal's shocking, "I think I see God when I look upon my lady nude." That was hair-raising blasphemy when written; but even more in the inner tradition of Tantra is Sordello's lovely:

> And if flee you not, Lady who has captured my soul,
> No sight is worth the beauty of my thought

Pound guessed (and admitting he was guessing) that this "yoga of male and female energies" had surfaced in medieval France after a thousand years of underground existence as Gnostic heresy. Louis de Rougemont, however, in *Love in the Western World*, presents an impressive body of evidence that the Troubadour yoga had been brought back from the Middle East by crusaders who learned it from Arab mystics, probably the more oddball Sufis.*

~•~

* Love in the Western World, Denis de Rougemont, Harper & Row, New York 1974.

~•~

Louis Culling, op. cit., claims that the tantric tradition in the West is of definite Sufi origin and is also coded into the *Rubiyat of Oma Khayaam*. This allegation is based, alas, on "inner teachings" of various occult orders and not on sources recognized by historians. Surely, there seems to be a tantric element in the 14th Century Sufi Mahmoud Shabistari who wrote, "In every atom a thousand rational beings are contained."

The Ordo Templi Orientis (of which Aleister Crowley was Outer Head for a quarter of a century) teaches the elements of Tantra in nine slow and carefully scheduled "degrees" of initiation; the first degree unambiguously attributes this tradition to Sufism in general and, in particular, to Mansur el Hallaj — a Sufi martyr who was stoned to death for proclaiming the eminently tantric (and vedantic) doctrine, "I am the Truth and there is nothing within my turban but God." (Some O.T.O. initiates think the true story of Mansur is the origin of the myth of Hiram in orthodox Masonry.) In my *Sex, Drugs & Magick:*

A Journey Beyond Limits (Falcon Press, 1988), I give some credence to all these theories, but suggest that a major role was also played by Hassan i Sabbah, founder of the Ishmaelian sect of Islam, who used both drugs and tantric sex to produce psychedelic experiences, which allegedly caused many to believe they had literally been privileged to experience Paradise while still alive.

This is the point at which most commentators on this Art tend to stumble or to wave their arms excitedly and start howling in rage. Some think all you have to do is adopt the "right attitude" during sex and — hey, presto — you are an alchemist or a magician or at least a Hermeticist of some sort. Others proclaim that all such yoga is "black" and "left-hand" and undoubtedly diabolical. While I cannot hope to dissolve the prejudices of the latter group in a short article, I can at least jar the naïveté of the former group somewhat.

Tantric yoga requires at least as much discipline as hatha yoga and as much capacity for loving and giving of oneself as bhakti yoga. To be effective at all, that is, the Tantra of sex must have the delicacy of a first-rate ballet troupe and the tenderness of true communion — in the religious sense of that term.

Aleister Crowley, our century's leading proponent of this yoga (and the teacher of Louis Culling, by the way) said this yoga requires "the nine and ninety rules of Art." Elsewhere Crowley expressed this in the mantram, which has many additional meanings outside Tantra, "Love is the law, love under will." One only knows if the art has been mastered if one comes to a state of consciousness in which one can immediately grasp, without doubt or hesitation, the meaning of another of Crowley's hermetic aphorisms, "Every man and every woman is a Star."

The power of Tantra may be indicated by the fact that Ezra Pound, who never studied this art under a Master, learned enough from his years scrutinizing Troubadour texts that, by 1933, in his essay on Guido Cavalcanti, he speaks of "magnetisms that border on the visible" and consciousness "extending several feet beyond the body." These are characteristic signs of passing from ordinary sex to meta-sex, from the crude act Shakespeare called a "momentary trick" (and D.H. Lawrence called "the sneeze in the loins") to tantric transcendence. What happens beyond those magnetisms and that expansion of consciousness is not worth discussing; those who know, know — and those who know not will simply not believe.

One might venture, however, that the mingling of yang and yin magnetisms tends to produce a synergetic third which burns up or consumes the original elements. Kenneth Grant, an oddball Crowleyan obsessed with menstrual magick ("the Mystery of the Red Gold"), speaks of this as the "bisexualization of both partners."*

~•~

* *The Magical Revival*, Kenneth Grant, Samuel Weiser, New York, 1974 p. 142.

~•~

More precisely, one can say that, in Chinese terms, active yang becomes passive yang, passive yin becomes active yin, and both tend to merge into the Dao, to re-emerge in new and unexpected forms. Crowley's notorious $2 = 0$ equation, which he alleged explained the universe and would eventually explain quantum mechanics, at least serves as a useful glyph for this stage of the alchemical mutation. And, although Crowley loved to play the bogie-man and terrorize the naive and nervous, one should take with some seriousness his warning when he says in *Magick*:

> The Cup is said to be full of the Blood of the Saints;
> that is, every saint or magician must give the last drop
> of his life's blood to that cup in the true Bridal chamber
> of the Rosy Cross . . . It is a woman whose cup must be
> Filled . . . the Cross is both Death and Generation, and
> it is on the Cross that the Rose blooms.*

~•~

* *Magick in Theory and Practice*, Aleister Crowley, Dover Publications, Ne York, 1976, pp. 41 — 42.

~•~

One has to be knowledgeable in both Freudian and Jungian analysis to understand this even dimly, until one has had the experience. But then everybody who did LSD in the 1960's knows a little about Death and Rebirth; we are not a totally unprepared generation for these Mysteries.

This begins to sound too metaphysical. The processes involved can be defined very materialistically, in terms of exercising to move the center of Consciousness from usual domination by the left brain hemisphere and the sympathetic (active) nervous system to balance between both hemispheres and a growing ability to relax into the parasympathetic (passive, receptive) nervous system. The old mystic terminology lingers on chiefly because it is poetically precise and psychologically highly suggestive.

It is, however, worth quoting Dr. J. W. Brodie-Innes, an initiate of the Hermetic Order of the Golden Dawn in England in the 1890's, who said of the relevance of traditional occult concepts:

> Whether the Gods, the Qlipothic forces or the Secret Chiefs really exist is comparatively unimportant; the point is that the universe behaves as though they do. In a sense the whole philosophy of the practise of Magick is identical with the Pragmatist position of Pierce the American philosopher.*

~•~

* For more writings of Brodie-Innes, see: *The Sorcerer and His Apprentice: Unknown Hermetic Writings of S.L. MacGregor Mathers and J. W. Brodie-Innes*, rd. R.A. Gilbert, Aquarian Press, Wellingborough, Northamptonshire, 1983.

~•~

In other words, we never know "the universe" per se; we know the universe as filtered through our consciousness, and when consciousness alters, the known universe alters. Crowley defined Magick as "the art of causing change by act of will," and Dion Fortune defined it as "the art of causing change in consciousness by act of will," and neither was over-simplifying or being cute. The traditional Aristotelian "Iron Curtain" between Mind and Universe has no meaning in magick, for the same reason it no longer has any meaning in quantum physics. As John Lilly wrote:

... if one plugs the proper beliefs into the metaprogrammatic levels of the (brain) . . . the computer will then construct (from the myriads of elements in memory) those possible experiences that fit this particular set of rules. Those programs will be run off and those displays made which are appropriate to the basic assumptions and their stored programming.*

~•~

* *Programming and Metaprogramming in the Human Biocomputer*, John C. Lilly, Bantam Books, New York, 1974, p. 50.

~•~

The Puritan looking at the Playmate of the Month sees something disgusting, awful, diabolical, and sinful; Pierre Vidal would see another manifestation of the glory of God. It all depends on the programs in the bio-computer. But all programs have a tendency to become self-fulfilling prophecies; a classic case is the sad, melancholy man who sits often in the dark, shunning sunlight, or walks around wearing dark glasses all the time, and gradually becomes even gloomier until he arrives at clinical depression. He has created the set and the setting for depression.

Conversely, those who achieve Divine Union with a beloved sexual partner tend to create their own self-fulfilling prophecies, and the most common effect is that all things become as beautiful as Vidal's nude lady was when he saw Her as God. This transmutation of experience is technically called "the multiplication of the first matter" and many alchemists said of it, wittily, that this "gold," unlike ordinary gold, could not be spent or used up, because the more of it you pass on to others, the more of it you find you still have.

All religions preach charity and forgiveness; but those virtues are hard to practice when you are surrounded by sons of bitches. When the alchemical "gold" is found, when consciousness mutates, you are surrounded by gods and goddesses, and the more of the "gold" you give away, the more comes back to you from an increasingly divine Mother Eagle. Quite simply, it is a short and almost inevitable step from Tantra to pantheism.

It is no accident that William Blake, who, like Shabistari, saw "infinity in a grain of sand," also penned the most searing indictment ever written of the puritan and ascetic hatred of Eros:

> Children of a future age
> Reading this indignant page
> Know that in a former time
> Love, sweet love, was thought a crime.*

~•~

* From "A Little Girl Lost," Songs of Experience, William Blake, Dover Publications, NY, 1992.

~•~

Old Man on a Balcony:
Views of Monterey Bay #20

Calm and quiet here

No anthrax or mad bombers...

Yet. ...but tomorrow?

Part IV
Q&A

Nothing is known. Everything is imagined.
— Federico Fellini

Nothing is true. All is permissible.
— Hassan i Sabbah

Hell, it's even more relative than Einstein realized.
— J.R. "Bob" Dobbs

Old Man On A Balcony:
Views Of Monterey Bay #21

Biggest damned raven

I ever saw flies howling

caw caw caw Lord Lord

Questions Answered

From a 1977 interview-by-mail with Neal Wilgus

Q: Would I be right in saying you probably lean more toward the libertarian form of anarchism than the classical leftist variety?

A: My trajectory is perpendicular to the left-right axis of terrestrial politics. I put some of my deepest idealism into both the Leftwing anarchism of Simon Moon and the Rightwing anarchism of Hagbard Celine in *Illuminatus!*, but I am detached from both on another level.

Politics consists of *demands*, disguised or rationalized by pseudo philosophies or bogus "social sciences" (ideologies). The disguise seems an absurdity to me and "should be" removed. *Make your demand explicit.* My emphasis is on whatever will make extraterrestrial migration possible — the sooner the better. I want to get the hell off Earth for the same reasons my ancestors left Europe: freedom is found on the expanding, pioneering perimeter, never inside the centralized State.*

~•~

* Afterthought 2004: I no longer even call myself an anarchist, since that kind of society seems much more far-off and dreamy than it did before 2000. With Bozo in the Oval Office, I would settle for a return to old-fashioned constitutional democracy. That seems pretty damned radical right now, doesn't it?

~•~

THOUGHTS TO PONDER

I never believed in God. Even as a child I thought if He did exist we should start a Class Action suit against Him.
— Woody Allen

In Spring 1981 we lived high up in the Berkeley hills and I did this conversation with Jeffery Elliot; Arlen read it and claimed I was stoned at the time.

Q: What made you want to become a writer?

A: As far back as I can remember, I wanted to be a storyteller. When I was 8 years old, I started drawing comic strips, which I circulated among other kids in the neighborhood. When I was 12, I "discovered" that there were books made up of nothing but words!

It seemed much easier to just write the words rather than having to do the drawings to accompany them. I wrote my first novel that year and, of course, I couldn't get it published. It was about a meek, mild reporter, somewhat like Clark Kent, who drank a potion which turned him into a virtual Superman-type character. His name was Danny Dingle, because it was a comedy rather than a melodrama. In my youthful naiveté, I thought I could sell it as a movie starring Danny Kaye. I wrote quite a few short stories in my teens, all of which were rejected. I knew I needed a money-making occupation until I became a success as a writer. As a result, I decided to pursue engineering and write in the evenings. Well, after five years as an engineering aide, I realized I couldn't be a writer and an engineer at the same time. It was too demanding in terms of time, so I decided to become, instead, an English teacher.

Along the way, I got married and ended up in the advertising business instead of teaching English. I spent about three years in advertising and then escaped, thank God, "relatively" undamaged. I've spent most of my life since then in various editorial positions at a number of publications.

I also worked at various times as a medical orderly, a salesman, a longshoreman, and an executive. I was an associate editor of *Playboy* for nearly six years. Once, I worked for a sweatshop in New York, where I edited five magazines simultaneously. Actually, this meant I wrote practically everything in the magazines under a variety of pen names.

They had a very low budget. I got $125 a week before taxes for "editing" and/or writing the five publications.

It took me an awfully long time to get my first book into print. In fact, I sold over 2,000 articles and stories to various magazines before landing my first book sale. I suppose I have more articles in print (or out of print?) than any other living author.

Q: Can you see in your writing any specific stylistic influences in terms of other writers whose work you admire?

A: Very definitely. I can easily look at my own prose and see whose voices are represented. There's a great deal of Ezra Pound, a great deal of James Joyce, a great deal of Raymond Chandler, a touch of William Faulkner, and a *soupcon* of H.L. Mencken.

Q: Did any of these writers prove helpful in the sense of teaching you about the process of writing itself?

A: Yes. For example, from Pound I learned that every sentence should have a life of its own. There should be no empty sentences. Basically, I see two types of writers: one type is interested in getting the damned thing done and sold, while the second type really enjoys writing and wants every sentence to have its own wit, its own small surprise. Pound converted me into the second type of writer. I want every sentence to contain a bit of pleasure for me and for the attentive reader; those who snooze simply lose.

From Faulkner, I learned how to write long sentences that are modern and swing. Henry James writes long, sometimes interminable sentences, but one gets lost in the syntax; one doesn't get lost in Faulkner. Joyce taught me a great deal about how to vary the tone of a paragraph and create emotional effects that are almost subliminal, and how to convey very subtle psychological processes. Chandler was a major influence, in the sense that there's not a single dull sentence in any of his books. I've tried to follow that practice in my own writing. It's odd, but I can't think of a single science-fiction writer who has significantly influenced my style of writing. What I have learned from science-fiction writers, though, is to have an open attitude towards the future. In this sense they've influenced my philosophy more than my style.

Q: What is it about writing that you find so personally rewarding?

A: Well, I think it's a sexy kind of controlled schizophrenia. It's also kind of yoga, especially novel-writing. Full-time fiction writing is a constant daily exercise in getting outside one's own head and thinking and feeling the way other people think and feel. I often think of story-telling in terms of Gurdjieff's work. Gurdjieff, the Russian mystic, devoted most of his energy to teaching his pupils how to get outside their own egos and see the world the way other people see it. I've become very interested in his work in the last four or five years, and it has occurred to me that what he is teaching is what every good novelist learns if he sticks with being a writer. One can't create characters who are simply variations of oneself; that gets boring after a while. One must go way out and create characters who are nothing like oneself. When one does that, one really learns something about humanity. In that sense, I think novel-writing is more educational for the novelist than for the reader, especially when the most "evil" villains I can imagine start making clever remarks and developing ideas of their own and really "come alive."

Q: Is a book fully organized in your mind before you start writing or does it take shape as it unfolds?

A: Sometimes I have a clearer idea of where I'm going than other times, but it always surprises me. In the course of writing, I'm always drawing on my unconscious creativity, and I find things creeping into my writing that I wasn't aware of at the time. That's part of the pleasure of writing. After you've written something, you say to yourself, "Where in the hell did that come from?" Faulkner called it the "demon" that directs the writer. The Kabbalists call it the "holy guardian angel." Every fiction writer experiences this sensation. Robert E. Howard said he felt there was somebody dictating the Conan stories to him. There's some deep level of the unconscious that knows a lot more than the conscious mind of the writer knows.

Q: Are you a meticulous writer? Do you agonize over word

choice and syntax?

A: I'm very meticulous, but I don't "agonize." It's all a lot of fun, and no more agonizing than anyone else's favorite hobby. It varies, however, according to what I'm writing. I've written some things as many as 16 times before I was satisfied with the finished product, but I enjoy myself the whole time. Sometimes, I enjoy myself so much that I collapse from exhaustion. I've been known to work from 16 to 20 hours and fall into bed with a very stiff back and wake up the next morning with an acute case of conjunctivitis. Even there, I enjoyed myself all the way through it.*

~•~

* Afterthought 2004: "If youth knew! If age could!" as some French writer said . . .

~•~

Q: Does writing come easily to you? Do the words flow smoothly and effortlessly?

A: Oh, yes. It comes as easily to me as tennis comes to a professional tennis player. It's my game. To me, it's the third best thing in the world — after sex and Chinese food.

Q: How do you feel about critics? Do their opinions affect you?

A: As William Butler Yeats asked, "Was there ever a dog that loved its fleas?" Critics have been very kind to me, personally. Of all the reviews of my published books, something like 90 percent have been highly favorable, so I have no personal grudge against critics.

On the other hand, in an impersonal way, I have a strong moral objection to nasty reviewers. Whenever I see a critic tearing a writer or actor or any artist to shreds in print, I feel a sense of revulsion. I write a lot of criticism myself, but I only review things I like. I don't admire people who like to tear other people apart.

I can only think of two unfavorable reviews I've written in my whole life, and I regret them.

People who like to write witty, nasty things about other people are not kindly or charitable, to put it mildly. We should all try to give out as much good energy to other human beings as we possibly can. I honestly believe that every bit of bad energy we put out has adverse effects that go on forever. I sort of accept the Buddhist doctrine of karma. The Buddhists believe that every bit of anger, resentment, hate, and so on that you send out passes from the target to somebody else convenient to the target, who then gets targeted, and so on, without stopping. The same is true of good energy: every bit of good energy one puts out makes someone else feel a little bit better. I think if people were really conscious of this psychological fact, they would try very, very hard to put out nothing but good energy, no matter what happened to them. They would certainly not be so casual about passing on bad energy. All the bad energy in the world builds up like a giant snowfall, until we have a huge war.* Nowadays, it can mean a total nuclear Armageddon.

~•~

* Yeah, Arlen got it right: I must have toked a bunch o'weed before delivering myself of that sermon...

~•~

This comes from traditional Buddhism, as I say, but I think it's materialistic common sense, too. One only needs to study human behavior to realize it. I regard those people who make a career out of being nasty as emotional plague carriers. Serial killers generally start out as children who torture animals; imagine how the average reviewer started out. Pulling wings off bugs?

Q: As you look back over those pieces you wrote early in your career, can you detect clear signs of stylistic improvement?

A: I hope so. I would rather be gored by a rhinoceros than see some of my 1950's pieces be reprinted now! Even some of my 1960's pieces, I hope, are lost forever.

Q: In what ways has your writing improved over the years?

A: I hope I'm less acerbic, less dogmatic, less "moralistic," and more charitable.

Q: Are you concerned that your work has didactic value, that people learn from it?

A: Absolutely! Didactic literature is very much out of style these days; if one is suspected of having a message, it's almost regarded as some kind of secret vice. I think, however, that all first-rate literature leans toward the didactic. The classic Greeks regarded Homer as didactic and allegorical to boot. Dante seems didactic. Shakespeare seems didactic. Melville seems didactic. Science fiction is the most didactic literature around; that's why I enjoy it so much.

All writers function as teachers, whether they're conscious of it or not, or whether they'll admit it or not. For example, take Mickey Spillane. He used to give interviews in which he said he only wrote books for money. However, if you look at his work, it's obvious he has very strong beliefs. He's always pitching them at the reader. They're rather fascist beliefs, but they're beliefs nonetheless, and he's a teacher, just like every other writer. Unfortunately, he's only teaching a violent, fascist morality.

Old Man On A Balcony:
Views Of Monterey Bay #22

Purple, vermilion:

Each part of the bay glitters

And none is just blue

More Questions Answered

1988 — with David Jay Brown in Los Angeles

Q: It is April 23, 1988, a significant day in Robert Anton Wilson's philosophy. What is the significance of 23?

A: Well, 23 has popped up in my life connected with so many synchronicities and weird coincidences that it must mean something. In several of my books, including the *Illuminatus!* trilogy and *Cosmic Trigger*, I have given examples of a tremendous number of coincidences connected with 23. Take today as an example, April 23: this is the anniversary of Shakespeare's birth, April 23, 1556 and his death, April 23, 1616. Also April 23, 1616, the same time Shakespeare died in England, Cervantes, author of *Don Quixote*, died in Spain. April 23, 1014 is when Brian Boru died; he was the first high king of Ireland to be a political as well as religious leader. He unified all Ireland and drove the Danes out, and on April 23, 1014 he was killed by one of the Danes after the battle of Clontarf, where he defeated the Danes for the final time, and liberated Ireland from foreign rule. August 23, 1170 is when the Normans came in, and Ireland has been under foreign rule again, in whole or in part, ever since.

On August 23, 1920 James Joyce was discussing coincidences with a friend in a Paris bar when he suddenly saw a giant black rat which scared the blue jesus out of him, by Christ; he fainted dead away. So that ties Joyce together with the invasion of Ireland, and Shakespeare, and Brian Boru. All of this is in *Finnegans Wake* by the way.

Q: You have a whole series of books focusing on the Illuminati. What is the Illuminati, and how did it become an inspiration for so many books?

A: Well, the Illuminati was a secret society in Europe in the 18th Century. A certain number of "paranoid" or at least unorthodox theorists believe the Illuminati still exists and has either taken over the world, or taken over most of the world, or something like that.

I discovered the anti-Illuminati literature in the late 1960's when there were all sorts of weird conspiracy theories going around. And then I discovered there were two ambiguities connected with the Illuminati. First, there are those who say the Illuminati doesn't still exist, versus those who say the Illuminati still exists; and then among those who say the Illuminati do exist, there are two schools of thought: those who claim they're the arch-villains of all history, and those who claim they're the heroes who are trying to liberate the human race from superstition and ignorance. And so, I decided a group that ambiguous — where we don't know whether they exist or not, and we don't even know, *if* they exist, whether they're the good guys or the bad guys — they're the perfect synecdoche, to me, for all the confusions of the age we're living through, and all of the rampant paranoia of our time.

Q: How did you first become interested in Aleister Crowley?

A: Sometime around 1969, I was having lunch with Alan Watts and I mentioned the *Illuminatus!* trilogy, which I was working on at the time, and the symbolism of the eye on the pyramid, which is the symbol of the Illuminati. And Alan said, that reminds me, the best book I've read all year is called *The Eye in the Triangle* by Israel Regardie, and I took Alan Watts very seriously. I mean, he was a very funny man, but when Alan said something was worth reading, I took that seriously, so I went out and bought *The Eye in the Triangle*, and it turned out to be a biography of Aleister Crowley. Israel Regardie was Crowley's secretary for a while in the 1930's. Then, later, he was a psychotherapist right here in Los Angeles. I got into correspondence with Dr. Regardie for several years, before his death, and learned quite a bit from him about Crowley's work.

Q: The average person would think of a magician as a side-show entertainer. What is a magician, in your definition?

A: Well, it's an ambiguous word. It can refer to prestidigitation, conjuring, other show business tricks, or it can refer to the ancient science of the magi, which is where the word magic comes from etymologically, it's the science of the magi. It's *the science of rapid, voluntary brain change, how to use the human brain for fun and profit.*

Q: That brings us to something you've written about called the HEAD Revolution: *H*edonic *E*ngineering *a*nd *D*evelopment.

A: The HEAD Revolution is my term for what's been happening since the 1960's, the discovery of newer and better technologies for rapid alteration of brain functioning. We've gone from psychedelic drugs, to biofeedback and Lilly isolation tanks, and a lot of fascinating new machines like the Mind Mirror, which is an accelerated biofeedback system that gives you a continuous profile of both hemispheres of your brain, and which frequencies they're working on.

I regard this as a great example of the *evolutionary function of stupidity*. When the government made psychedelic research illegal in the 1960's (scientific, open, aboveboard research I mean — that did not stop research — the research just went underground, together with a great deal of partying and hell-raising and whatnot with those drugs). I thought it was the stupidest thing the government ever did. But in retrospect I think stupidity *has an evolutionary function*, because when they stopped that research, all the leading researchers in the field went into other areas, and so we've discovered dozens of other ways of rapid brain change.

Lilly worked on his isolation tank; others went into biofeedback; Stan Grof, who came to this country seeking scientific freedom because he felt he didn't have enough scientific freedom in Czechoslovakia, and over here they told him he couldn't do any more LSD research, so he went to work on breathing techniques and the effect of sound on the brain, and has developed some very interesting post-Reichian, post-yogic techniques of brain change. So, by and large, the stupider the establishment is, the smarter the rebels become. *Establishment*

stupidity is the greatest spur to creativity in evolutionary history.
That's why I think Reagan has been a godsend to this country.
He's brought more stupidity to Washington than anybody in my
lifetime, and there's been a tremendous upsurge of creativity
while he's been in there.

Q: In the 1970's you and Leary came up with the SMIILE
formula, which stands for Space Migration, Intelligence Increase
and Life Extension. Do you still find those three things to be
important?

A: Very much so. Space migration *feels* tremendously exciting
to me, because it's the opening of a new frontier. Historically,
every time a new frontier has opened, there's been a big upsurge
of creative energies, a Renaissance effect, a creativity boom, and
the human race badly needs that at this point. Also, I think most
of the energy problems that it's fashionable to worry about will
be solved when we get out of the closed system of one planet
and start dealing with many worlds. When we have hundreds
and hundreds of space colonies dotted all over the earth-moon
system, or as far out as the asteroid belt probably, then there
won't be any more energy problem, there's so damn much
energy out there compared to the energy available on the surface
of the Earth. And it will also solve the population problem; more
and more people will be migrating into space, I'm sure. I want
to go myself — some people think that's whimsical in a man my
age, but I'm expecting rejuvenation technology will be along in
the next 15-20 years of bio-tech research.

Q: The Life Extension part of SMIILE.

A: Yes, I figure 20 years from now, I'll be 20 years younger
instead of 20 years older.

Q: Do you have a favorite of the books that you've written?
I think my personal favorite right now is the *Schrödinger's Cat*
trilogy.

A: Bless you, sir — that's about to be reprinted, I'm happy

to say. But when it first came out it got more bad reviews than anything else I've ever written; it only got two good reviews I ever saw. The *LA Times* said it was "hilarious, multi-dimensional, a laugh a paragraph," something like that. *New Scientist* in England had the other good review, they said it was "the most scientific of all science-fiction novels." Everybody else bum-rapped it. One sensitive soul got so furious that he actually wrote three denunciatory reviews of it for three different sci-fi magazines. Like he would have buried it with a stake through its heart if he could have . . .

After that, it went out of print quickly in this country and for seven years the only money I made from it came from the German and English editions.*

~•~

* It has remained in print even in America since the second edition, and some years even outsells *Illuminatus!* Caloo Calay! O frabjuous day! And, as for that guy with the three bad reviews, every now and then I remember all the snotty things he said and I sob all the way to the bank.

~•~

THOUGHTS TO PONDER

The fundamental article of my political creed is that despotism, or unlimited sovereignty, or absolute power, is the same in a majority of a popular assembly, an aristocratical council, an oligarchical junta, and a single emperor: equally arbitrary, cruel, bloody, and in every respect diabolical.

— John Adams

1994 — with James Nye in London

Q: What are your current views on the alien abduction phenomenon?

A: Jeff Mishlove has edited an enormous book called *The Roots of Consciousness* which examines classic studies in parapsychology over the last hundred years. Jeff has a masters in criminology, and the only Ph.D. in parapsychology given by the University of California. He's made a study of the phenomenon and concludes that there are various layers to it.

There are people who think they've been meddled with by "visitors"; others who think that relatives took them to satanic rituals where they were sexually abused and sacrifices occurred; and others who think that relatives abused them.

Jeff's conclusion is that they were probably sexually abused in childhood and this created a situation — a response to trauma — in which their fantasy life is just as "real" as their ordinary life, and they're always working on variations on their traumatic memory. The abusers — "real" or "imagined" — become aliens, devils, incubi or succubi. That's one kind of case.

Others, I think, start out as sleep paralysis — a state I have experienced twice in-my 62 years. In pure sleep paralysis, you simply feel paralyzed and don't know whether you're dreaming or awake. In other cases, this is accompanied by a nightmare-like fantasy; in my two cases, this merely consisted of a fearful sense that something awful was in the room. In each instance, I awoke before it went further. But I think for some reason it might escalate to a "real hallucination" — lovely oxymoron! — in which the "something awful" becomes any kind of monster you have in your fantasy library — aliens, demons, whatever.

Q: What about apparent physical phenomena connected with visitation — radiation burns, spirit rappings? The Elizabethan magus John Dee reported strange knockings which proceeded his visitation by "angels," and Strieber also alleges hearing knocking patterns . . .

A: In my book *The New Inquisition* I describe Persinger's theory that there are transient energy fluctuations in the Earth's electromagnetic and gravitational fields which may account for poltergeist disturbances, cars stalling, televisions turning themselves on and off, ball lightning — a great deal of the UFO experience. Persinger also describes how this might affect the brain and create hallucinations. I think Persinger has an explanation for much of the phenomenon, but not quite all. We are surrounded by equipment whose effects on us are not fully known. One of Philip K. Dick's favourite themes was: How do we know that our brains aren't continually being altered, that the reality we experience isn't entirely programmed? The violence of *Total Recall* is not PhilDickian, but they really got the mood right in the scene where the hero is told what he *thinks* he's experiencing on Mars is being done to him in a laboratory, on Earth.

Q: I once had a dream communication from [Philip K.] Dick: "Experience of telepathy does not necessarily indicate psychosis"!

A: That sounds like Phil! Ray Nelson was going to collaborate with Phil on a novel when Phil died. Nelson then began having dreams in which Phil started dictating the plot — so he's working on it and going to publish it as a joint novel! Another friend of Dick's is D. Scott Apel who co-edits my *Trajectories* newsletter. He's also working on a novel in dream collaboration with Dick. In the first dream, Phil told him that "the secret is in the centre of Disneyland." The curious thing is that another friend goes to Disneyland once a year, takes acid and talks to Mickey Mouse. Whoever is in the suit gives answers to this fellow's questions that seem profound enough to satisfy him. He is the only one I know whose god is visible, tangible and responsive.

Q: Dick thought at one time that he might have temporal lobe epilepsy — a type which might prompt visionary experiences.

Strieber also tested (negatively) for TLE, and I understand it is one of the parts of the brain Persinger is interested in.

A: One of Phil's therapists suggested that sexual abuse by his grandfather might have been the root of his problems, so this ties Phil in with current theories of the abduction phenomenon. But Phil had a much more developed mind than some of these victims and drew a whole cosmology out of it — one of the most fascinating world views I've ever studied. I often think his ideas make more sense than Christianity or Hinduism, or atheism or Forteanism, and then I think "this is the ravings of a madman, how did I get sucked into this!" But then I read more, and start to wonder again . . .

Q: I often wonder how much social isolation has to do with this. I'm not just thinking of Biblical prophets and hermits, but people in solitary confinement who sometimes start hallucinating within hours . . .

A: And yet some people do very well in solitary. Timothy Leary said it was one of the most productive periods of his life. He said the only person he had to talk to was the most intelligent person he knew. He had a great time philosophizing about the universe and his role in it.

It's very strange that Leary's books don't sell well, but he does well on the lecture circuit. We've done a double act together: the Laurel and Hardy of the futurist intelligentsia — or the space cadets, if you like. Leary's books on psychology and cosmology are very far out; generally they are regarded as proof that his brain is blown by all the drugs he's done. A few people I know understand them — we think they're brilliant, but maybe our brains have been blown by those drugs, too. He's also writing very successful computer programs. For someone who's supposed to be brain damaged by drugs, he's pretty good at designing software.

Leary and I appeared at the Libertarian Party Convention in Chicago. Coming back on the plane we met Guns and Roses, who love him — everyone knows Leary. And Tim got drunker and drunker on his bottle of Scotch, and finally he says "Fuck it! I'm gonna have a cigarette!" You're not allowed to smoke on U.S. airlines anymore, so the whole of Guns and Roses gathered round to conceal him. At this point, one of the stewards sees Leary's smoking and comes over, and he says to Tim, "I just want to tell you I think you're right about everything!" When we got off the plane, Leary spotted a wheelchair and got a Joyce scholar to push it for him through the airport. I was a bit drunk, too, by then, so as we raced through the crowd, I pointed to Leary in the wheelchair and shouted "Chromosome damage, chromosome damage!" Wonderful night, wonderful . . .

Q: What's your connection with the Church of the SubGenius and its deity J.R. "Bob" Dobbs?

A: Well, Rev. Ivan Stang told me I was one of his main inspirations — but maybe he says that to all writers he wants to get on the good side of. There are a lot of my ideas in the SubGenius mythos, so maybe "Bob" was named after me . . . Maybe I should start using the inverted commas?

Q: In your second volume of autobiography, *Cosmic Trigger II*, there is a hint of resignation. You say that you would like to be shot into space and listen to Scarlatti. Have you given up on mankind?

A: The book was an attempt to present different sides of my personality as they've developed in time, and so you get the past mixed up with the present.

The past does not always unfold chronologically. It's the same with ideas — some I held for a long time, some I held for just one afternoon. The book's an attempt to show that there is no consistent ego. It's a Buddhist book. So the resignation was just a mood that George Bush [Sr.] put me in around the time of the Gulf War.

Q: One of the recurrent themes of your writing concerns belief . . .

A: Not believing in anything, not disbelieving in anything — that may be one of the most important of the ideas in my books, though I hardly invented it.

It's characteristic of modern physicists to have that attitude. It also ties in with Fort's notion that the product of minds is not acceptable as subject matter for belief — except temporarily.

CSICOP — the Committee for the Scientific Investigation of Claims of the Paranormal — for instance are profound believers in conventional paradigms. They call themselves "skeptics," but Catholics are just as skeptical — only about different things. Everybody has an area of belief and an area of skepticism. CSICOP's dogmas are as rigid as anyone else's. I heard a bloke from CSICOP denouncing chiropractors on the radio. I got so pissed off I called in and quoted the Office of Technology Assessment of the National Science Institute in Washington. They regard something as scientifically confirmed if it has had a period of randomized double blind experiments which have been published in several refereed scientific journals. By that standard, 85% of American medicine hasn't been verified, so CSICOP is in no position to throw stones at chiropractors.

Q: Much of your early writing is influenced by Aleister Crowley. Do you have any reservations about him?

A: In *Cosmic Trigger I*, I said that Crowley's philosophy is a combination of anarchism, fascism, and anti-Christian propaganda, which is not very congenial to my form of Libertarianism. So I've always tried to make a distinction between his method and his philosophy. He is part anarchist, part fascist — and I like the anarchist part.

Q: One Crowleyite told me that Crowley's magick is "qliphophthically booby-trapped."

A: I've heard that — I don't agree with it. I've done a lot of Crowley rituals and I don't see any sign yet that I've been obsessed, possessed or otherwise taken over by qliphophthic energies or entities. I think it's a paranoid anti-Crowley idea that's been spread, and like much else in that field, has become a self-fulfilling prophecy. If you're worried that Crowley's system is booby-trapped, and you start fooling around with it, you're likely to suffer hallucinations that you are being attacked by demons. Similarly, the fears of the dangers of LSD can precipitate a bad trip.

Q: In *Cosmic Trigger I*, you hypothesize about apparent telepathic communication emanating from Sirius. What's your view about those experiences now?

A: Sirius seems to have been rambunctious at the time. Doris Lessing wrote *The Sirian Experiments* around the same time I was having my Sirius experience. Phil Dick had his extraterrestrial experience (which for one reason or another, he connected with Sirius) about the same time. I used to think he got the idea after he read *Cosmic Trigger I*, but one of the recent biographies of Phil makes it perfectly clear that he connected his experience with Sirius before he read *Cosmic Trigger*. So that makes it even more interesting . . .

Q: The composer Karlheinz Stockhausen may have got his notions about Sirius from Edgar Varese, who was involved with the late 19th Century Parisian Rosicrucian revival, and perhaps got it from there — or from the writings of Paracelsus with whom he was fascinated. I wonder if the Rosicrucians are the source for Varese — especially with the importance of Sirius to occult groups such as the OTC. and A ∴ A ∴ which you have traced?

A: Well, there are a lot of occult traditions connected with Sirius. Among other things, Sirius is the brightest star in the sky, so if people are going to focus on anything out there — especially in the ancient world — Sirius would be very important. Particularly in Egypt, where it happens to rise just at the same time the Nile starts its annual flooding. I mention in *Cosmic Trigger I* something I picked up from Theosophy: just as in yoga you activate the heart chakra and then move the energy up to the crown chakra; this is happening to the "Cosmic Being" which is trying to move the energy up from our Sun to Sirius.

In Dublin I met somebody who told me — on the basis of God knows what authority besides his own imagination — that above the 33rd degree of Masonry, unknown to the world, there is actually an illuminated inner circle which is in touch with Sirius. I thought I'd invented that myself, but this guy is telling me this like it's an inner secret of Masonry! But maybe that's what Hugh Kenner calls an "Irish fact," which is quite unlike an English fact, an American fact, or a French fact, and has no connection with a scientific fact. An Irish fact has the wonderful Daliesque fluidity of a melting clock and the Joycean uncertainty of a rubber inch.

Q: When did Robert Temple's book *The Sirius Mystery* come out in relation to your experiences?

A: Well, it came out after I had my experiences (which I first attributed to Sirius — and then to the Pookah, a giant white rabbit from County Kerry — depending on which metaphor suited me at the time). His book came out after the experiences, and just at the point when I was giving up Sirius as an explanation for my experiences, and more inclined to look at it in terms of brain processes: the left hemisphere and the right hemisphere talking to each other, learning to communicate. So I was just about through with the Sirius model, and then Temple's book came out trying to show that there had been connections between Earth and Sirius for about 4,000 years! So it did make me look back and reconsider the Sirius aspect of it. And then along came Phil Dick's novel VALIS!

Q: So the Sirius model could be a screen for something more personal?

A: That's what I think most of the time. Every now and then something about Sirius comes to me from somewhere and I start thinking, "Well who knows, maybe I should take it literally?" But that's 5% of the time; 95% of the time I tend to look at it as neurological evolution.

Q: How then do you account for the Dogon tribe of Mali knowing about Sirius B, the dwarf companion to Sirius which cannot be seen by the naked eye — and was only photographed using the most powerful telescopes in the early 1970's?

A: I don't account for that; I regard that as a mystery. I remember that a writer in CSICOP's journal *The Skeptical Inquirer* pointed out that the Dogon could have learnt about this from a Jesuit missionary or a wandering explorer, or a merchant who digs astronomy — and I thought, yeah, all of that is possible. But then the writer concludes that therefore we don't have to take it seriously. Hell, the writer's mother could have got knocked up by the grocer or the delivery boy, or the ice man, or the postman — therefore we don't have to consider the hypothesis that his conception might have been due to the guy actually known as his father!

I didn't bother sending that additional bit of skepticism to them because I knew they wouldn't print it. They're very selective about what they doubt.

Q: Temple also seems to have been at pains to point out that the Dogons got their information from ancient Egyptian sources as well — so the question is really how did the Egyptians know of Sirius B's existence?

A: I have an open mind about these things, but don't have any dogmas. I await further enlightenment.

c. 2000 — with Sean Casteel

Q: You have an excellent sense of humor that keeps a reader engaged . . .

A: Without a sense of humor, life is utterly unbearable on this barbaric planet.

Q: Yeah, I know what you're saying. In your introduction to *Everything Is Under Control* [Harper, 1999], you quote a poll that says three out of four people believe the government is engaged in at least some kinds of conspiracies. Then you go on to say the government also mistrusts the people it governs. Would you expound on that vicious circle here?

A: Sure. The people mistrust the government for a variety of reasons: some of them psychological, some of them sociological. We'll come to that later. For the present, we'll just say that one of the reasons is that the government has been caught repeatedly telling outrageous lies, under both Republican and Democratic administrations going back to the 1950's. And, as a matter of fact, you can find some pretty outrageous lies even earlier than that. Eventually, recognition of this does dawn on a large percentage of the population.

Q: Then you went on to say that the government also mistrusts us.

A: The government has no idea who we are. This is what I call *the burden of omniscience*. The government is supposed to know everything, but the power they wield guarantees that they generally know nothing. They never hear anything that doesn't suit their prejudices because nobody dares to tell them. The top echelon of the government has so much incredible power that everybody is terrified of it. So nobody ever tells it the truth. They tell it always and only whatever they think will keep it from going ballistic. So the people at the very top are told flattering lies filtered through several layers of flattering liars who've been lied to by those below them.

I have been conducting workshops on neurolinguistics and general semantics for a long time — four decades. And I frequently ask audiences, "Has anybody ever told the complete and utter truth without reservations to anybody from the government?" Nobody ever puts up their hand. Nobody claims to be that trusting and docile and submissive. Everybody lies a little or hides a little when dealing with the government. People lie as much as they think is necessary to survive, to go on living without getting this beast on top of them. *The government is armed and dangerous.*

And so the government has no idea who we are or what we want. So they distrust us profoundly, because every time they write laws they think we're going to like, we don't like them. And so they're continually running into opposition from us. And they don't think we have any right to meddle in our own affairs anyway, to begin with, because they're supposed to be the governors. We're only supposed to be the subjects or the serfs. The Constitution says they're our servants, but none of them believe it. They think they're our Masters, and they act that way.

Q: You also talk about the government's response to its own inability to trust us is to create further oppressions which then amplifies the mistrust of the people, and it becomes like a vicious circle.

A: The more they spy on us, the more paranoid more people become about them. When they spy on our very innards, our bladder and urine, we're beyond the stage of the Gestapo or KGB; we're in the realm of Kafka. And the more paranoid the people become, the more they're likely to resort to er um hostile gestures like the Oklahoma City bombing, for instance. And something even worse than that may be coming down the pike. Most people in this country don't trust the government, are terrified of it and kind of wish it would go away. And the government, accordingly, doesn't trust us. As Bertold Brecht once said, "Why don't they find another people and go govern them?"

But they don't want to find another people to go govern. They insist on trying to govern us even while they don't trust us. So they're spying on us more and more to see if we're plotting to get rid of them. I think most of us would like to get rid of them, but only a few nuts think it's possible or can be achieved by dynamite, but the government thinks we're all potential bombers. They know we hate them. They know most of us don't even bother voting, for instance. They just don't know when our passive disgust might turn into violent revolution. That's not totally irrational; we ourselves don't know how many Timothy McVeighs there are among us.

Q: What about the idea of people needing some kind of conspiracy to justify their day-to-day misery? That something is lurking out there that's responsible for all their personal pain?

A: That's what I call the "blame game." When you have problems, there are two approaches. One is to try to solve the problem. The other is to find somebody to blame for it so you don't have to go to all the trouble of solving the problem. And with humans being largely a bunch of lazy bums, the second solution is much more popular. Don't try to fix the problem, find somebody to blame for it. That is why there are so many totally nutty conspiracy theories floating around.

Q: How much credence do you lend to the idea that genuine aliens could be involved in some of these conspiracies in real-world-terms? Do aliens exist for you, and do you think they conspire with the government?

A: I think the literal form of that model, brought forth by Bill Cooper and William Moore and others of that persuasion, is a wonderful metaphor, a great plot for a science-fiction story. But I can't take it literally. I just can't believe in it. The aliens in these scenarios come right out of bad 1950's science-fiction B-movies. I'd find it easier to believe that Snow White and the Seven Dwarfs were piloting all the UFOs . . . or the Three Stooges . . .

On the other hand, the idea that there are forces we don't

understand involved in some of the shenanigans on this planet does have a certain plausibility to it. The more you look into these things, the more you feel that there is a player on the other side. I feel like Thomas Henry Huxley, the great agnostic — a guy who was an enemy of religion all his life — and yet in one passage in one of his essays, he says we're like people playing a chess game, where the pieces are the phenomena of the universe, the rules of the game are the laws of nature we've discovered so far, but the player on the other side is still invisible. I classify UFOs, and the paranormal in general, and Fortean phenomena as acts of the "player" on the other side that we don't understand yet.

Q: You say at the end of the book that you wish all the conspiracies you had written about were as easy to dismiss as the Zionist Occupied Government conspiracy. What conspiracies do you have a hard time dismissing? What are the top two or three that seem possible to you?

A: The Multi-Conspiracy Model, which I heard from Timothy Leary and later from a District Attorney of, I think, Santa Barbara, whom I met at Big Sur. It's also the model used by historian Carl Oglesby.

This theory holds that any town, once it gets beyond being a one-horse town out of the Westerns — any town that has a bank and a grocery and a lot of real estate and a lot of people, even before it becomes a big city — there are always a minimum of 24 gangs fighting over who's going to dominate the town and own most of the real estate and make most of the profits. So they're all conspiring against one another.

When you get up to the size of a whole state, there are 24 bigger conspiracies, or 30 maybe. When you get up to the nations, there are God knows how many of them. They're all conspiring and they're all willing to break the law whenever it's in their interest. They even lie. I know you get called paranoid for saying it out loud, but bankers and politicians do tell lies sometimes.

Roberto Calvi, who was one of the bankers in one of the

biggest conspiracies, the P2 conspiracy in Italy, often said, "Read *The Godfather*. That shows you how the world really works." In other words, all power groups act fundamentally like the Mafia. And the Mafia is not a monolithic conspiracy. It is a conspiracy or secret society that hangs together part of the time and makes war on itself part of the time. Calvi worked intimately with the Mafia and with Arab terrorists and international bankers, and he thought they all operated like Don Corleone.

Q: So you're talking then about a multiple conspiracy that's mostly directed at making money?

A: Exactly. I think that there are multiple conspiracies and occasionally five or six of them will join together to make a Mega-Conspiracy for a given period of time to accomplish a given result. But I don't see any evidence that they've all worked together since the dawn of time to the present. Mostly they've been fighting with one another.

Q: Do you see everything as a conspiracy?

A: No. Somebody once accused me of claiming that everything is subjective, but I don't make statements about "everything," I only make statements about sombunall things. I suspect conspiracy is very prevalent behavior on this backward & barbaric planet. It even precedes humanity. Lions conspire — one lion will frighten a herd of antelope to get them running in a certain direction where the other lions will be waiting there to eat them. That's a conspiracy against antelopes, and I'm sure the antelopes are very pissed off about it. "Damned lions, can't trust those motherfuckers no way."

Ants conspire, they seize territory and drive off interlopers; rats have very vigorous conspiracies — when a rat from a strange pack gets into a house they'll hunt him down and kill him. It's just like the Mafia: "We don't like you moving in on our territory."

Q: Is it possible for a conspiracy to be benign?

A: I have to give you a "Yes but" answer on that.

One difference between a conspiracy and an affinity group is that when me and my friends do it it's an affinity group and when someone we don't like does it it's a goddam conspiracy. Conspiracies run the literary world, the art world, etc.; marijuana arrives here due to conspiracies; etc. Modern "liberal" intellectuals are the first and only group to ever believe that conspiracies never happen. That's like claiming it never rains or snows; we just see other things falling and we mistake them for rain and snow . . .

c 1996 — A chat with Randy Lee Payton

Q: Why do you claim you don't believe anything?

A: "The map is not the territory," as Korzybski said. Any map you make of the city you live in can't show the whole city. It would have to show you, and it would have to show you drawing the map, and it would have to show you drawing a map of the map . . . so every map is a simplification.

And words are like maps . . . and how much can you put in a sentence? And because of this a lot of modern scientists believe we should drop the word "is" entirely because "is" tends to lead us to confuse our verbal categories in our heads with the non-verbal reality that we experience. So I try to practice describing what I've actually seen rather than saying "is"; instead of saying, "There is a drunk coming down the street," I might say, "I see a man approaching who looks drunk to me." Or you can say. "I see a man approaching who may have a broken leg and needs help." You make yourself realize there are alternative explanations. Once you say "is" you stop thinking about alternative explanations.

Q: Does this kind of mechanistic thinking, though perhaps serving an evolutionary function during the industrial period, only serve to hurt us all in this information processing era?

A: Yes. You take something like obscenity. There's no way of saying how much obscenity exists in a book, a painting, a film, etc. We don't have an obscenometer. You can't point an obscenometer at a movie and say "Oh this has 50 chambers of obscenity. Oh this one has 75 chambers, and hey, this one went all the way up to 100 chambers!" So if we don't have any measurements, we don't have anything to talk about . . . When we're not talking about anything out there measurable, we're talking about our own neurological reactions we probably learned from our parents. So when we say, "That movie is obscene," what we mean is "My parents wouldn't have liked that movie." So you should say that, instead of deluding yourself that you're talking about the movie.

Q: You've been writing and talking for some time, Dr. Wilson, about an emerging society where high technology is put in the service of abundance for all. Alvin Toffler believes we're halfway between the old industrial model and the emerging, high tech information processing society. Do you agree?

A: I think we're there. The problem is the people who run our society can't figure out how to make the adjustment because they're still thinking in terms of an economy of scarcity. Actually, measurably, we've had an economy of abundance since 1974. There's been more than enough, but our rulers and owners just don't know how to run the new information society because the market and everything will jump in spooky ways when everybody realizes there's plenty to go around. *Since the 1930's the State has paid farmers not to grow food while people are starving.* Now if anyone tells you that this economy makes sense ask them, how sane is a world where people are starving in one place and over here people are being paid not to grow the food to feed them. How can anyone describe that as sanity?

Q: Do you think that such a post-scarcity society will make censorship superfluous in a lot of ways because censorship is based on ideological power grabs . . . ?

A: Censorship is chiefly intended to kill brain cells. When you don't get enough information, brain cells start dying, and anything that comes between the brain and potential information is killing brain cells. This is necessary in a scarcity economy so people won't figure out that hey, there's a crowd over there who are eating all the food while we're starving. The best thing is to keep people stupid, but since we're past that stage of evolution we don't need social institutions designed only to keep the people stupid, we can allow them to develop their intelligence to the full now. As a matter of fact, developing our intelligence to the full may now not only be "allowed," but it probably will prove to be a vast benefit for all of us.

Q: It is said that Clinton's current sex scandals are the result of a right-wing conspiracy against him. Do you think there is any truth to that idea?

A: Some. But there is also the media frenzy for scandal. The President's sex life used to be taboo, but the taboo has broken down. Like all taboos, as soon as it gets broken down, you have a period of kind of sociopathic chaos where there are no rules at all. Eventually a new set of rules will have to be established. Meanwhile, I wouldn't run for President. I wouldn't run for dogcatcher. I don't want anybody going over my life the way the lives of politicians get examined these days.

Q: My reaction was that I couldn't believe my ears half the time. You're sitting there watching the evening news and they're talking about the President's semen stains.

A: (laughs) It is like he's a suspect on "NYPD Blue." Everybody in Washington knew about Kennedy's sexual romps, but their editors wouldn't print it. Now it's open season on politicians. Well, they deserve it.

Old Man On A Balcony:
Views Of Monterey Bay #23

ANOTHER MIDNIGHT HAIKU

Black Darkness only:

I see nothing but I hear

Rain and wind and waves

Still More Questions Answered

and now a 2002 romp with Paul Krassner

Q: You've written 34 books with the aid of pot. Could you describe that process?

A: It's rather obsessive-compulsive, I think. I write the first draft straight, then rewrite stoned, then rewrite straight again, then rewrite stoned again, and so on, until I'm absolutely delighted with every sentence, or irate editors start reminding me about deadlines — whichever comes first. Hemingway and Raymond Chandler had similar compulsions but used the wrong drug, booze, and they both attempted suicide. Papa succeeded but poor Ray didn't and just looked like a sloppy alcoholic. (He tried to shoot himself in the head and missed.) Faulkner also had obsessive components and died by falling off a horse, drunk. I don't think booze is a very safe drug for us obsessive-compulsives. Almost as bad as becoming known as a Sage. By the way, Congress should impeach Bozo and impound Rumsfeld.

Q: The piss police read *High Times*. What would you like to tell them?

A: "You are all equally blessed, equally empty, equally coming Buddhas." But some of them are such assholes, it will take a long time to get from there to here.

Q: Columnist Clarence Page recently wrote about the DEA raiding "a legitimate health co-operative [WAMM, the Wo/Men's Alliance for Medical Marijuana] that was treating more than 200 patients, some of them terminally ill, in Santa Cruz. Snatching medicine out of the hands of seriously ill patients sounds like terrorism to me. In this case it was federally sponsored and taxpayer-financed." Tell me about your own relationship with WAMM.

A: Long before I needed WAMM, Valerie Corral, the founder, came regularly to my *Finnegans Wake* reading/rapping group and I considered her incredibly bright. As I learned about her WAMM activities, distributing pot to terminal cancer and AIDS patients, sitting with them, giving love and support during the death process, I decided she was also a saint. I never thought I would become another WAMM patient. My post-polio syndrome had been a minor nuisance until then; suddenly two years ago it flared up into blazing pain. My doctor recommended marijuana and named WAMM as the safest and most legal source. By then, I think I was on the edge of suicide; the pain had become like a permanent abscessed tooth in the leg. Nobody can or should endure that. Thanks to Valerie and WAMM, I never have that kind of torture for more than an hour these days. I pop one of their pain pills and I'm up and back at the iMac in, well, if not an hour, then at most two hours. By the way, Congress should impeach Bozo and impound Rumy. Or did I say that already?

Q: I think you did.

A: Well, it bears repeating.

Q: When the City Council staged a public giveaway of medical marijuana, a DEA agent asked, "What kind of message are city officials sending to the youth of Santa Cruz?" How would you answer him?

A: "The powers not delegated to the United States by the Constitution, nor prohibited by it to the States, are reserved to the States respectively, or to the people."

I didn't invent that; I found it in the back of my dictionary, in a dusty old historical document called "U.S. Constitution," which Bozo seemingly has never heard of, but it's supposed to be the rules of our government. I wish more people would look at that document, because it has a lot of other radical ideas that seem worth thinking about; it's based on the Massachusetts constitution written by John Adams. Look it up before the Bush Crime Family forces dictionary publishers to remove it. Congress should impeach Bozo and impound Rummy. Or does this begin to sound like an echo chamber?

Q: How does all that tie in with your new book, *TSOG*? First, what does TSOG mean, and how do you pronounce it?

A: TSOG means Tsarist Occupation Government and I pronounce it TSOG, so it sounds like a monster in a Lovecraft story. The book presents the evidence that ever since the CIA-Nazi-Tsarist alliance of the 1940's, the Tsarists have taken over as the "brains" of the Control System and America has become a Tsarist nation, with the Constitution only known to those who peek in the back of their dictionaries, like I did. Hell, we even have an official Tsar and he has the alleged "right" — or at least the power — to come between my doctor and me, and decide how much excruciating pain I should suffer before dying.

What next? Is the Tsar going to rule on controversial questions in physics and astronomy? In mathematical set theory? In biology? Believe me, there's no Tsar mentioned in the Constitution. Personal doctor/patient matters are left to the individuals. You see, this was once supposed to be a free country, not a Tsarist despotism.

Q: You were brought up as a Catholic and became a Marxist when you were 16. What disillusioned you about each of those belief systems?

A: Their rigidity. All rigid Belief Systems (B.S.) censor and warp the processes of perception, thought and even empathy. They literally make people behave like badly-wired robots. Philip K. Dick noticed this too, and worried a lot about the possible robots among us. Some people think he was crazy, but I've never met anybody with rigid beliefs who seemed fully human to me. Phil got it right: a lot of them do act like robots. Especially in government offices and churches. Gort, Bozo barada nikto, dig?

Q: What was the purpose of what you call the Christian conspiracy?

A: Well, I regard the Bill of Rights as the result of a conspiracy by the intellectual freemasons of the Enlightenment Era. It's always had a precarious existence because of the rival Christian conspiracy to restore the dark ages — Inquisitions, witch-hunts and all. With the Tsarist take-over, the Christians appear to have won. Not a single clause in the Bill of Rights hasn't gotten either diluted or totally reversed.

Q: Why are you so skeptical about organized skepticism?

A: Like I keep saying, rigid Belief Systems frighten me and make me think of robots, or "humanoids" — some kinda creepy mechanism like that. Organized skepticism in the U.S. today contains no true skeptics in the philosophical sense. They seem like just another gang of dogmatic lunatics at war with all the other gangs of dogmatic fanatics, and, of course, with us model agnostics also. Look at the Committee for Scientific Investigation of Claims of the Paranormal. They never do any Scientific Investigation at all, at all. Why? My guess is that, like the Inquisitors who refused to look through Galileo's telescope, they have a deep fear that such research might upset their dogmas.

Q: What's the basis of your obsession with Hannibal Lecter?

A: Hannibal Lecter, M.D., please. In the books, he seems one of the greatest creations in literature to me. I admire Thomas Harris more than any novelist since James Joyce. Everything about Dr. Lecter is likable and even admirable except that one Nasty Habit, but that habit's so intolerable, even to libertarians, we can never forget it even when we find him most likable and most admirable. A paradox like that can inspire Ph.D. candidates for 1,000 years. I mean, how can you resist a psychiatrist who tells a lesbian patient, as Hannibal did once, "There's nothing wrong with being weird. You have no idea how weird I am" — and really means it? In the films, of course, Dr. Lecter also has the stupendous contribution of intelligence and eerie charm only Anthony Hopkins can project. By the way, God bless Valerie Corral and God damn Asa Hutchinson.

Q: I thought you don't believe in God?

A: I have no "beliefs," only probabilities; but I was not speaking literally there. A poetic flourish, as it were.

Q: I know you don't believe in life after death, but I'm intrigued by the notion that, during 42 years of marriage, you and Arlen imprinted each other's nervous systems. Could you elaborate on that?

A: I don't "believe" in spiritualism, but that does not keep me from suspecting an unbreakable link between those who have loved deeply. To avoid sounding esoteric, let me put it in nitty-gritty terms. I literally cannot look at a movie on TV without knowing what she'd say about it. For instance, if a film starts out well and ends up a mess, I can virtually "hear" her saying, "Well, they had one Story Conference too many . . ."

Q: Would you relate the tale of Arlen and the Encyclopedias?

A: She liked to collect old encyclopedias from second-hand bookstores, and at one point we had eight of them. When I wrote my first historical novel — back in 1980, before I was online — I used them often as a research tool. For instance, I learned that the Bastille was either 90 feet high or 100 feet or 120 feet. This led me to formulate Wilson's 22nd Law: "Certitude belongs exclusively to those who only look in one encyclopedia."

Q: How has the Internet changed your life?

A: It has felt like a neurological quantum jump. Not only does the word processing software make my compulsive rewriting a lot easier than if I still had to cut my words on rocks or use a typewriter or retreat to similar barbarism, but the e-mail function provides most of my social life since I became "disabled." I do most of my research on the World Wide Web, get my answer in minutes and don't have to hunt laboriously through my library for hours. It has improved my life a thousand ways. I also have a notion that Internet, as a feedback system, will eventually replace government, a no-feedback system.

Q: How do you discern between conspiracy and coincidence?

A: The way Mr. and Mrs. Godzilla make love: verrrrry carefully.

Q: A dinner party was scheduled for March 31, 1981, the day after an assassination attempt on Ronald Reagan, which, if successful, would have elevated Vice President and former CIA chief George Bush to the presidency. The dinner was immediately cancelled. It would have been held at the home of Neil Bush, and a guest was to be Scott Hinckley, brother of the would-be killer. Hinckley's father and Bush were friends and fellow oil industrialists. A PR firm issued a statement: "This horrible coincidence has been devastating to the Bush Family. Our condolences go out to all involved. And we hope to get the matter behind us as soon as possible." Congressman Larry MacDonald was the only legislator who demanded an investigation, but his plane crashed. Whattaya think — coincidence or conspiracy?

A: To me, it looks at first glance like coincidence by about 75% probability. I mean, who would be dumb enough to use an assassin with such obvious links to his employers? But then again, the Bush Crime Family seem to think they can get away with anything, from S&L fraud to stealing an election in the clear light of day with the whole world watching. They must have an even lower opinion of the intelligence of the American people than I do. Maybe I should change the probability down to about 50%. I guess this does deserve further investigation by somebody who doesn't fly in airplanes.

Q: Ishmael Reed said, "The history of civilization is the history of warfare between secret societies." Do you agree?

A: Yes and no. I would say there is no history, singular; only histories, plural. The warfare between secret societies is a history, one that both Ishmael and I have explored. There also exists a history of class war, a history of war (or competition) between gene pools, a history of primate/canine relations, etc., ad infinitum. None of them contradicts the others, except in the heads of aristotelian logicians, or Ideologists. They each supplement all the others.

Q: You and I have something in common. Lyndon LaRouche has revealed the truth about each of us: You're really the secret leader of the Illuminati; and I was brainwashed at the Tavistock Institute in England. Do you think he actually believes such things, or is he consciously creating fiction, just as the FBI's counter-intelligence program did?

A: I still don't understand some of my computer's innards and you expect me to explain a bizarre contraption like the brain of Lyndon LaRouche? I can only hazard that he seems more a case for a bile specialist than a psychiatrist.

Q: What was LaRouche's factoid about the Queen of England?

A: He said Liz sent Aldous Huxley and Alan Watts over here to destroy us with Oriental religions and drugs, so England could become the top Super-Power again. If you took Liz and England out and put Fu Manchu and the Third World in her place, it would make a great matinee thriller. I think Bozo lives in that film with Mickey and Goofy and Osama bin Laden and Darth Vader.

Q: What's the most bizarre conspiracy theory you've come across?

A: A group called Christians Awake claims Ronald Reagan was a Gay freemason and that he filled the government and courts with other Gay freemasons. I suppose they let Clarence Thomas in as a concession to the Gay Prince Hal lodge.

Q: And what would be the least known conspiracy theory — I mean, that you know of?

A: The Church of Positive Accord believes — and I think they make a damned good case — that the God of the Bible is corporeal, not spiritual. In udder woids, he eats and shits just like you and me. And, contrary to my 1959 heresies, he definitely has a penis. He even has boogers: they proclaimed that in an interview with [SubGenius Church reverend] Ivan Stang. They point out that all "spiritual" ideas of God derive from Greek philosophy, not the Bible, and claim that gaseous Greek god has been promoted by a conspiracy of intellectuals. Just re-read the Bible with that grid and it makes sense, in a Stone Age sort of way. He walks, He talks. He loves the smell of beef cooking. He hates Gay people and shellfish. He's a serial killer. And in the sequel He even knocks up a teen-age chick.

Q: Your readers can't always discern — when you write about the Illuminati, for example — whether you're sharing information or satirizing reality. Does it make any difference?

A: To quote Madonna, "I'm only kidding — not." Add my Celtic sense of humor to Niels Bohr's model agnosticism and out comes my neo-surrealist novels and "post-modern" criticism.

Q: I've had many occurrences of satirical prophecy, where something I invented turned out to become reality. Has that happened with you?

A: Well, in *Illuminatus!* (published 1975), terrorists attack the Pentagon and only succeed in blowing a hole in one of the five sides. Sound familiar? Also, in *Schrödinger's Cat* (published 1981), terrorists blow up Wall Street. I don't regard either of those "hits" as precognition or even "intuition," just common sense. It seemed obvious to me that the TSOG could not run amok around the planet, invading and bombing damned near everybody, without somebody firing back eventually.

Q: Here's a confession. In my article on the conspiracy convention in *High Times*, I did a reverse of satirical prophecy. I had once asked Mae Brussell, the queen of conspiracy researchers, why the conspirators didn't kill her, and she explained that agents always work on a need-to-know basis, but they would read her work and show up wherever she spoke, in order to get a peek at the big picture, because it was "a safety valve for them," she said, "on how far things are going." I asked, "Are you saying that the intelligence community has allowed you to function precisely because *you* know more than any of *them*?" And she replied, "Exactly." Well, in my *High Times* satire, I put those words into the mouth of somewhat fraudulent conspiracy researcher David Icke. Anyway, my question is, do you think the conspirators allow *you* to live because you know too much?

A: I doubt it. I don't think they've ever heard of me. They don't read books.

Q: After my *High Times* column on the Prophets Conference, in which I referred to you as "the irreverent bad boy at this oh-so-polite conference," why were you disinvited from speaking at future Prophets Conferences?

A: A lot of my fans think I got booted for lack of respect for His Royal Fraudulency George II. I take that as an assertion beyond proof or disproof. The managers said it was for finding a Joycean epiphany in a Spike Lee movie. I take that as an assertion beyond even comprehension.

Q: I'd like to hear about your — perhaps psychotic? — experience with higher consciousness and the resulting epiphany.

A: I have had not one but many *seeming* encounters with *seemingly* non-human intelligences. The first was a Christmas tree that loved me — loved me more than my parents or my wife or my kids, or even my dog. I was on peyote at the time. With and without other drugs — for instance by Cabala — I have *seemingly* contacted a medieval Irish bard, an ancient Chinese alchemist, an extraterrestrial from the Sirius system, and a giant white rabbit called the pook or pookah from County Kerry. I finally accepted that if you already have a multi-model ontology going into the shamanic world, you're going to come out with multi-model results. As Wilson's Fourth Law sez, *"With sufficient research you will find evidence to support your theory."* So I settled on the magick rabbit as the model nobody could take literally, not even myself. The real shocker came when I discovered that my grandmother's people, the O'Lachlanns, came from Kerry and allegedly have a clan pookah who protects us from becoming English by adding periodic doses of weirdness to our lives.

Q: The dedication in my book, *Murder At the Conspiracy Convention and Other American Absurdities*, reads: "This one is for Robert Anton Wilson — guerrilla ontologist, part-time post-modernist, Damned Old Crank, my weirdest friend and favorite philosopher." Since these are all terms you've used to label yourself, would you explain what each one means?

A: Well, I picked up "guerrilla ontology" from the Physics/Consciousness Research Group when I was a member back in the 1970's. Physicists more usually call it "model agnosticism," and it consists of never regarding any model or map of Universe with total 100% belief or total 100% denial. Following Korzybski, I put things in probabilities, not absolutes. I give most of modern physics over 90% probability, the Loch Ness Monster around 50% probability and anything the State Department says under 5% probability. As Bucky Fuller used to say, "Universe is non-simultaneously apprehended" — nobody can apprehend it all at once — so we have no guarantee that today's best model will fit what we may discover tomorrow.

My only originality lies in applying this zetetic attitude outside the hardest of the hard sciences, physics, to softer sciences and then to non-sciences like politics, ideology, jury verdicts and, of course, conspiracy theory. Also, I have a strong aversion, almost an allergy, to Belief Systems, or B.S. — a convenient abbreviation I owe to David Jay Brown [*Virus: The Alien Strain and Brainchild*, New Falcon Publications]. A neurolinguistic diet high in B.S. and low in instrumental data eventually produces Permanent Brain Damage, a lurching gait, blindness and hairy palms like a werewolf.

Then I started calling myself a post-modernist after that label got pinned on me in two different books, one on my sociological works and one on my science-fiction. Then I read some of the post-modernists and decided they were only agnostic about other people's dogmas, not their own. So then I switched to Damned Old Crank, which seems to suit my case better than either of the previous labels. Besides, once my hair turned snowy white, some people wanted to promote me to a Sage, and I had to block that. It's more dangerous to a writer than booze. By the way, Congress should impeach Bozo and impound Rumsfeld.

Q: Since you believe that the universe is indifferent, why are you an optimist?

A: It may have genetic origins — some of us bounce up again no matter what we get hit with — but as far as I can rationalize it, nobody knows the future, so choosing between pessimism and optimism depends on temperament as much as probabilities.

Psychologist John Barefoot has studied this extensively and concludes that optimists live about 20% longer than pessimists. When the outcome remains unknown, why should I make the bet that keeps me miserable and shortens my life? I prefer the gamble that keeps me high, happy, and creative, and also increases life span. It's like the advantage of pot over aspirin. Pot not only kills pain better, but the High boosts the immune system. High and happy moods prolong life, miserable and masochistic moods shorten it.

Q: Recently, when I spoke at a college campus, a student asked what I wanted my epitaph to be. I replied, "Wait, I'm not finished." What do you want *your* epitaph to be?

A: I have ordained in my will that my body will get cremated and the ashes thrown in Jerry Falwell's face. The executor of my will should then shout one word only: "Gotcha!"

PART V

ON MY WAY OUT

Believe nothing, no matter where you read it, or who said it, no matter if I have said it, unless it agrees with your own reason and your own common sense.

- Gotama Buddha

Escape From CNN

No fakes or deceits:
Bay, clouds, birds, trees: All
Doing what they do.

Cheerful Reflections on Death and Dying

I wrote this c. 2001 for some online zine that quickly went kerflooey.

Wavy Gravy told me about a guy who asked a Zen Master,
"What happens after death?"
The roshi replied, "I don't know."
"But, you're a Zen Master!"
"Yes, " said the roshi, "but I'm not a dead Zen Master."

I don't understand why people fear death — although of course I see good reasons to fear the process of dying.

Dying often involves a great deal of prolonged pain, and in this country at least may drain your life savings into the bank accounts of the A.M.A. Both prospects seem equally terrifying — especially if you hoped to leave a decent estate to your children.

One can avoid these deplorable conditions, however, by moving to a civilized country with a national health plan and legal help to assist you in suicide if you have reached a condition where you can't do it yourself. I personally intend to move to Nederland in the event that a painful, expensive and prolonged death seems inescapable. The medical banditos have made enough money out of me already; I refuse to enrich them further on my way out.

But as for death, and what — if anything — comes after death, I see no cause for apprehension whatsoever.

I consider the alternatives in order:

Most people through most of history have believed that after death comes rebirth (reincarnation). I think most people, planet-wide, still believe that. It fails to terrify me. If I get reborn as a cockroach, I intend to hide in the vicinity of somebody's computer and write poems on the keyboard at night, like Archy, the famous roach who left his verse in the typewriter of Don Marquis. If I get reborn as a human, I might meet my wife Arlen again and love her again and marry her again. That sounds great to me.

Other rebirths, as a tree, say, or a blue whale, also seem more entertaining (and educational) than frightening.

Unfortunately, I have no good reasons to believe in reincarnation, although I'd sort of like to. I include it only for the sake of completeness.

A sinister rumor, widely believed in the Occident, holds that after death we may go to a place called Heaven. From all the descriptions I've read, it sounds dreadful to me. It seems to have a population made up entirely of some gang of Christians; the experts on Heaven disagree about which conglomeration of Christians will qualify, but they always seem to think that they personally belong to that elite group. An eternity with people that conceited seems intolerable to me, but fortunately I am not a Christian so I won't be consigned to such a boring place.

An even more nefarious report appears in the United States Marine Corps hymn:

> If the Army and the Navy
> ever looked on Heaven's scenes
> they would find the streets were guarded
> by the United States Marines

A place where every street is guarded by Marines sounds like a particularly vicious police state, especially if Christians run it, and I definitely don't want to go there, even for a visit. I wouldn't even wish it on my worst enemy, if I had any enemies. (Some people hate me for the books I write, but I refuse to hate them back, so they don't count as enemies.)

Fortunately, as noted, I don't qualify for Heaven, with all its harps and fanatic Christians and martial law by Marines.

An equally terrible idea, which has terrified millions, claims that some of us will go to a place called Hell, where we will suffer eternal torture. This does not scare me because, when I try to imagine a Mind behind this universe, I cannot conceive that Mind, usually called "God," as totally mad.

I mean, guys, compare that "God" with the worst monsters you can think of — Adolph Hitler, Joe Stalin, that sort of guy. None of them ever inflicted more than finite pain on their victims. Even de Sade, in his sado-maso fantasy novels, never devised an unlimited torture. The idea that the Mind of Creation (if such exists) wants to torture some of its critters for endless infinities of infinities seems too absurd to take seriously.

Such a deranged Mind could not create a mud hut, much less the exquisitely mathematical universe around us.

If such a monster-God did exist, the sane attitude would consist of practicing the Buddhist virtue of compassion. He seems very sick in His head, so don't give way to hatred: try to understand and forgive Him. Maybe He will recover his wits some day. (I wrote "He" instead of the fashionable "He or She" because only male Gods appear to have invented Hells. I can't think of a single Goddess who ever created a Hell for people who displeased Her.)

A fourth alternative after-death scenario involves merger with "God" or with "the Godhead" (the latter term seems more popular). This idea, which seems Hindic in origin, currently enjoys vast popularity with New Agers.

I see nothing terrifying here; in fact, I suspect I would enjoy it, based on my previous experiences in which this merging/melting seemed to take place on LSD. An infinite Acid Trip in which the whole universe seems like your body: who could fear that (except Republicans)?

The fifth and, as far as I know, the last thinkable alternative holds that after death comes total oblivion. This has either terrorized or angered many intelligent writers (e.g., Bertrand Russell and Jean Paul Sartre, who seem to have hated "life after death" for not existing, just as they remained permanently pissed off at "God" for not existing). Sorry: it doesn't seem terrible to me at all. If I become totally oblivious, I won't know about it (by definition of oblivion). How can you feel, terrified of something you can't experience?

Besides oblivion means freedom from "all the ills the flesh is heir to," from bleeding piles to cancer, including even bad reviews of my books.

Living in New York or Los Angeles seem much worse than not living in Oblivion.

Although I have a few opinions, or hunches, I have no dogma about what happens after death. But none of the above alternatives seem really unpleasant, except the ones that seem too absurd to take seriously.

As some Roman wrote:

> Nothing to clutch in life.
> Nothing to fear in death.

On My Way Out

Bozo and the TSOG
both seem far far away from
my bay and my clouds

AFTERWORD

by Paul Krassner

Filmmaker Luis Bunuel once said that he made movies to give himself something to do between birth and death. So, then, Robert Anton Wilson's final published book — diverse topics in *Email to the Universe* — serves as a documentary of his multi-dimensional imagination and genius. He died on January 11, 2007 at the age of 74. The prolific author and countercultural icon had been suffering from post-polio syndrome. Caregivers at his bedside read aloud all of his late wife Arlen's poetry, and e-mailed to me that "He was quite cheered up by the time we left. He definitely needed to die. His body was turning on him in ways that would not allow him to rest."

In his final blog on January 6, Wilson wrote: "I don't see how to take death seriously. I look forward without dogmatic optimism, but without dread. I love you all and I deeply implore you to keep the lasagna flying." Actually, it was expected that he would die seven months earlier. On June 19, 2006, he sent this haiku (with one syllable missing) to his electronic cabal:

Well what do you know?
Another day has passed
and I'm still not not.

Bob Wilson and I originally became friends in 1959, when his first published article graced the cover of my irreverent magazine, *The Realist*. It was titled "The Semantics of God," in which he suggested that "The Believer had better face himself and ask squarely: Do I literally believe that 'God' has a penis? If the answer is no, then it seems only logical to drop the ridiculous practice of referring to 'God' as 'he.'" Incidentally, Bob's byline in that piece was the first time he used Anton as if it was his middle name. He then began writing a regular column, "Negative Thinking."

In 1964, I ran another front-cover story by him, "Timothy Leary and His Psychological H-Bomb," which began: "The future may decide that the two greatest thinkers of the 20th Century were Albert Einstein, who showed how to create atomic fission in the physical world, and Timothy Leary, who showed how to create atomic fission in the psychological world. The latter discovery may be more important than the former; there are some reasons for thinking that it was made necessary by the former. Leary may have shown how our habits of thought can be changed."

Wilson took that notion as his personal marching orders, altering the consciousness of countless grateful readers of his 35 books — from *Sex, Drugs & Magick* to *Everything Is Under Control: An Encyclopedia of Conspiracy Theories* — all written with the aid of that good old creative fuel, marijuana. He once told me about his creative process: "It's rather obsessive-compulsive, I think. I write the first draft straight, then rewrite stoned, then rewrite straight again, then rewrite stoned again, and so on, until I'm absolutely delighted with every sentence, or irate editors start reminding me about deadlines — whichever comes first."

Bob originally became a dedicated pot-head in 1955. But, a few years before his death, he told the audience at a Prophets Conference, "I haven't smoked pot in about twelve . . . hours, and I want you to know it's great to be clean." He enjoyed peppering his presentations at such distinguished New Age events with "motherfuckers" and "cocksuckers," and was disinvited from participating in future Prophet Conferences because, said the organizers, "What we feel to be important to your insights are being lost to the audience when packaged in hard and harsh language."

Wilson once described his writings as "intellectual comedy." He told an Internet database, Contemporary Authors: "If my books do what I intend, they should leave the reader feeling that the universe is capable of doing something totally shocking and unexpected in the next five minutes. I am trying to show that life without certainty can be exhilarating, liberating, a great adventure." He called his philosophy "Maybe Logic," which became the title of a documentary about him.

Stephen Gaskin, founder of The Farm commune, wrote, "I had the good fortune to visit with Robert at his house and meet his wife. When I saw the beautiful relationship between them, I understood why the sex scenes in his books are so nicely written that they stand out above everyone else's sex scenes that I've read.

"One of my next encounters with him was standing on the sidewalk of a cold November day in Amsterdam waiting for a taxi. He didn't have enough of a coat, and he was standing in the cold with his collar turned up and his hands stuck in his pockets. It was a while after his wife had died and he looked quite forlorn. We collected him up, put a warm coat on him, and put a joint in his mouth. It was a real hoot to get to be friends with one of my very favorite writers. His *Illuminatus!* trilogy is a benchmark in science-fiction and contemporary paranoia."

Wilson wrote his own obituary in an autobiography, *Cosmic Trigger*: "According to reliable sources, I died on February 22, 1994 — George Washington's birthday. I felt nothing special or shocking at the time, and believed that I still sat at my word processor working on a novel called Bride of Illuminatus.

"At lunch-time, however, when I checked my voice mail, I found that Tim Leary and a dozen friends had already called to ask to speak to me, or — if they still believed in Reliable Sources — to offer support and condolences to my grieving family. I quickly gathered that the news of my tragic end had appeared on the Internet: 'Noted science-fiction author Robert Anton Wilson was found dead in his home yesterday, apparently the victim of a heart attack. [He] was noted for his libertarian viewpoints, love of technology and off the wall humor. Mr. Wilson is survived by his wife and two children.'"

R. U. Sirius, co-author of *Counterculture Through the Ages*, writes, "Robert Anton Wilson enjoyed his first death so much, he decided to try it again. As the result of medical expenses and problems with the IRS, he found himself in a financial squeeze towards the end of his life. Word went out and the Internet community responded by sending him $68,000 within the first couple of days. This allowed him to die with the comfort, grace and dignity that he deserved.

"He taught us all that 'the universe contains a maybe.' So maybe there is an afterlife, and maybe Bob's consciousness is hovering around all of us who were touched by his words and his presence all these years. And if that's the case, I'm sure he'd like to see you do something strange and irreverent — and yet beautiful — in his honor."

In 1974, I stopped publishing *The Realist* because I ran out of money and taboos. In 1985, I re-launched it in a newsletter format. For a feature story in the born-again *Realist*, I contacted Bob Wilson. There was a one-inch news item about a convention in Italy of the Married Roman Catholic Priests Association, representing 70,000 priests who had married in defiance of the Vatican. I gave the clipping to him.

"Bob, should you choose to accept this assignment, I'd like you to cover this event as though you had actually been there."

Wilson wrote his report, and even I almost believed that he had actually gone to the married priests convention. Next, there was a tiny news item about the first International Orgasm Conference, and I assigned him to cover that event too, as though he had actually been there. *The Realist* was back in apocryphal business. This time I published the final issue in 2001. But Robert Anton Wilson is still alive in the form of his literary legacy. May he rest in lasagna.

Paul Krassner is the author of *Confessions of a Raving,
Unconfined Nut: Misadventures in the Counterculture*
The first version of this essay was published on boingboing.
com. Paul rewrote a little and made some additions to the essay
for this edition of *Email to the Universe*.

What Critics Say About Robert Anton Wilson

A SUPER-GENIUS . . . He has written everything I was afraid to write

Dr. John Lilly

◎

One of the funniest, most incisive social critics around, and with a positive bent, thank Goddess.

Riane Eisler, author of The Chalice and the Blade

◎

A very funny man . . . readers with open minds will like his books.

Robin Robertson, Psychological Perspectives

◎

Robert Anton Wilson is a dazzling barker hawking tickets to the most thrilling tilt-a-whirls and daring loop-o-planes on the midway of higher consciousness.

Tom Robbins,
author of Even Cowgirls Get the Blues

◎

STUPID

Andrea Antonoff

◎

The man's either a genius or Jesus

SOUNDS (London)

◎

Wilson managed to reverse every mental polarity in me, as if I had been dragged through infinity. I was astounded and delighted.

Philip K. Dick, author of *Blade Runner*

◎

One of the leading thinkers of the modern age.

Barbara Marx Hubbard, World Future Society

◎

A male feminist. ..a simpering, pussy-whipped wimp.

Lou Rollins

◎

SEXIST

Arlene Meyers

◎

The most important philosopher of this century . . . scholarly, witty, hip and hopeful.

Timothy Leary

◎

What great physicist hides behind the mask of "Robert Anton Wilson?"

NEW SCIENTIST

Does for Quantum Mechanics what Durrell's
Alexandria Quartet did for Relativity, but Wilson is
funnier.

John Gribbin, physicist

OBSCENE, blasphemous, subversive and very,
very interesting.

Alan Watts

Erudite, witty and genuinely scary.
PUBLISHER'S WEEKLY

Deliberately annoying.

Jay Kinney

Misguided malicious fanaticism.

Robert Sheafer, Committee for Scientific
Investigation of Claims of the Paranormal

The man's glittering intelligence won't let you rest.
With each new book, I look forward to his wisdom,
laced with his special brand of crazy humor.

Alan Harrington, author of *The Immortalist*

Mosbunall* Books By Robert Anton Wilson

1972 Playboy's Book of Forbidden Words

1973 Sex, Drugs and Magick: A Journey Beyond Limits

1973 The Sex Magicians

1974 The Book of the Breast (now 'Ishtar Rising')

1975 ILLUMINATUS! (with Robert Shea)

    The Eye in the Pyramid

    The Golden Apple

    Leviathan

1977 Cosmic Trigger I: Final Secret of the Illuminati

1978 Neuropolitique (with T. Leary & G. Koopman)

1980 The Illuminati Papers

1980-1 The Schrodinger's Cat Trilogy

    The Universe Next Door

    The Trick Top Hat

    The Homing Pigeon

1981 Masks of the Illuminati

1983 Right Where You Are Sitting Now

*Adaptation of "sombunall" – see reference

HILARITAS
PRESS

Publishing the Books of Robert Anton Wilson
and Other Adventurous Thinkers

www.hilaritaspress.com

CPSIA information can be obtained
at www.ICGtesting.com
Printed in the USA
LVHW020052100222
710601LV00013B/983